Slut-Shaming,

Whorephobia,

and the

Unfinished

Sexual Revolution

SLUT-SHAMING, WHOREPHOBIA, AND THE UNFINISHED SEXUAL REVOLUTION

MEREDITH RALSTON

McGill-Queen's University Press
Montreal & Kingston • London • Chicago

ISBN 978-0-2280-0665-7 (cloth)
ISBN 978-0-2280-0798-2 (ePDF)
ISBN 978-0-2280-0799-9 (ePUB)

Legal deposit second quarter 2021
Bibliothèque nationale du Québec

Printed in Canada on acid-free paper that is 100% ancient forest free
(100% post-consumer recycled), processed chlorine free

Funded by the   Financé par le
.Government   gouvernement
of Canada   du Canada

Canada Council   Conseil des arts
for the Arts   du Canada

We acknowledge the support of the Canada Council for the Arts.
Nous remercions le Conseil des arts du Canada de son soutien.

Library and Archives Canada Cataloguing in Publication

Title: Slut-shaming, whorephobia, and the unfinished sexual
   revolution / Meredith Ralston.
Names: Ralston, Meredith L., author.
Description: Includes bibliographical references and index.
Identifiers: Canadiana (print) 20210118512 | Canadiana (ebook)
   2021011858X | ISBN 9780228006657 (cloth) | ISBN 9780228007982
   (ePDF) | ISBN 9780228007999 (ePUB)
Subjects: LCSH: Women—Sexual behavior. | LCSH: Stigma (Social
   psychology) | LCSH: Sex workers. | LCSH: Prostitution. | LCSH: Rape
   culture. | LCSH: Sex.
Classification: LCC HQ29 .R33 2021 | DDC 306.7082—dc23

This book was designed and typeset by studio oneonone
in 11/14 Minion.

For Lucy, Amanda, Maria, and Anna

Contents

PART ONE

The "Good Girl" Problem

Chapter One

Rape Culture and Slut-Shaming

Question: which of these things is not like the other?

1 In 2020, Harvey Weinstein was convicted of rape and sexual assault in New York, and sentenced to twenty-three years in prison, after more than eighty women accused the former movie mogul of abuse, harassment, and rape. Accusations against him in 2017 spurred the #MeToo movement when thousands of women took to Twitter to describe their own experiences of sexual assault.[1]

2 Larry Nassar, the USA gymnastics doctor, was sentenced to 40 to 170 years in prison in 2018 for abusing more than 150 young women and girls. Between 1997 and 2015, seventeen official complaints were made to administrators at Michigan State University about students being molested during treatment. Nassar was able to convince the university that sticking his fingers in the women's vaginas (ungloved and unlubricated) was medically necessary. Nothing in the reports exonerating him mentioned his erections and the grunting that the women and girls reported.[2]

3 The National Survey of Sexual Health and Behavior found that 91 per cent of men but only 64 per cent of women had an orgasm during their last sexual encounter. The study also claims that between 5 and 10 per cent of women have *never* had an orgasm.[3]

4 Rehtaeh Parsons, a young woman in Halifax, Nova Scotia, attempted suicide (and was eventually taken off life support) when video of her being

sexually assaulted while intoxicated and throwing up out a window was passed around her high school, and she was slut-shamed into changing schools, leaving school, and finally trying to kill herself. The perpetrators were later charged with possession of child pornography, not sexual assault.[4]

5 Robert Pickton, a British Columbia pig farmer, was found guilty of six counts of first-degree murder of women who had disappeared from Vancouver's Downtown Eastside. More than sixty, mainly Indigenous, sex workers had gone missing before the police decided a serial killer might be on the loose and searched his property. DNA from the women was found all over his farm.[5]

I haven't done a survey on this but I wouldn't be surprised if many people pick #3 as being "not like the others." The first two have to do with rape culture, male privilege, and women not being believed; the fourth about rape culture, the negative effects of slut-shaming (and not being believed); the fifth with rape culture, racism, victim-blaming, dehumanization (and not being believed). Number 3 may appear out of place because orgasms and the lack of pleasurable sex are, of course, different from sexualized violence. I'm going to argue throughout this book, however, that these facts and events are actually closely interrelated and have similar causes.

The question really should be: what do these things have in common?

Rape Culture, Slut-Shaming, and Whorephobia

Rape culture is defined as a society that normalizes and trivializes sexual assault; that perpetuates various rape myths that the victim asked for it, she was dressed for it, she wanted it, she was drunk; the reportedly widespread sexual assault of young women on college campuses and the slut-shaming and victim blaming that go along with it.[6] As Kate Harding puts it, rape culture *rewards* men for their sexual conquests "while condemning women for expressing any sexual impulses at all. A culture in which a young woman's supposed friends will videotape her being violated and then use it as evidence that she's a 'slut.' A culture in which most victims of sexual assault and rape never report it because they fear they won't be believed – and know that even if they are believed, they're likely to be mortified and harassed, blamed and shamed, throughout a legal process that ultimately leads nowhere."[7] One of the worst aspects of rape culture is that it becomes normalized to blame the victim when something bad happens. It's not the rapist's fault; it is the fault of the one who allowed herself to be raped. This is the signature effect of rape culture. As Harding puts it, rape culture's "most devilish trick is to make the average, non-criminal person identify with the person accused, instead of the person reporting a crime."[8] She outlines the examples of the Steubenville, Ohio, football players who assaulted an unconscious teenager and the gang rape of an eleven-year-old in Cleveland, Texas, to illustrate how the sympathies of the community were for the most part with the perpetrators – what Kate Manne has brilliantly called "himpathy."[9]

Why is this? Why aren't victims of sexual assault believed until dozens of them come forward claiming the same thing? Why are victims blamed for their own assaults? Why are women slut-shamed for behaviour that is lauded in men? In the course of this book I hope to answer these questions by looking at the causes and consequences of rape culture, slut-shaming, and whore stigma.[10] I became convinced, in the course of completing research for a film on escorts in the United States called *Selling Sex*,[11] that we won't be able to deal fully with the problems of rape culture and slut-shaming until we deal with whore stigma and, relatedly, the negative treatment of sex workers. And until we eradicate the stigma around sex work itself, we won't be able to eradicate the stigma around sex in general and female sexuality in particular.

Both slut-shaming and its more extreme counterpart whorephobia (the hatred of and discrimination against sex workers) result from the continuing sexual double standard between men and women and the good girl/bad girl distinction between women themselves. Slut-shaming works as a way to embarrass, humiliate, and "police" women and girls for real or suspected sexual activity that is not considered socially acceptable. Shaming works very effectively, as we will see, to control and constrain women's behaviour. A less familiar term than slut-shaming, "whorephobia" refers to the hatred and stigmatization of actual whores and women who are perceived as whores because of their "promiscuous" behaviour. Like homophobia or fat-phobia, whorephobia allows people to shame, taunt, look down on, and marginalize women who don't conform to traditional gender roles, in this case, by selling sexual services for a living. It has a profoundly negative effect on women who sell sex, of course, as well as all other women who see and understand the phobia around selling sex or of being overtly sexually active. The "good girls" do their damnedest to try to protect them-selves from judgement and abuse by being good, as if that will shield them from harm.[12] By blaming and shaming the bad girls, whorephobia allows bad girls to be treated badly and by extension controls the behaviours of the good girls – what I will discuss as "good girl privilege."

Slut-shaming and whorephobia, then, are both about the control of women's sexuality. Until we eliminate the shame of the actual whore, we won't eliminate the shaming of women's sexuality in general or the negative consequences for women who can be framed as "whores." As Melissa Gira Grant has bluntly written, "so long as there are women who are called whores, there will be women who are trained to believe it is next to death to be one or to be mistaken as one. And as long as that is, men will feel they can leave whores for dead with impunity."[13] This book will demonstrate the damaging connections between slut-shaming and whorephobia, show how whorephobia contributes directly to the fear and degradation of women's sexuality, and argue that overcoming the sexual double standard and good girl privilege/bad girl stigma is the unfinished sexual revolution for women.

The sexual double standard is not a new phenomenon and authors have been writing about the problems of the sexual double standard for at least forty years. But the problem remains. In fact, some argue that it's getting worse rather than better because of social media and cyber bullying.[14] Books have dealt with the sexual double standard by way of the history of sex,[15] the history of courtesans,[16] the history of the vagina,[17] the concept of slut bashing,[18] the lack of orgasm equality,[19] and the need for intimate justice.[20] Whether the authors are dealing with "good" sex or "bad" sex, the "good" vagina or the "bad" vagina, the "good" girl or the "bad" girl, the common denominator is the sexual double standard: women's sexuality is somehow bad or threatening, sex for women is dangerous or degrading, and men's sexual desires are more important and natural than the sexual desires of women or – as Peggy Orenstein and Leora Tanenbaum have pointed out – of girls. Girls' sexuality is all about sexiness: about looking sexy and pleas-ing boys. Boys' sexuality is about their own pleasure and "scoring" as much as possible.

This dichotomy shouldn't be that surprising because along with the continuing double standard during the sexual revolution of the 1960s and 1970s there was a real lack of focus on women's pleasure.[21] Women were free to be more sexual, but many women had little information about their own bodies' capabilities, and the books that were available (like *Our Bodies, Ourselves*) were seen to be "obscene, antifamily and anti-Christian."[22] While it sounds absurd to modern ears, we needn't think we've come so far. In 2019, the inventors of a hands-free female vibrator called Osé had an award for innovation rescinded by the Consumer Technology Association in the United States because of rules against "immoral, obscene, indecent, profane" products. At the same time, the organization allowed Virtual Reality pornography and other products aimed at men to be displayed. As the product's founder stated, "When you call something obscene just because it has to do with a vagina, technology as an industry starts to lose out."[23] As do women. Almost fifty years after the release of *Our Bodies, Ourselves*, it seems some of us are still uncomfortable with the "obscenity" of female sexuality and prefer the sexual double standard where female pleasure is considered obscene, but men's pleasure is not.

Other issues remain. The clitoris itself wasn't fully mapped or understood until the late 1990s,[24] and the idea that vaginal orgasms were the "mature" kind put pressure on women to have the "right" kind of orgasm, if they weren't faking it to begin with. Fortunately, the lack of focus on women's pleasure has begun to change. There have been several recent books concentrating on the importance of the female orgasm and female biology – books like *The Vagina Bible*, *Come as You Are*, *O Wow*, *Closer*, and *Becoming Cliterate*. These books are about the biology of female orgasm, and how-to manuals for women not having, but hoping for, orgasms,[25] and there are books that attempt to demystify female genital anatomy itself.[26] *The Pleasure Gap* by Katherine Rowland[27] is explicitly about how and why there is generally less sexual fulfilment for American women than for men. Critics of some of these books argue that while an orgasm is important it's not as important as, let's say, pay equity for most women.[28] Putting aside the important revelation that some women, unlike men, need to be taught how to orgasm and what this means for the necessity of explicit sex education for girls (as I will argue in chapter 8), this critique trivializes the consequences of the sexual double standard when we see the connection with the problem of sexualized violence. If women are tainted by sexual activity and seen as sexual gatekeepers,[29] then we understand how rape has historically been seen as a problem for women and their male guardians, not the male rapists – rape was "a crime against the husband, father, or male guardian of the woman rather than against herself."[30] To this day, women in rape culture are "spoiled" by the act of rape and discounted by the myths of rape and so the crime goes unreported, underreported, and assessed as "unfounded" by many police departments.[31] Women are simply not believed. Or they are blamed for the violence because of what they were wearing, how much they had to drink, and their decisions to engage in any sexual activity at all.[32] The relationship between rape culture and slut-shaming will be explored more fully in chapter 2.

This book deals with the political and philosophical consequences of the sexual double standard and good girl/bad girl binary for all women and especially for "bad girls." What I will argue is that the lack of sexual equity, i.e., orgasm equality and "intimate justice" for women, is a direct result of the continuing sexual double standard, and the good girl/bad girl dichotomy, and that until these two pillars of women's experiences are understood and eliminated women will not have sexual, orgasmic equality.[33] Further, as wonderful as it is that we are getting to a critical mass of authors and scholars writing about the problems of slut-shaming and the need for intimate justice (see all of the authors above), we have to go much deeper in our analysis, showing how and why the sexual double standard and Madonna/whore distinction continues and, more radically yet, showing how the stigma against sex workers and sex work reinforces and helps to create slut-shaming and whorephobia in the first place. Until we end the stigma against sex workers, we won't end slut-shaming or rape culture.

And this puts many people who are interested in social justice issues in a dilemma. It is much easier to condemn sex work as a practice and particularly condemn the clients of sex workers than to look at how our continuing stigma against sex work contributes to the sexual double standard. If the main problem with sex work is the harm to women and children (and no one denies that there is harm done to many people involved in prostitution) then understandably the solution for many feminists is to eradicate prostitution, as it was for me at one time. Antiprostitution activists and radical feminists are clear about this. They don't want to normalize or destigmatize sex work. They want clients to be criminalized and sex workers to be given the resources they need to get out of the trade. What to do with the sex workers who don't want to be rescued is a point of contention because, as we will see, antiprostitution activists believe that these sex workers don't exist or that they are somehow deluded and brainwashed by the sex industry.[34] Prostitution, in this view, is "something which is done to the poorest, most disenfranchised females on the planet, bar a few high-profile exceptions of the 'happy hooker' variety."[35]

The legal and philosophical problems with continued criminalization of sex work will be explored in the second part of this book. In particular, I will outline how I believe the work of antiprostitution activists inadvertently reinforces the stigma against sex workers and the sexual double standard, by reinforcing our stereotypes and stigmas about sex. If we didn't think women are somehow damaged by their (consensual) sexual activity (why else would they become "bad girls" or need to be rescued) or that men are more sexual than women (so that women who are sexually active are seen as deviants and men simply need to control themselves better), then perhaps we wouldn't have a stigma against sexually active women *or* men who go to sex workers. The more we vilify sex work, the more we marginalize those who participate in it. The more we marginalize any group of people, the more we allow abuse and violence to fester. The negative effects of whore stigma will be discussed in chapter 3.

If slut-shaming can only end when whorephobia ends, then we have to end the stigma against the actual whore. Continuing the quest to eliminate sex work by vilifying (and criminalizing) the clients and making victims of the "prostituted" women will not end whore stigma because it continues the separation of women into good and bad categories, as inadvertent as that may be (prostituted women/chaste women being the good girls and voluntary sex workers/sexually active women the bad). The antiprostitution claim that women cannot consent to sex work (because it is inherently exploitative) also fundamentally undermines the bodily autonomy of voluntarily working sex workers. I am not arguing that antiprostitution activists want the women who choose to be sex workers to be harmed. Rather, I am arguing that by actively encouraging the stigma against sex work, these activists are promoting whore stigma. It is not in abolishing sex work, then, that we will end the stigma but in creating conditions for the work to be done with respect and dignity. The escorts I interviewed taught me that what can be done – and should be done – if we want to eliminate the horrendous abuse of some women working in the sex trade is to eliminate whore stigma for all women.

A Note on Methods and the Story of *Selling Sex*

The research for this book has been in the making for at least twenty-five years. While working at a homeless women's shelter in Halifax in the 1980s and 1990s and on a development project in the Philippines on sex tourism from 1995 to 2004, I explored the many negative sides of sex work. My documentary *Hope in Heaven*, about sex tourism in the Philippines, profiled a young bar girl and solidified my standing at the time as an antiprostitution scholar and activist.[36] The film was used by Canada Border Services, the RCMP, and antitrafficking groups to educate people about the horrors of sex trafficking; nothing I had seen at that point had indicated that any good came of prostitution. For most of my research career, I studied survival sex workers[37] who, as the name implies, were working on the streets for food and housing, in Halifax and Toronto, and young bar girls in Angeles City, Philippines, who were hoping to escape poverty by marrying a Western man. So, with these women and girls as my research subjects, I thought choice and empowerment for sex workers was nonexistent.

Hope in Heaven was clear in its emphasis on bar girls as the victims of Western men and concentrated on the issues of social injustice, inequality, and poverty. After the film was broadcast on CBC in 2007, however, I was challenged by sex worker advocacy groups to broaden my focus and look at the positives of sex work and the harms of criminalization. To say I was sceptical is an understatement. My main questions in the original film proposal for my second film on prostitution, *Selling Sex*, had to do with whether or not selling and buying sex are inherently problematic: Is it the financial exchange that makes prostitution a problem? Is it the nature of sex itself? Why is it so gendered? Why do men go to sex workers? What policies have the best outcomes for the sellers of sex? On paper, the intention of the film was to outline the good, bad, and ugly of sex work, but when I'm honest with myself I realize that I really intended only to pursue the bad and the ugly because at the beginning of the process I couldn't see what was good about sex work. What could possibly be the value of sex work?

However, as I met more and more women who chose to do sex work, it was harder and harder to say they were all suffering from false consciousness or were victims of violence. I interviewed approximately thirty sex workers or former sex workers in Las Vegas, New York, New Orleans, Vancouver, Halifax, Toronto, and Amsterdam from 2010 to 2014. Only four sex workers agreed to go on camera for the documentary and those are my primary informants in the film. I recognize that this group of cisgender women is not a representative sample by any means, as all but one were white women, aged twenty-five to fifty-five, all having at least high school educations, some had been to college, and two had advanced degrees. All of the sex workers I interviewed were lower middle-class in their families of origin (though I would describe the four main interviewees now as solidly middle-class because of the incomes generated from their sex work), and three reported being queer or bisexual. I also interviewed Norma Jean Almodovar (better known as the "cop to call girl"), Carol Leigh ("Scarlot Harlot" and the originator of the term "sex work") and Xaviera Hollander (the original "happy hooker") in their capacity as former sex workers and well-known activists. I interviewed three executive directors of antiprostitution organizations, two antiprostitution academic researchers, and one executive director from a (relatively neutral) sex work advocacy group. I interviewed seven pro–sex work researchers, a male sex surrogate and a female sex surrogate/tantric sex teacher, and three male clients, although only one agreed to go on camera. Of the researchers, I have on-camera interviews with Dr Laurie Shrage, Dr Catherine Hakim, Dr Christine Milrod, Dr Tamara O'Doherty, and journalist Melissa Ditmore. I did not interview male sex workers, though their perspectives and experiences will be elaborated through secondary sources for contrast purposes. I did not interview transgender or street-based survival workers for the film, though I have in past projects. Those interviews from my previous research in Halifax in the 1990s and the Philippines in the early 2000s will inform this book[38] but the perspectives of male, transgender, and street-based sex workers will be illustrated mainly through secondary sources.[39] As part of filming, I also did person-on-the-street interviews in Las Vegas and had open discussions with my women's studies and political studies classes in Halifax, one of which was filmed with the students' permission. Those who didn't want to participate sat off to the side and were not on camera or audiotaped. All of the students quoted in this book are from the filmed classes. All participants signed ethics consent forms from the university for interviews and legal clearance forms for the film stating that their image and words could be used in all media forever, i.e., films, books, articles, podcasts, etc. All names of the participants and their representative organizations (if any) were given pseudonyms when the film became a book, except for the five researchers mentioned above.

My Main Characters

I met my main character at a media-training workshop for sex work activists in New York when I started the project in 2010. I was asked by the main organizer to do a session on documentary filmmaking, so I did a ninety-minute introductory class on creating documentaries. The nine cisgender women (there were no male or trans women workers at the session) had been chosen by the organization because they wanted to be advocates for their profession and lobby for the decriminalization of sex work. I met the organizer (who will be profiled below) when she was in Halifax giving a talk sponsored by a local sex worker's advocacy group, and I introduced myself to her after her talk. I mentioned the film I had done on sex tourism in the Philippines, and the new one I was preparing to do on prostitution globally, and she asked if I was willing to talk to women who were not exploited and had a different experience of sex work. Would I like to meet sex workers who are activists and talk about their experiences? I was sceptical but intrigued, and I agreed to come. At the workshop, there was a high-end escort from Las Vegas, a dominatrix from New York, three escorts from the Midwest, a representative from a sex work advocacy group in Washington, DC, two women from California, one working in pornography and one from St James, a well-known sex work advocacy group in San Francisco, and an exotic dancer from New York. The purpose of the weekend was to enhance the women's media skills. As practice, they produced a public service announcement for the organization.

One of the participants was very interested in speaking to me, and I had my first interview with her in New York. She ended up becoming my lead character. I followed her from the workshop in New York to a Desiree Alliance conference in Las Vegas to her hometown as she worked in her local antitrafficking organization and did sex worker advocacy. She had started an online advocacy group and wanted to lobby for the decriminalization of prostitution (and for reproductive rights) in her state. For privacy and safety reasons, as I will explain below (and for all the other participants), I am not using her real name, her working name, or identifying her hometown. I'm calling her Lucy and she comes from a medium-sized town in the Midwest.

Lucy has had many different experiences in sex work, from massage parlours to outcalls to a brief stint in a brothel. She is now an independent escort working from her website. I found her very down to earth, self-confident, and articulate. She told me she considered sex work her calling and that her goal in going to the workshop was to improve her speaking skills so that she could give a talk at her local antitrafficking conference about the *value* of sex work. She wanted to educate people, I will repeat, about the value of sex work – to an audience of antiprostitution activists, missionaries, and law enforcement personnel.[40] Given my experience seeing the hostility between these groups and sex worker advocacy groups I was extremely impressed with her bravery and commitment. I followed her around for almost a year and got to know her well, and we've kept in touch via email since. Over this period her goal didn't change nor did her story. She told me that sex work is something that she loves doing, she has done it for eighteen years without any problems, she has never had any violent clients, and she liked her clients who were mainly regulars.

Lucy started in sex work when she was twenty-two years old. She was then working as a sous chef in a restaurant and had racked up a lot of debt. She wanted a second job and answered an ad for a lingerie model, thinking, naively as she said, that it was just a way for men to see what something would look like on a live model, that they'd then take home to their wives. She went to the little hole in the wall where the interview was being held and immediately knew what was going on:

> Cheap lingerie tacked on the wall, three girls sitting on, like, slip-covered couches watching *Oprah* and smoking cigarettes and over the time it took for the owner to get there to actually interview me, I had this conversation in my head. Cause I sat there for about a half

hour going, okay, I know what this is. Can I do this? And I'm like, I need the money, but beyond that I was also, I was always very open and free with my sexuality so, you know, some might say promiscuous, but I have always enjoyed just exploring my sexuality and so, I'm like, why not get paid for it? I love sex, you know and so by the time he'd gotten there and we'd had our conversation to get hired I was, like, yah I'm going to try it and see what happens. If I don't like it, I can walk away. And so that's what I did. And within less than a year I had my credit card debt paid off, I went to Europe and backpacked in Europe for a month.

Lucy was in and out of sex work in her twenties but kept coming back to it both as a lifestyle and as a way of making money. She had the support of her friends and family who knew what she did, and when I met her she had two homes (one for business purposes), a car, and a big airstream trailer, which she proudly travels around the United States in by herself. Sex work has worked well for her. She pays taxes as an entertainer and has avoided trouble with the law. She is warm and friendly, extroverted, loves her Rottweilers and thought it was very funny that I did not. Lucy believes that most sex workers are just like her, "the silent majority" that "blend[s] in with mainstream America." As she says, "We're minding our own business and we keep out of trouble." Sex workers like Lucy feel they can't publicize what they're doing because it's illegal, so no one hears their positive stories.

I came to admire Lucy in many ways: her body confidence, her sexual confidence, and her ability to connect with people. She believed that sex work was a calling for her. She wanted to change people's view of sex from something that was bad – except, perhaps, under certain conditions like marriage or even love – to an inherent good. She wanted people to recognize the *goods of sex*:[41] until sexuality is valued as a good in and of itself, sex work won't be valued, and women will continue to be caught between Madonna and whore. When women finally start to value sex, she said, they'll want to go to sex workers too. It became a compelling argument for me to think about and dissect. As she shared her stories with me over several months during which she prepared to give her talk on the value of sex work,

I came to see her as a woman who embraced her sexuality in a way most women I know could never imagine. She embodied the positive aspects of sex work, and she saw herself as a service provider and therapist.

Amanda (again all names have been changed) was a friend of Lucy's and was doing her PhD in anthropology at a university in Chicago when I met her. She had been a sex worker in her early twenties until being arrested by two undercover police officers. She said that experience was by far the worst aspect of sex work that she had ever encountered. She and a colleague had worked together and had two customers. They had agreed to switch hotel rooms partway through the encounter and to have sex with both clients. The clients turned out to be undercover police officers and arrested Amanda and her colleague after the services were complete. She said it was the most humiliating moment of her life. Other than those police officers, she didn't remember any bad clients, but she did say that her arrest experience got her into sex work activism. The police officers did not face any consequences for what they had done even though it was illegal in the state where she was working both to have sex for money and for police officers to have sex with prostitutes. She was handcuffed and taken to the police station and made to sit in the main foyer for all to see, shamed and humiliated:

> I mean it is absolutely devastating to get arrested. It's embarrassing, you know they handcuff you, and you have to sit outside exposed to the public … It's a shameful thing and it hurt … I don't think that any prostitute should ever be arrested, but since prostitution is illegal, it is understandable for me when, you know, we make the deal and you arrest me. You don't get to have sex and arrest me. That's such a violation, such a violation of my human rights.

Amanda got into sex work, like Lucy, in a roundabout (and some might say, fraudulent) way. She answered an ad for a dancer, as Lucy had for lingerie models, but, as she states, "it turned out to be for more than dancing." The position was actually for sex work but because of its illegality it couldn't be advertised as such. She had been very sexually active as a young woman and was having a lot of anonymous sex anyway, so when she realized she could get paid for sex she would have been having anyway, she was thrilled.

Amanda got out of the business after being arrested and went back to school, but she felt that what she had been doing had value for herself and her customers and told me she would work again if it were legal.

Maria was doing her PhD in religious studies when I met her, and she wanted to tell me her story after hearing me speak at a conference and hearing that many people think all prostitution is violence against women. That had not been her reality and she wanted to tell me about her positive experiences. She had worked as an escort in Los Angeles, putting her ads in the back pages of newspapers and magazines. She specialized in disabled men and felt that she was part of a helping profession. She only got out of the business when she realized that her life would be ruined if she were arrested. Prostitution wasn't the problem for her; the criminal justice system was. As she said, if it was legal she'd still be doing it. She also had a very "healthy sexuality," as she put it, and enjoyed having sex with "strange men" – men she didn't know initially or have a relationship with. She couldn't understand why people thought this was so strange. She was married and her husband knew that she had worked as an escort. She said her family tried to make her ashamed of what she had done but she wasn't.

> I was very religious. I went to Catholic School until I was in ninth grade and my Catholic education was very important to me ... It instilled in me a lot of values that I believe I brought into my sex work. But at the same time, there were certain understandings of sexuality or sexual repression that were also part of my Catholic education and when I was fourteen years of age and had my first sexual experience, I felt, "this is so beautiful, how can it be wrong?" And so, I don't say I left the church entirely but I started questioning the church more and trying to understand why would this be wrong? [Sex] should be celebrated in and of itself.

Anna's story is different again, and she is an example of someone who has worked both on the streets and as an online escort. She started out on the streets of Vancouver's infamous Downtown Eastside as a teenager, and although she had some close calls she was not harmed, physically. She worked for housing and to put herself through school, not for drugs, which she says is the real killer on the streets. She regrets her time on the street and would never do it again. "It was a bad idea because it was unhealthy and really, really, like unrewindable things could have happened, right? So that's what makes it a bad idea." After finishing university, she found work in the United States and began supplementing her income with online sex work. She says the experiences were completely different and emphatically states, "prostitution wasn't the problem; the circumstances were the problem." The second time around she made more money, had more control over clients, and her time was her own. She thinks sex work is a job like any other, and she volunteers at a sex worker rights group, advocating for the health and safety of sex workers. She believes prohibitionists[42] are well intentioned, but they do nothing to help sex workers since their goal is to keep the work illegal and stigmatized in hopes it will be eradicated. As she says, "even those who are having a terrible time of it don't want the men criminalized. They want money and if they don't have sex work, what will they do then?" She did sex work solely for the money and as a means to an end. She currently works for the New York State government and is married with two small children.

Getting to know these women (and the many others I interviewed who are not in the film) made me confront my own biases about sex work and sex workers. I came to admire their honesty, confidence, and openness. They were kind and funny, and saw the humanity of their clients and the good intentions of antitraffickers trying to save them, even when it was clear they didn't want or need to be saved. In fact, in the documentary, I chose to take out the interviews with the antiprostitution activists and scholars entirely because they came across so badly compared to the escorts. It would have seemed as if I was making fun of them – juxtaposing their comments about how all prostitution is violence against women and a human rights violation with the escorts' comments that they liked having sex with strange men. Or when antiprostitution interviewees claimed that disabled people just shouldn't ever have sex if it meant paying someone, even if that someone was willing and able to provide. The comments came across as inflexible, ableist, and (frankly) mean. Next to the compassion of the women who specialized in disabled men, I felt the comments had to be removed. The need to do justice to both sides became impossible, so in the film I became the stand-in for the antiprostitution side both to explore the issues and come to terms with my own ambivalence about telling the story. I became a character in the film, exploring the two sides and showing how I came to understand the connection between sex work and women's sexual autonomy.

I conducted the interviews between 2010 and 2014, spending a year following the main character and getting to know her, but even after all that time with these women I didn't want to believe what the interviews were telling me. I delayed the film for several years because I couldn't accept what they were saying: that their problems weren't related to the work they were doing; their problems arose because of criminalization, the stigma of the job, and the beliefs of others, like myself, "who thought they couldn't possibly be doing this work and enjoying the work," as one of the interviewees put it to me. The film was finished in 2016 and premiered at two film festivals. As the film was being prepared for broadcast, I got an email from Lucy.

Film to Book

Although Lucy enthusiastically agreed to go on camera and I developed the whole documentary around her, she was so harassed after she came out as a sex worker that she subsequently did not want anything to do with sex work activism. The harassment, as I will detail in chapter 3, was not from a client but from someone who had found her online sites and took it upon himself to shame her for what she did for work. She was able to get a restraining order against him but not before he set a small fire in her garage and stalked her. She shut down her websites and stopped doing any sex work activism. I had sent her a rough cut of the film in 2015 for her review and told her about the film festivals. When I sent her the final film for broadcast in 2016, she sent me an email saying she was no longer involved in activism and asked me to take out anything that would identify her in the film. Because she was the main character that was impossible and though she said she understood and it was her fault for agreeing to it in the first place, I could not in good conscience go through with broadcasting the film even though, as she pointed out, she knew she had signed legal clearances (as had all others in the film) for me to use her image.

I decided to turn the film into a book because I still thought I had a valuable tale to tell about sex work and women's sexuality, I had hundreds of pages of transcripts, and I could mask everyone's identity in a book – sex workers and prohibitionists. If I couldn't show it visually, then I could expand what was a forty-eight-minute broadcast-hour documentary into this book, elaborating on all the themes just touched on in the film (as I had after *Hope in Heaven* came out in 2007 and my co-author and I wrote *Reluctant Bedfellows* in 2009). I also thought the dilemma of the now-aborted film (of sex workers "coming out" and getting threatened) made a perfect case for why these stories are so necessary. Because sex workers are marginalized and criminalized worldwide, it is very difficult for them to come forward to tell their stories, though some bravely have.[43] As Lucy puts it, "Because of the stigma of it, of course we're also not allowed to talk about it. So even for those of us that have a great working experience and find empowerment and fulfillment through sex work, there's not a lot of opportunities or outlets for us to talk about that publicly with people that are not involved in sex work itself and talk about that honestly. And so no one hears those stories." I am telling their stories and the story of how I came to understand sex work as connected to the control of women's sexuality in a way that, hopefully, does not further damage these women's lives or bring unintended consequences upon them.

But because of the stigma faced by sex workers, many people simply won't believe their experiences. As the executive director of an anti-child-exploitation group in Canada said to me, "The buying of a body is a human rights violation ... even if they [the women] don't see it that way and are involved in this in a fashion where they don't see they're being victimized, the reality is at the end of their life when they're getting more mature, they will see themselves clearly as a victim or start victimizing others in order to live." She firmly believed that women involved in prostitution don't know their own interests or have been taken in by the patriarchy and sex/porn industry.

I, however, will argue that it is difficult to meet these women and hear their stories (either in person or via the film and hopefully this book) and not come away from the encounter changed in some way. (Thus, several antiprostitution scholars who saw the film as a rough cut said it was "dangerous.") The women I interviewed convincingly argued that they chose sex work over other types of work and that they did not feel exploited, degraded, or desperate. Rather, they led me to look at sex work from an empowerment perspective. Can a person buy or sell sex with dignity, integrity, and respect for the other? These women certainly seemed to. Not only did they enjoy the money that came with sex work, but they, more controversially, actually enjoyed the work itself.[44] They were advocates of female sexuality, pleasure, and sex positivity, even as they worked in the sex trade. I came to the conclusion that for some women in some circumstances, sex work is a viable, lucrative work option, and an expression of their sexuality. That's the short version of a very long transition and one I write about in this book.

Sex Work to Rape Culture

Rather than concentrate on the bad experiences of women in sex work, which I have done in the past, I talked to almost thirty women who have had good experiences with sex work and began asking different questions. What can these stories tell us about what makes a good sex work experience? What do these experiences tell us about what can be done about bad sex work practices? What makes a good customer? How can sex work be done with respect and dignity? What are the linkages between seeing women as victims and the control of women's sexuality? Why is the idea of women enjoying sex for money so disgusting for so many people? Why is stigma against sex workers so prevalent and how do we overcome that stigma? Starting from the perspectives of women selling sex as a career (Lucy as I mentioned calls sex work her calling) tells us about the ways it can be done with safety, respect, and dignity. And knowing the optimal conditions for sex work can help make the life and work of more marginalized sex workers better too, as the women I interviewed always pointed out.

I am not arguing that sex work is easy work or that sex workers do not face huge problems in this whorephobic world. I am not arguing that all clients are good or that pimps don't exist or that exploitation in the industry doesn't exist. It does. And these conditions do tremendous harm to some women. But by ignoring the experiences of those who have chosen sex work and believe that selling sex has been a good experience for them, we are not able to sort out what makes sex work a better (or worse) job than a minimum wage job, for instance. We are not able to figure out what conditions would make sex workers safer or how the stigma and criminalization of the work is a real problem for many women working in the sex trade. And we won't understand how the negative treatment of women selling sex affects all women.

What are the unintended consequences of continuing to stigmatize sex workers? I will argue this specific stigma reinforces the deep-seated stigma about sexually active women generally and allows men *and* women to police women's sexuality with impunity (see Leora Tanenbaum's work for wonderful examples of women slut-shaming other women and monitoring their behaviour). As I say at the end of the film (spoiler alert!), I'm amazed that I didn't recognize the misogyny behind restricting women's sexual autonomy and the choice to be sex workers because I really didn't understand the connection between slut-shaming and whore stigma.

Weaving in history, pop culture, interviews, archival research, newspaper accounts, and anecdotes from person-on-the-street interviews, student discussions, and personal reflections, this book will look at the origins of rape culture and the damaging ways it is reinforced through slut-shaming and whorephobia. How does slut-shaming control women's behaviour and lead to treating bad girls badly? How and why does whorephobia negatively affect the lives of girls and women? In popular culture, in daily news items we see this whorephobia at work. Whether it is an explicit article about a serial killer targeting sex workers because of their vulnerability or a cyberbullying account of yet another young woman who was slut-shamed to the point she commits suicide, the effects of whorephobia and slut-shaming are all around us.

Outline of the Chapters

The chapters that follow will show the connection between sex work and whorephobia, the slut-shaming that we see on college campuses today and in the mainstream media, the cyberbullying around women's sexuality, and the #MeToo movement response. In part 1, I examine the unfinished sexual revolution for women as an "unrealized ideal" (as a reviewer said in response to the book), and connect the issues of women's sexual pleasure, slut-shaming, bad girl stigma, and good girl privilege.

Chapter 2 describes the contemporary problem of slut-shaming and shows how the sexual double standard maintains the longstanding Madonna/whore dichotomy for all women (boys are never sluts and there is no equivalent negative language about "promiscuous" men). I show the negative effects of the double standard on women and girls, particularly on young women who have been labelled sluts through sexualized violence directed at them. Why is the stigma placed on the young women and not on the men who have raped or slut-shamed them? Why are women blamed for the violence against them? I examine the concept of rape culture (and the corresponding rape myths) and explain the advantages and disadvantages of good girl privilege. I begin the discussion of how and why the sexual revolution of the 1960s is unfinished for women.

Chapter 3 explains the origins of bad girl stigma and good girl privilege and how they both function, even today in our sexualized culture. I show how the stigma of sexually active women has changed over time and how it is still used to police all women. This chapter includes the history of sex work, the origins of the stigma against sex workers, and the related history of the Madonna/whore dichotomy. I demonstrate how the concept of a sexual double standard is racialized and varies according to class and show how the stigma around sex work and sexual double standards affect women and girls who are *not* sex workers.

In part 2 I examine the perceived problems of sex work through the eyes of the women I interviewed to see if sex work is as irredeemable as some antiprostitution activists claim. I look at why the issue of women's sexual pleasure particularly in commercialized sex is such a problem for many people. Does sex work have value in society as the women I interviewed maintained? Can destigmatizing sex work undermine the sexual double standard? I consider three aspects of sex work that are problematized by prohibitionists: the role and implications of money, men, and morality. I present antiprostitution arguments as they relate to these three issues and outline the responses of sex workers I interviewed.

Specifically, chapter 4 takes on the problem of money in commercialized sex and the dilemma of sex work as work. I examine the issues of class, capitalism, low wage work, and the shame of "dirty work" to show how choice and agency are manifested for the women interviewed. I explain the philosophical debates around sex work and explore the potential value of sex work. Chapter 5 looks at the critical question of male power and abuse within sex work. I address the issues of male entitlement and violence and, crucially, how the women I interviewed were able to work in safety. I look at the motivations and characteristics of the buyers of sex and profile a long-time client of Lucy's. Chapter 6 argues that the sex problem is in reality a morality issue (distinguishing between "good sex" and "bad sex" and criminalizing paid sex as "bad sex") and shows how the continuing double standard of male and female sexuality is the most likely cause of the ongoing stigma around sex work. Rather than being victimized by their sex work, the women I interviewed enjoyed the work and viewed sex work as an economic and lifestyle issue. Their enjoyment of the work was a big part of why they did sex work, as difficult as that is to believe for many people because of the victim narrative prevalent today in terms of sex work.[45]

In part 3, I look at what remains to be done to achieve sexual equity for women. Chapter 7 looks at the need to decriminalize sex work. Ensuring that women are not criminalized or working in a criminalized environment is the first step towards ensuring their health and safety and better working conditions. I look at the arguments for and against the Nordic model (where the buyers, not sellers, of sex are criminalized) and show how the continuing criminalization of sex work negatively affects sex workers. I argue that the Nordic model, in fact, reinforces whore stigma by reinforcing the idea that women are dirtied and degraded by sex. Chapter 8 looks at orgasm (in)equality and the need to destigmatize sex. In order to end slut-shaming we have to end whore stigma because in order to eliminate the sexual double standard we have to eliminate the stigma against women and sex, generally. There is a deep-seated bias against sexually active women that is unlikely to disappear in my lifetime, and part of the challenge is to end "good girl privilege." In this last chapter, I outline in more detail what I learned from escorts about what needs to happen in terms of freeing women's sexuality. They were all convinced that "orgasm equality" is the final frontier in the struggle for women's rights by celebrating female sexuality, particularly female pleasure, encouraging women to embrace their sexuality, and by eliminating the traditional Madonna/whore dichotomy and the sexual double standards between men and women. I argue that to have sexual equity between women and men, society needs to eliminate the main barriers to women's pleasure: socialization to be good girls, lack of explicit sexual education, sexual stigma, and shame of the body.

Slut-Shaming, Whorephobia, and the Unfinished Sexual Revolution outlines what needs to be done for the next sexual revolution for women. I show the connections between the sexual double standard, the criminalization of sex work, and the controlling of all women's sexuality; the connections between whorephobia and slut-shaming that explain violence against sex workers and why the public is reluctant to see it as a human rights issue. I look at the contempt for women's sexuality in general and the stigma associated with women who are ironically "free" with their sexuality, like sex workers, and the consequences for those of us with good girl privilege. In the end, I want to be able to answer what I see as the fundamental question: is it in *eliminating* sex work that we will help women be free from sexual stigma, exploitation, and abuse or is it in *destigmatizing* sex work and *normalizing* pleasurable sex for women that will help eliminate exploitation and abuse by ending slut-shaming and whore stigma? As the women I interviewed taught me and as I hope to show in this book, the disgust, fear, and anger surrounding the issue of sex work says a tremendous amount about our disgust, fear, and anger about female sexuality in general.

Chapter Two

Sexual Double Standards and the Unfinished Sexual Revolution

Many women (and girls) in North America will probably remember the first time they were called a slut or heard the word used against another woman and the shaming, negative effect of the word – Peggy Orenstein claims that virtually every young woman she interviewed had been called a slut at some point.[1] My first encounter with the words slut, whore, and cunt (all on the same day!) was as a young tween almost forty years ago at a movie theatre. The film was *Saturday Night Fever* and I went to see it with my father and best (male) friend because it was R rated and we were too young to get in without an adult (turns out, given the subject matter, we were too young to see it, period). At any rate, I'm sure my poor father had no idea what it was about and only expected a cool dance movie. It was excruciatingly embarrassing (I'd actually use the word horrifying) for several reasons I understood only many years later when I watched the film as an adult. The movie is a perfect example of how people discard a woman's respect and dignity, literally making her a throwaway woman, because of having sex. The John Travolta character (Tony) has a friend, Annette (who clearly wants to be more than friends with Tony), and he tells her, emphatically, that girls have to choose between being a nice girl and a whore. When Annette asks why she can't be both, Tony replies, "You can't be both. I mean that's the thing a girl's gotta decide early on. You gotta decide whether you're gonna be a nice girl or a cunt." For him it was clear that girls have to decide which they'll be so boys will know how to treat them, i.e., with or without respect. And when later in the movie, Annette has sex with two of his friends in the back seat of the car, partly to fit in and be cool and make him jealous (even then I knew there was a blurred line of consent when the second friend thinks he can just have sex with her too – while she's crying!), Tony says sadly to Annette words to the effect of, so now you're (just) a cunt. Now, you're not a nice girl and now we know how to treat you, i.e., badly like the slut you are. Because you see, the sexual double standard and the Madonna/whore view of women gives men (and other women) licence to treat sluts (or perceived sluts) badly. The "good" girl of the movie gets Tony, wins the big dance competition with him, is treated with respect by Tony and his friends, and lives happily ever after in her new loft in Manhattan.[2] So while most people remember *Saturday Night Fever* as a dance movie with great Bee Gees disco music, I remember it for the cautionary tale about poor Annette. "You a nice girl or a cunt?" became a touchstone for me without me even knowing it. I clearly did not want to be a c-word with all the horrors that came with it, and without consciously making that decision, I became a classic good girl.[3]

Slut-Shaming and the Sexual Double Standard

The power of the slut condemnation and the continuing sexual double standard is still with us today forty years after that movie came out. Well after the sexual revolution, women still have to choose some version of "nice girl/prude" or "bad girl/slut" because, as Tony so bluntly stated, you can't be both. Choosing which you'll be gives men, and other women, cues as to how to treat you, i.e., with or without respect. This contradiction is wonderfully captured in both Peggy Orenstein's *Girls and Sex* and Leora Tanenbaum's *I Am Not a Slut*: girls are perpetually caught between being "prudes" and socially irrelevant, and being "sluts" and socially ostracized. That boys never have to make this choice is a defining characteristic of the sexual double standard. Men and boys are perceived as naturally more sexual than women and girls, and male heterosexual appetite is not problematized. There are no pejorative equivalent words for male slut or whore. The words are uniquely applied to females.

Leora Tanenbaum first started exploring the nature of slut-shaming twenty years ago in her 2000 book *Slut!* She wrote about the reasons for it and how to solve it but if anything, as she writes in her updated version in 2015, the problem has become worse in the years that have passed with the rise of social media and cyberbullying.[4] Orenstein[5] agrees, writing that the sexual double standard is alive and well, even as it has adapted to twenty-first-century technology and social media. Everyone she interviewed knew that a boy who had sex with multiple girls in a week would be congratulated and seen as a player. A girl who did the same thing would be a slut and severely punished.

Educating people about slut-shaming has not prevented it from happening. Being more aware hasn't stopped it. Many sex education classes now include consent issues in the curriculum. So why is it still okay for a boy to have multiple sex partners and not okay for girls? Why are girls slut-shamed to the point of suicide for behaviour that is high-fived in boys? Why are they vilified and the boys are not? The double standard has morphed a little over the last twenty years. Virginity and purity aren't the same ideals for most young women today and in fact for some teens virginity is now equated with being a prude. Orenstein wonders if the double standard is actually worse because now it's not just about being a good girl; it's become worse to be a virgin than a slut because then you're "too ugly to fuck." But the stigma of the slut hasn't disappeared.

I often ask my students if they think there is still a sexual double standard, thinking that surely things have changed since my day and the overt good girl/bad girl dilemma of Annette. They all know what I am talking about and have all experienced examples of the double standard from friends, family, and boyfriends. Says Lori, "I think [it] is just the whole double-standard stereotype like men aren't worried about, 'oh no my girlfriends, everyone's going to think I'm a slut,' but girls are always worried about that. Like they don't want to have a bad reputation or anything." Most of them believed they were socialized to want to be good girls and to police other girls' behaviour. Says Jane, "women are conditioned to kind of conceal that, their sexual side, you know, 'they're a bad girl or they're not [respectable]' so it's different because you're not as free to express that."

The students also confirmed what Orenstein calls the "sexiness" factor: girls are supposed to be sexy and look hot, but that doesn't mean they should actually act out their sexuality. Looking good is more important than how they feel because their sexual pleasure is secondary to the boy's pleasure.

Says Kyla, "I mean the girls tend to dress more provocative just for that role, but they're not actually going through [with] the act. I mean if a girl sleeps with a bunch of guys last weekend and tells her girlfriends, that's not acceptable. And if a guy does it, then he's a stud." Says Alison, "I think there's almost like a mainstreaming of wanting women to look like prostitutes because you even have Christian Louboutins – I believe the red soles on the shoe has some significance with French prostitutes. And there is almost a pressure to dress a little more provocatively but I don't think women still want to be viewed as a slut, so it's a weird mix." A weird mix indeed.

Slut-shaming and cyberbullying have become the twenty-first-century way to punish and control women's sexuality. The girls interviewed by both Orenstein and Tanenbaum face the consequences of trying to be sexual and good girls at the same time: facing the double bind of being sexually active and slut-shamed simultaneously. They don't want to use contraception because that will mean they are prepared for sexual activity and therefore they are sluts. The young women can't imagine sex without being drunk so that the sex can be seen as spontaneous and not planned, i.e., so that they're not sluts. But unplanned sex can be dangerous sex – with risks of both STIs and pregnancy – in addition to the concerns of blurry consent between people having sex while drunk.[6]

The young women Orenstein and Tanenbaum interviewed are not imagining that they'll be targeted as sluts for using contraception or being prepared for sex. The conservative radio host Rush Limbaugh infamously called a university student a prostitute because she wanted birth control paid for by her insurance plan: "What I said yesterday about Susan Fluke, or Sandra Fluke, whatever her name is, the Georgetown student who went before a congressional committee and said she's having so much sex she's going broke buying contraceptives ... if we're paying for this it makes these women sluts, prostitutes, now what else could it be?"[7] Hello, misogyny?

In this age of social media and smartphones, slut-shaming has become much more visible. Revenge porn, distribution of unauthorized images of naked girls and women, hacking celebrities' photos and then using them to shame the victims is more and more common and is another way to shame women and make them feel badly about themselves. Or force them to resign from high profile positions. Thirty-six years after Vanessa Williams (the first African American Miss America in history) had to give up the title of Miss America when nude photos of her were published, Congresswoman Katie Hill had to resign after her ex-husband released nude photos of her and disclosed an affair.[8] The resulting online slut-shaming really makes one wonder if any positive changes have happened in almost four decades.

Sexting is common amongst teenagers, but the negative effects are solely on the girls. As Tanenbaum has shown, men and boys sext pictures of their private parts not because they think women are going to be physically aroused by their penis pictures but mainly as a form of harassment. They often bully women and girls to send them intimate pictures in return. It's not just teenagers, unfortunately. Anthony Weiner, the former Democratic congressman, pled guilty in 2018 to sexting with a teenage girl and acknowledged he had a problem that has cost him his job and marriage.[9]

Most concerning, as many of the respondents in Orenstein and Tanenbaum's books state, is the idea that once you've had sex with someone it's like you can't say no again. You lose your ability to say no to anyone. You become a slut. And sluts deserve punishment. As Kate Harding puts it sarcastically, it's as if people in rape culture believe that "once your vagina is open for business, it's not like having a penis in there is anything new or shocking,"[10] so what's the big deal anyway. Women's right to bodily autonomy is not always assumed, to put it mildly. There have been numerous examples in North America of slut-shaming severe enough to drive girls to suicide: Rehtaeh Parsons, Amanda Todd, Felicia Garcia, Audrie Post, and Cherice Moralez.[11] These girls were ridiculed and humiliated by people they believed to be friends when photos of the incidents in which they were involved were circulated via social media. They were blamed for the abuse and notoriety: You went to his house. You were drunk. You were dressed like a slut. What did you think was going to happen? The blame is put on the victim, not the rapist – the signature effect of rape culture.

Victim blaming is prevalent generally in our culture. Our so-called "lizard brains"[12] are primed to take in bad news more readily than good in order to find out what happened and figure out what we might be able to do to prevent it from happening to us; our "imaginations tend to fill in uncertainty with worst-case scenarios."[13] What did they do wrong? How did they bring this upon themselves? Why were they out so late? Why were they drinking so much? We can make ourselves feel better by saying to ourselves, that's not going to happen to me because I don't get that drunk, I don't go out that late by myself, I don't do whatever – fill in the blank. In this way, we can feel that we're bringing some order to a chaotic world and that gives us "psychological comfort."[14] But in a sexist, patriarchal world, unless you're the "good victim" you're asking for trouble.[15]

Even progressives can be caught up in victim blaming. In 2020, twenty-two women successfully won a lawsuit against a porn website based in San Diego and were awarded $12.7 million for being victims of fraud and co-ercion. "Some of the women testified that although they agreed to perform sex on camera to earn money, including paying for college, the subsequent publicity ruined their lives and careers. At least one considered suicide ... the women alleged, they were victims of an orchestrated system of harass-ment, threats and public humiliation by defendants who made sure friends, family, college and work colleagues saw the online films."[16] An acquaintance in Los Angeles was incensed that these women got any money "for being stupid" as she said (echoing the brutal online comments I saw). The women agreed to have sex on camera for money and they should have known the films would be put online. There was no sympathy whatsoever for the fraud or for the threats or humiliation, no curiosity that the men in the films were not targeted for harassment or slut-shamed because of their participation, no empathy for the women at all because of their stupidity in making the films in the first place. The problem, of course, goes beyond a lack of em-pathy. Victim blaming is a crucial component of rape myths, which come from the sexual double standard.

Rape Culture and Rape Myths

Rape myths are ideas about women and sexual assault that have been ac-cepted by media, courts, and the general public, ideas suggesting that women are to be blamed for their own sexual assaults and which can dis-credit women in court. Shannon Sampert argues that she found six main rape myths in media coverage of sexual assaults:[17] women lie about being assaulted (when the statistics say less than 4 per cent are falsely reported); it is the victim's behaviour that led to the rape (victim blaming of the sort already mentioned re why did she go to his house?); men can't control themselves (using a biological argument that men just can't stop themselves once things get going); "good" men don't rape (this one was very common and insidious – the idea that good family men or talented young athletes couldn't possibly have committed rape – and furthers the claim that women are lying. These [good men don't rape] articles also showed more sympathy for the men or boys who were accused of rape than the victims; i.e., why is she trying to ruin this poor boy's life?); perpetrators are viewed as Others (focus on immigrants or men of colour as the perpetrators); and, more recently, perpetrators are increasingly female (making use of titillating stories of sex between young female teachers and their underage students when we know that perpetrators are overwhelmingly male).

Kate Harding uses a similar group of seven beliefs that signify rape culture: "she asked for it; it wasn't really rape; he didn't mean to; she wanted it; she lied; rape is a trivial event; rape is a deviant event."[18] She counters all of the rape myths – myth-busting she calls it but summarizes the underlying problem as follows: "As long as our image of a 'real' rape victim is still a naïve, sexually inexperienced, able-bodied, middle-class white woman conked over the head and dragged into an alley by a large, gun-wielding, brown man, other types of people who report rapes are at risk ... of being humiliated and degraded."[19] Examples of these assumptions are not hard to come by.[20] In 2019, a judge in New York excused an accused rapist because he came from a "good" family (and because it wasn't "traditional rape," as the judge put it, since she was drunk) even though the accused sexually assaulted a drunk girl, recorded it on his phone, and sent it out to his friends with the caption, "when your first time is rape." Echoing Harding's argument, the article points out yet another problem with the judicial system: its history of treating "privileged white kids with leniency while coming down hard on poor minority offenders."[21]

What these six (or seven) rape myths do is instil in the general public the ideas that rape is less of a problem than it is, that women can't be believed, and only bad, "othered" men rape. They play an important role in the appalling statistics about conviction rates for sexual assault in Canada and lead to more victim blaming.[22] The sexual double standard in fact encourages victim blaming because at the heart of rape culture is the idea that women are the sexual gatekeepers and are responsible for controlling whether sexual interactions happen or not.[23] "In a rape culture, girls are supposed to be the pure ones, the responsible ones, the ones putting the brakes on all adolescent sexual overtures, regardless of their own desires."[24] If women are not successful in repelling men's advances, then that is their fault, too, in this twisted logic.

Another problem is what assumptions we make when we victim blame. "If the real crime of rape is the violation of another person's autonomy, the use of another person's body against their wishes, then it shouldn't matter what the victim was wearing, if she was drinking, how much sexual experience she's had before"[25] because it's not about sex, it's about power. "But if the real crime of rape is sullying a pure woman with the filth and sin of sex – making her 'damaged goods' in the eyes of other men – then of course it matters whether she was a virgin, and what kind of situations she willingly 'put herself' in … What matters is that she displayed a clear pattern, in both her everyday behavior and her reaction to a man overpowering her, of not wanting sex. Not ever, from anyone."[26]

Being blamed and shamed (for being in a bar, for wearing a low-cut top and miniskirt, for getting drunk) means being blamed for the violence against you, the victim. It's a no win. No matter how "good" you are you can always do something you shouldn't and then you are blamed. As Lindy West writes, "This is how society has always functioned. Stay indoors, women. Stay safe. Stay quiet."[27] No wonder women join abstinence groups, wanting to be good girls, thinking this will protect them.[28] Women see how bad girls are treated in the media, by their peers, and by society and want to avoid being humiliated and shamed for their sexual conduct. Sexual violence itself works as a threat to women and acts to control their behaviour out of fear of becoming a victim, as Susan Brownmiller pointed out back in 1975.

Jessica Valenti has vividly illustrated this good girl/bad girl connection in her book on the United States' obsession with virginity and its negative effects on young women. In *The Purity Myth*, Valenti describes the cult of virginity in America and shows how it reinforces the sexual double standard between men and women. By ascribing a crisis to the rise of hookup culture and the purported negative effects on young women's sexuality, conservative organizations in the United States are trying to roll back the clock on traditional gender roles. By promoting abstinence education and purity balls, modesty, and "saving" yourself for marriage, Valenti argues, appeals to a 1950s moral and gender code only reinscribe the good girl/bad girl dichotomy and continue the slut-shaming that has become so prevalent in the conservative backlash of the 1990s and 2000s. Using truly appalling examples of men controlling their daughters' sexuality until they can transfer them to their husbands (the meaning, after all, behind fathers "giving away" their daughter to the new husband at marriage), she documents the linkages between purity balls and virginity pledges, abstinence-only education and teen pregnancies. The United States still has the highest rate of teen pregnancy in the Western world. Other disturbing examples of the purity myth and "virginity fetishism" include remarks by a politician about the circumstances under which he would grant abortion rights to a woman: she would have to be a virgin, saving herself for her husband, and violently raped by a stranger.[29] This is an extreme example of the good girl/bad girl dilemma, but Valenti argues that it keeps women in line with the fear of becoming a bad girl such that even other women fear and disassociate from bad girls. She argues that the "fear of becoming that 'impure'" woman means that some "women work hard to present themselves as 'pure'... If they can paint other women as 'impure,' then they're safe from criticism."[30] Good girls think they're protected and police themselves in order to continue being good girls, but the good girl/bad girl dilemma is a trap. The sexual double standard means that men and women are held to different sexual standards and slut-shaming results. This leads to the dichotomy between good girls and bad, in the futile attempt of good girls to distance themselves from bad girls and protect themselves. The sexual double standard may be between men and women but the good girl/bad girl binary works against women themselves. While Valenti doesn't label this dilemma, what she is describing is the contradictions of good girl privilege.

"When I Became a Sex Worker, I Gave Up My Good Girl Privilege"

I hadn't seen the term "good girl privilege" until I saw this tweet in late 2019 from Veronica Valenta, a former sex worker and now attorney in the United States. When I went looking for academic references for the term (as opposed to the usual good girl/bad girl binary), what I found were mainly references in feminist blog posts and websites – about critiques of celebrity feminists like singer Taylor Swift, model Emily Ratajkowski, and NBA star Steph Curry's wife Ayesha. The term was used to show how these women benefited from "being appealing and palatable to men" and how they used "the myth of the 'classy' woman's superiority" to judge other women, thereby reinforcing the good girl/bad girl division.[31] Good girl privilege in these examples was accepting patriarchal messaging that says that certain women deserve respect and others don't based on what they wear or how they comport themselves.[32] For example, in a positive response to a Twitter post by Ayesha Curry, a woman agreed with Curry's statement, "Everyone's into barely wearing clothes these days huh? Not my style. I like to keep the good stuff covered up for the one who matters" by writing, "Modesty is always respected, and you receive the respect that you deserve by dressing modest." The blog poster Candice Benbow objected strongly to Curry's original post, writing that Curry had "leaned right back into her pretty good girl privilege" as a light-skinned, successful Black woman married to a wealthy Black man, and "held up as the epitome of young Black Christian womanhood."[33] In Benbow's analysis, given her role as an influencer, Curry's message was dangerous to other Black women like herself because "Black men consistently hold her up as the kind of woman, wife and mother other Black women should be."[34]

The phrase "good girl privilege" named the missing link for me in what I had been writing about for years – the problems of slut-shaming and whorephobia, of the sexual double standard and the Madonna/whore binary. By identifying the privilege of the "good girl," I could connect the dots between all of these seemingly disparate terms by seeing it as the counterpoint to bad girl stigma – there's a reason good girls want to be good or be seen as good. Good girl privilege both benefits and hinders those who have it (unlike other privileges like white, male, heterosexual, middle-class, able-bodied, or cisgender privilege where there is little to no downside to the holders of the privilege themselves) and challenges us to think about the problems for those who don't have it and why.

Some women benefit from good girl privilege by receiving respect and protection for being good girls, as Valenti has demonstrated in her work. They are treated well by men and authority figures when they conform to being a good girl and the privilege is usually invisible to them, as it is with most privilege. Good girls actually end up policing themselves in hopes of retaining the respect and protection. "Patriarchal cultures must work to suppress and limit women's bodies by policing women's comportment, sartorial choices, movement in public spaces and participation in political life and the generation of meaning. This patriarchal delimitation includes the reduction of women's sexual agency within discourses framed around fear, violence and safety."[35]

Good girl privilege is highly correlated with class and race privilege as Sojourner Truth pointed out in 1851: "That man over there says that women need to be helped into carriages and lifted over ditches and to have the best place everywhere. Nobody ever helped me into carriages or over mud puddles, or give me any best place, and ain't I a woman?"[36] As her words demonstrate, white, middle-class women were seen by white, middle-class men as delicate flowers who needed protection, and men used this justification to avoid giving women the vote – Truth spoke the famous words at a women's rights convention. Her words speak directly to the issue of intersectionality – the white men did not consider her a woman, seeing only her Blackness – but also to the double bind of being good. Women are only "protected" if they play the part and behave themselves, which is the main problem with good girl "privilege": it is a convenient and highly effective way for schools, religions, families, and men to control girls' behaviour – for the benefit of the schools, religions, families, and men.

The pressures to be a good girl and the level of societal coercion that goes into making good girls are impressive. Greer Litton Fox developed her theory of how "good girl" status is used to control women back in 1977. She doesn't use the word privilege because for her being a good girl is mainly negative. According to Fox, the good girl is "chaste, gentle, gracious, ingenuous, good, clean, kind, virtuous, noncontroversial, and above suspicion and reproach,"[37] and it takes a lot of overt and subtle effort by societies as a whole to ensure these characteristics. She argues that there are three ways that societies have controlled women and helped to make them good girls: confinement, protection, and "normative restriction."[38]

The first two categories are less common today in the West but still occur. Confinement means to restrict women's movement in various ways, and protection is about the need to chaperone women when they are out in public. This is mainly because of a cross-cultural fixation on virginity and purity, female obedience, and control of women's sexuality.[39] Most cultures have had restrictions on women's sexuality to some extent or another. Physical restraints like chastity belts in the Middle Ages or foot binding in China (abolished in 1911) had the effect of confining and restricting women's movement and behaviour. Clitoridectomy (more commonly called female genital mutilation/cutting – FGM/C) was (and still is in some countries) another way to restrict women's sexual pleasure and freedom. By removing the clitoris itself, women lost their ability to feel sexual pleasure and with it much of the potential incentive to stray outside the marital relation.[40] Not satisfied with physical restraints, men and society in general restricted women's minds with religion and culture, shaming women's sexuality and bodily functions as bad, and separating women into categories based on marital and virginal status. Women became the gatekeepers of male sexuality, and family honour became tied to female chastity.[41] As Valerie Hudson et al. write,

> the value of a woman in many cultures soon becomes associated with the state of her sexual relations. If she is chaste before marriage, and perfectly sexually faithful after marriage, her sexual relations build the group. If her sexual relations and attendant behavior, such as manner of dress, do not conform to this model, her activities are viewed as bringing chaos and instability to the group. Thus the need to protect a woman becomes more and more associated with the need to protect her chastity – not her life, not her freedom ... In this way, the honor of her family and her group becomes associated with her sexual behavior in an almost one-to-one correspondence. This is especially true for the men of her family: the chastity of their female kin is their honor.[42]

The third way to control women (normative restriction), Fox argued, is different from confinement and protection in that "the method of administration of control is largely internal – self-control through the internalization of values and norms – rather than externally imposed."[43] Girls are socialized to be good; that behaviour is reinforced by parents, peers, and schools, and girls come to impose the restrictions on themselves, rather than by an external agent. Fox argued that socialization structures are put in place to ensure that women are "nice" and "ladylike."[44] Good girls are rule followers, don't ask for what they want, and never want to inconvenience anyone. More than forty years later, as author Elizabeth Gilbert puts it, many women still suffer from the Miss Congeniality likeability trap: the "captivity of niceness" of being a good girl.[45] Good girls are socialized to be polite, passive, and silent and to always put other people first, being as nonthreatening as possible. "All the time, as a woman you're supposed to be nice. Like, 'Look at me, I'm a nice chair' or whatever, I'm smiling and not dangerous."[46] Kate Manne calls out the dangers of this internalized misogyny when writing about why women put up with coercive or bad sex: "the shame and guilt women often feel for not protecting a man who mistreats us. We do not want to hurt him or let him down; we want to be a good girl."[47]

The downsides of good girl privilege explain some of the issues surrounding the US gymnastics scandal and the gymnasts' decades-long abuse by Dr Larry Nassar. These elite gymnasts were physically strong and powerful, able to do amazing feats with their bodies. But they were also the ultimate good girls and became the "perfect prey."[48] As Abigail Pesta puts it, the gymnasts "had been taught not to question, not to make noise, they were told to fall in line."[49] They had no voice, no physical boundaries (because of the hands-on coaching and spotting) and were told to push through their pain and never complain. They had been socialized to obey and not question the coaches or doctors. They were told to be good, to be quiet, and to work hard and they'd get to the Olympics. They weren't believed when they did disclose, and they were gaslighted into believing it was all in their heads and that they were crazy.[50] There was a lot of abusive treatment generally in the gyms, which allowed for an environment for sexual abuse to fester, encouraging the girls to put up with more and more abusive behaviour from Nassar. Nassar even abused them in front of their parents, which led them to being further groomed for when they were alone with him. Even those who asked themselves, "Is this normal?" were led to believe that it was by their parents, coaches, and other gymnasts.[51] They were good girls and did what they were told.

Normative restriction means that women themselves buy into the good girl frame and police their own and other women's behaviour. Women's sexuality and behaviour is controlled through ideas of appropriate behaviour, appearances, and clothing, seeing these as a way to not entice or arouse men. Consider dress codes in schools where girls are told to cover up so they don't distract the boys, as if it's women's fault that men are aroused and can't control themselves. Or consider the case of the eight-year-old girl in Guelph, Ontario wearing only swim trunks told to cover up at a public pool and made to feel sexualized and ashamed of her body because others were sexualizing her nonexistent breasts. In this case, any girl over the age of four had to cover herself. As one mother said at the time, the policies "send a message to young girls that 'their bodies are somehow provocative and shameful and should be covered.'"[52]

So the "privilege" is a double-edged sword. Girls who don't conform to the good girl construct are severely punished, says Fox:

> To such women are reserved some of the most sophisticated forms of punishment devised by social groups. In addition to forfeiture of personal physical security, the not nice woman becomes the target of ridicule, ostracism, and psychological punishment directed not so much at her behavior as at her person. The group withdraws its approval from her and attacks the worthiness of her self; it negates her moral existence as part of itself, and by so doing it absolves itself of the responsibility for the fate of its "unworthy" members.[53]

Catherine Hakim, a researcher interviewed for the film, had a violent memory of her own education into what it meant to be a good girl:

> I remember when I was a teenager the great fear was to ever be labelled as a slut or a whore. I remember the first time I ever put lipstick on, very pale, pink lipstick, my father almost murdered me because he decided this was sluttish and whatever. I've never forgotten it ... Somehow, I was prostituting myself by wearing a pink lipstick. I can't remember how old I was but you know somewhere around thirteen or fourteen. I was not a child, but it was just the idea that you would even do such a thing, just so ingrained into me that was the lowest of the low, how can you sink so low? The whole system was that way. So that you were constantly holding yourself back and saying I can't do this or I shouldn't do that or this is inappropriate.

I understood the Madonna/whore binary intellectually but didn't see the connections in my own life or history – how I had been raised to be a good girl (even to the point of being an obedient gymnast) and to have an absolute horror of being a bad girl – until I met Lucy and the other escorts and saw my own socialization through Fox's theory. As Fox states, many women police and restrict their own behaviours in hopes of being good and avoiding being bad. She points out the double bind for women: women's behaviour can be policed by everyone but their failure is seen to be the individual woman's fault.

> Social control through normative constructs has the virtue of sub-tlety; it gives the appearance of nonrestriction and noncontrol, thus reducing the potential for resistance. Because it operates through the mechanisms of shared values, norms, and understandings – which are universally accessible to both sexes, to all ages, races, and socio-economic strata – all persons can be involved as control agents. En-suring adherence to the norms of control becomes everybody's business. In contrast, failure to comply to the norms is solely the fault of the individual woman; thus it follows that responsibility for the negative consequences of noncompliance is that of the transgressor alone. The victim, in other words, will have earned her fate.

Fox writes above that these norms transcend race or class in terms of controlling women's behaviour, meaning that being nice and ladylike are not just goals for middle-class white girls, though as I will outline in chapter 3, bad girl stigma is definitely racialized and class-based. Being a good girl can help to mitigate class or racial inequalities. In an article entitled "Mak-ing 'Good Girls': Sexual Agency in the Sexuality Education of Low-Income Black Girls," Clarissa Froyum describes how teachers relied on good girl tropes in an abstinence class to try to protect the girls from their perceived vulnerability but instead reinscribed traditional gender roles. "Adults viewed girls as vulnerable because they were black and low-income; they thought the girls were subject to racial stereotyping that heightened the importance of being a 'good girl.' In response, they tried to promote sexual agency among girls as a way to mediate their sexual vulnerability. They did so, however, by extending gendered discourses that equated sexual restraint with being 'good girls,'" i.e., through abstinence.[54] Well-meaning Black educators, having experienced racism themselves, thought that being seen as good girls would mitigate the racism that the girls faced. "They feared that fitting the stereotypes by appearing to be poor, bad girls and 'hos' facilitated this white racism."[55]

Class and race remain important variables in the good girl/bad girl binary since middle-class and white women have advantages historically, economically, and socially in being seen and accepted as "good girls" and using that to their advantage. They tend to get the benefit of the doubt from authorities and have the privilege of not being followed around in stores or being thought of as a sex worker while walking on the street. "The policing of female sexuality is something bourgeois women talk about often, with little understanding that what exists largely in the realm of metaphor for them remains, for poor women, a very literal and criminalizing surveillance of how they present themselves when they leave the house."[56] Another study showed that middle-class, female university students use slut-shaming to call out their working-class fellow students and shame them for their "promiscuity." "High-status women employ slut discourse to assert class advantage, defining their styles of femininity and approaches to sexuality as classy rather than trashy ... For high-status women – whose definitions prevail in the dominant social scene – slut discourse enables, rather than constrains, sexual experimentation. In contrast, low-status women are vulnerable to public shaming."[57]

Good girls are undoubtedly rewarded but it is also a straightjacket of control. Whether it is perfectionism or anorexia, conformity or denial, good girls constrain themselves, thinking, consciously or unconsciously, if I am perfectly good, then I can protect myself. If I am perfectly good, no one will hurt me. Men will respect me and know their boundaries with me because bad things only happen to bad girls. Good girls don't want to give up their good girl "privilege" because they see how the bad girls are treated. It is why girls police other girls and what they wear and how they behave.[58]

Sexual double standards and socialization to be "good girls" exist cross-culturally as well. In Turkey, for instance, boys are encouraged to "show their penises to relatives and neighbours and to be proud of this, whereas girl children are warned that it is shameful to expose, even by mistake a quick glimpse of their underwear while playing."[59] The shame of the body and sexuality is only socialized into the girls. "Women's negative associations with their bodies and sexuality are later further exacerbated by the importance given to preserving virginity until marriage and customary practices in some regions such as displaying a bloodstained sheet as proof of the bride's virginity on the 'first night of marriage.'"[60]

In Indonesia, women who are tattooed "can be labeled as promiscuous or disreputable and not worth marrying."[61] A nineteen-year-old young woman started wearing a face-covering veil and is having her tattoos removed because "she feels Indonesian men treat her with respect when she is fully covered … 'I saw the eyes of men and boys no longer looking at me in a disgusting way,' she said. 'Suddenly for the first time I felt respected. I wanted to keep wearing the hijab and I felt like I was a different person, an honorable person.'"[62] Only by covering up and being "good" could she be respected by men and feel safe.

Mona Eltahawy's work illustrates how women in some Islamic cultures are abused "by a toxic mix of culture and religion that few seem willing or able to disentangle lest they blaspheme."[63] Without restraint women are seen to be "just a few degrees short of sexual insatiability"[64] and "the walking embodiment of sin."[65] She argues that women's behaviour and movement is controlled even though it's actually men who are viewed as unable to control themselves. We have curfews on women, she says, but we're not telling men not to rape or assault women. Why are women responsible for men's desires? She writes that men hate women "because they need us, they fear us, they understand how much control it takes to keep us in line, to keep us good girls with our hymens intact."[66] There are many similarities with Valenti's work on purity culture in the US. Victim blaming is part of purity culture because rape brings shame to women, not to the men who rape them. Eltahawy believes that women are brainwashed to believe it's their fault. Why didn't you resist? How could you let them do that to you? And then after years of drilling it into you that sex is dirty and a sin, she says, how are you to suddenly enjoy sex?[67] Most parents don't want girls to learn about sex or female sexual pleasure, and she calls passionately for a "revolution of the mind."[68]

The Unfinished Sexual Revolution

Though sexual mores have certainly loosened over the years, the distinction between good and bad women has remained. We still don't have any equivalent (negative) language for men who are "promiscuous." Men who revel in their sexuality are not judged as bad people or bad fathers or bad husbands because they enjoy sex, unless they get caught in adultery or if they are transgressing with a sex worker. Men are not judged as harshly for their sexuality, as it is assumed to be part of their natural male identity. This particular double standard was infuriating to the women interviewed. Says Lucy,

> Ultimately it does not devalue who we are as a person because we revel in our sexuality. That we can be sexual and embrace that all we want and still be smart and intelligent and all of those other things. And we need to help learn how to have those conversations where women can be honored for being mothers, for being daughters, for being citizens in our community, upstanding citizens that are aware of what's going on and involved, but also very sexual and not afraid to want to explore their sexuality with other consenting adults.

Why is this so difficult to imagine for so many people? What happened to the sexual revolution? How is the sexual revolution "unfinished"? The 1960s and 1970s were a time of great change in terms of sexual liberation for both men and women in the Western world, partly because of the introduction of the birth control pill, which gave women control over their own fertility. "The uncoupling of intercourse and reproduction involved a radical transformation of the conditions of female sexuality."[69] Men had always had more access to sex outside marriage than women, but the development of the birth control pill enabled women to separate sex for procreation from sex for recreation, thereby removing women's worry about controlling their own reproduction.[70]

Much has been written about the counterculture elements of the 1960s with an increased drug culture, student activism, and freedom from repressive cultural norms. Veronique Mottier writes of the 1960s as an explosion of movements for the freedom of the individual and freedom for marginal-

ized groups because of the various civil rights movements, including an-
tiracist activism, women's liberation, and anti–Vietnam War protests. The
sexual revolution went a great distance towards bringing sexuality out into
the open and exposed certain segments of society to a variety of sexual
practices. And it was a revolution in many ways. Sexual norms began to be
questioned. Young people looked at their parents' attitudes towards sexuality as old-fashioned and rebelled accordingly. Women were encouraged
to throw off the old moral shackles that had kept them sexually monogamous and embrace their sexuality – just as men had always been encouraged to do.

Amongst these calls for change and the rise of social movements, the
women's movement as a "second wave" came into existence. From the beginning, sexuality was contested within the women's movement. Should
women embrace their sexuality or was heterosexual sex another tool of the
patriarchy? Should women become political lesbians and reject men entirely?[71] Second-wave feminists were divided about the importance of sexuality and particularly lesbianism and this created divides between liberal
feminists who were interested in equal rights in the public sphere and radical feminists who were concerned with sexuality and reproduction. And
the emphasis on sexuality tended to be on the acceptance (or not) of different sexual orientations and lesbian identity, as opposed to "orgasm
equality" within a heterosexual relationship.[72] Although today LGBTQ+
rights are taken for granted in most social justice movements, they were
controversial in the early part of the second wave because of the "lavender
menace," that lesbianism was too radical for the goals of liberal feminists.[73]
Some second-wave feminists worried about what we would now call "respectability politics" – that if the movement was taken over by more radical
elements it wouldn't appeal to the majority. Feminists, it was thought, had
to be "good girls" to get the respect and attention of the more powerful –
no burning of bras or making spectacles of themselves.

The second wave also began the very polarizing debates about the "sex
wars" on pornography and prostitution that continue to the present day.
On the one hand, some "sex positive" feminists saw the potential in freeing
sexuality and opposed censorship;[74] other antipornography feminists like
Catherine MacKinnon and Andrea Dworkin focused on sexuality as *the*
site of women's oppression. The feminist sex wars continued into the 1980s

and became focused on the questions of whether pornography and prostitution were bad for women: What does it mean to be sexually empowered?
Can pornography be feminist? Is prostitution bad for all women? Should
we eliminate prostitution and pornography or celebrate women's autonomy? These ideological divides continue to this day.

As much as women were encouraged to "be like men" in their sexuality
(in terms of being as uninhibited and as sexual as men), women still be-
longed to a culture of sexual repression and sexual double standards, where
the good girl/bad girl dichotomy was alive and well: with the added pressure
to be seen as sexy and available. So individual women may have heeded the
call to embrace their sexuality, but in reality, as many authors have argued,
the birth control pill did as much for men as for women, in terms of getting
access to women sexually.[75] With no reproductive worries, there was more
pressure on women to be sexual and to see themselves as "square" if they
didn't acquiesce. And remember this was still a time when it was illegal to
give contraception to single women, when you had to have a marriage license to rent a hotel room, when access to abortion was not legal anywhere
in the Western world. What was lacking in this sexual revolution was emphasis on women's pleasure. As Mottier states, "The sexual revolution was
nothing like the 'fulfilling love and sex between equal partners' which the
free love feminists had imagined."[76] There remained cognitive dissonance
around being hyper sexualized on the one hand and still restricted by the
double standard on the other.

The 2016 documentary *She's Beautiful When She's Angry* records important aspects of the second wave of feminism, particularly in the 1970s, and
reminds us how far we've come in just forty years. At the time, discussions
of the female body and female sexuality were considered obscene and
women in general were not encouraged to know their own bodies. While
some feminist consciousness raising groups did infamously explore their
genitalia with mirrors and a Boston women's collective began publishing
Our Bodies, Ourselves, as a resource for women's health, these resources
were not mainstream and did not reach the average woman. *Our Bodies,
Ourselves* was called "filthy trash" by evangelical Jerry Falwell in the 1970s
and banned from some US schools.[77] Sex education classes, such as they
were, focused on anatomy and prevention of disease and pregnancy. To this

day, sex education rarely includes learning on pleasure in sexuality, which would be seen as encouraging promiscuity. So it is not surprising that we are still defending our rights to control our bodies, our reproduction, and our sexuality.

The problem wasn't just for women's sexual liberation but for sexual minorities as well. For conservatives the sexual revolution of the 1960s was a disaster: it led to promiscuity, breakdown of the family, loss of morality, loss of religion, the rise of feminism, gay rights, and the undermining of traditional, monogamous, heterosexual families.[78] The AIDS crisis of the 1980s further entrenched conservative values around sexuality and particularly sexual minorities like gays and lesbians. The gay rights movement had to contend with people's discomfort with imagining gay sex, particularly gay male sex. In the 1980s at the height of the AIDS crisis, the illness was seen by many on the right as being God's punishment. The AIDS crisis renewed the association of sexuality with disease, danger, and moral panic about the "gay plague."[79] The crisis took over the dialogue about sexuality and brought the sexual revolution to an abrupt halt. Freedom and live-and-let-live attitudes were out; morality was back in, with its emphasis on abstinence and purity for women. The sexual revolution was over. It wasn't until 2003 that the US Supreme Court struck down antisodomy laws, in effect decriminalizing gay male sex. The change in attitudes has been swift, historically speaking, even if many people in the US and Canada are still homophobic and opposed to same-sex marriage. Times have changed but there is still something about sex that makes many people very uncomfortable.

In truth, the sexual revolution had never removed the sexual double standard or the Madonna/whore distinction. Women still faced the good girl/bad girl dilemma (and the consequences of being a "bad girl") and the sexual double standard where male sexuality was understood to be natural and insatiable while women were seen as the gatekeepers of and to male sexuality. If men managed to scale the gate, then women were to blame. So even though more and more women were sexually active and society itself became more sexualized, the norms surrounding good girls and bad were not eliminated, putting women in a double bind of damned if you do, and damned if you don't.

Women and Sex: Part I

The unfinished sexual revolution, then, is about how to overcome the continuing double standard in terms of male and female sexuality and rectify
the lack of emphasis on women's pleasure in sex. Describing "the male in
the head," many authors have shown how young women emphasize their
partner's pleasure at the expense of their own,[80] ensuring he climaxes, and
know little to nothing about how their bodies work or how to give themselves pleasure: "male preferences are instead interiorized and actively re-
produced by women."[81] Peggy Orenstein has shown how oral sex is
something that girls and young women do for boys willingly but they are
reluctant to have reciprocated because of their own internalized disgust
with the female body. There is such a lack of knowledge about the female
body and such a sense of shame around its normal functioning that it leads
girls to engage in behaviour that is not reciprocal, not mutual, not pleasurable for them. They think it's gross for a boy to have to "go down there."

And again, if we think girls are just too sensitive or prudish or are mis-
reading the culture, think of the pop culture icons who reinforce this
shame. Robert Pattinson, of *Twilight* fame and a huge Hollywood star, says
in a *Details* interview that he "hates" women's genitalia: "I really hate vaginas. I'm allergic to vagina."[82] DJ Khaled says going down on women is emas-
culating and gross. Real men (the kings!) don't do it.[83] These are just two
examples of the ways in which women's bodies are shamed and oral sex is
not to be reciprocated.

The consequences go beyond good or bad sex or mutuality. Suzanne
Moore writes of the decline of women and girls going to get pap smears in
the United Kingdom because they are embarrassed by their "private parts"
and think they're too hairy and smelly.[84] This obviously can be life threatening. If women are not screened during pap tests, they have a higher risk
of cervical cancer. Again, it's not just happening in Canada or Europe. In
one community in Mexico, "women did not undergo any kind of gynae-
cological examination, and the resulting complications ... were a significant
mortality risk. These women simply couldn't open their legs because their
beliefs wouldn't allow such a thing."[85] The women were put at significant
risk because they had been taught to be ashamed of their bodies and they

couldn't "overcome the shame of opening their legs, a shame that had been systematically inculcated by 2000 years of Judaeo-Christian culture."[86] Much needs to be done to educate girls about the pleasure of their bodies, but this learning is actively discouraged when girls are still being shamed about their own body parts. Parents and school boards who think that they are protecting their daughters from engaging in sexual behaviour by not educating them about women's pleasure are in fact encouraging a male-focused sexual experience. When Jocelyn Elders in 1994 dared to suggest that masturbation should be discussed in sex education classes, she had to resign as surgeon general of the United States.[87] The debates as to whether or not to vaccinate girls and boys against the human papillomavirus (HPV) in Canada also demonstrate our reluctance to recognize the future sexual activities of girls in particular. Many parents and conservative religious school boards refused to get their girls vaccinated because it might lead to promiscuity. They are willing to risk their children getting cervical or oral cancer so that the threat of an STI will remain in place to discourage sexual activity.

Whether parents and teachers do it out of love, concern, fear, or simple double standards, we have continued in the twenty-first century to make girls fearful and worried about stigma relating to their sexuality. "A study of adolescent girls ... found that some were paralysed with fear of the dangers of having sex, both in terms of their reputation, and in relation to the risks of pregnancy and disease."[88] Being paralyzed with fear means they are much less likely to explore their sexuality and find out what is pleasurable for them: to even see the value of sexuality outside of it being a commodity. What might the connection be between this continuing stigma towards sexually active girls and their ambivalence in embracing their sexuality? What accounts for women not having an orgasm ever or assuming it won't happen every time?[89] In 2020, a reality series on Netflix about women's sexuality that is trying to dispel "the shame many women feel about their genitalia ... led to yet another collective Twitter meltdown" for its portrayal of multiple women's vulva and a woman masturbating on camera.[90] Houston, we (still) have a problem.

We may have come to a turning point in the West in regards to sexual assault, consent, and slut-shaming. Discussions of rape culture abound in the media and on campuses, and women are saying more and more that they're not going to take the double standards and slut-shaming anymore. They won't be shamed for what they wear, how much they drink, or who they sleep with. Women are seeing clearly how they have been silenced by the shame around rape and how that silence keeps them shamed. Unfortunately, all the "yes means yes"[91] consent education in the world won't be effective in ridding us of slut-shaming and rape culture if we don't deal with the underlying sexual double standard and good girl privilege.

What is the relationship between rape culture, purity balls, the cult of virginity, slut-shaming, and FGM/C? These are all ways to control women's sexuality – sometimes out of concern for the sexualization of girls and worry about the harm to women but mainly because of the double standard of sexuality between men and women. Valenti's work shows how nonvirgin women are still punished in myriad ways by the state and she demonstrates how the sexual double standard hurts bad girls. When bad girls are so marginalized that predators and police discount their existence, they become throwaway women. Their horrible fates are seen to be their own fault; they are blamed for their own abuse – because what can you expect when you make the choice to be a sex worker or get in a cab alone while drunk or pick up a guy at a bar.

Most researchers believe it will take generations to transform the sexual double standard. We are up against millennia of socialization, religion, and biology in our quest for sexual equity. Kate Harding claims that rape culture took hold in the 1990s with the publication of two popular books on the differences between men and women (John Grey's *Men Are from Mars, Women Are from Venus*; and Deborah Tannen's *You Just Don't Understand Me: Women and Men in Conversation*) but the history of rape culture, slut-shaming, and whore stigma goes back a lot further than that.

Chapter Three

The Origins of Bad Girl Stigma and Good Girl Privilege

In July 1982, a woman's body was found in the Green River near Seattle. More than fifty women who worked the strip or were teenage runaways disappeared before DNA evidence revealed the identity of the man responsible decades after the fact. The so-called Green River Killer finally confessed to murdering forty-eight women but later said it was more like seventy-one – he had killed so many he had lost count. At Gary Ridgeway's sentencing in 2003, he was asked to confess his crimes as the prosecutor read his statements:

> "I wanted to kill as many women I thought were prostitutes as I possibly could." Is that true? "Yes."
>
> "I picked prostitutes because I thought I could kill as many of them as I wanted without getting caught." Is that true? "Yes."[1]

This is whorephobia. When a group of people are so dehumanized that no one cares if they are dead or alive, society has a problem. There are numerous, horrific examples of violence against sex workers by predators like Gary Ridgeway, the Yorkshire Ripper, and Marcello Palma of Toronto who killed three sex workers in one night on Victoria Day in 1996. "Mr Palma told his psychiatrist he had sex with people described then as 'prostitutes, transvestites and homosexuals' and admitted he thought about killing people, especially 'street people' or 'scum.'"[2] Robert Pickton, the notorious serial

killer targeting sex workers in Vancouver's Downtown Eastside, was convicted of killing six women when their DNA was found on his pig farm, but
he is believed to have killed almost fifty women over a twenty-year period.
Because the women he killed used drugs and were mainly Indigenous
women who worked in the sex trade, for years the police did not take their
disappearances seriously. Even with testimony from other women who had
been abused at his farm and the growing numbers of missing women, the
police did not finally act until they raided his farm in 2002 looking for illegal
firearms. They found evidence of his gruesome killings when body parts
and DNA were located all over his farm.

Dehumanization allows us to dismiss a whole group of people and not
see them as people who are like us but for their different choices and different life experiences. When researchers or journalists say they want to
"humanize" a group of people, what they mean is that they want to show
others why we should be concerned about them, why we should care about
them, why they are just like us. This shouldn't be necessary, of course, but
it is. When we allow sex workers to be continually dismissed and disre-
spected, we allow their humanity to be questioned. And when their humanity is questioned, there is a lack of concern when they die. The stigma
around sex workers leads to their dehumanization and their dehumanization leads to the continuing stigma. It's a vicious cycle.

When you marginalize any group whether they be Muslims, people who
use drugs, trans people, Indigenous peoples, or sex workers you send a message to others that those you marginalize don't deserve respect and you give
license to others to treat them badly. When Trump says that transgender
people can no longer serve in the United States military, it endangers transgender people by sending a message to others that they can be mistreated
and that they don't deserve the same respect and the rule of law.[3] Marginal-
izing others creates a culture of hatred and allows others to hate as well. It
emboldens people who may have these views to act on them. Violence
against Indigenous women becomes commonplace and normalized, so the
response of the community and police reflects that with victim blaming.[4]
Violence against Black men in the United States by police is rampant and
the murder of George Floyd in May 2020 galvanized the Black Lives Matter
movement in protest of the dehumanization of Black people. The violence
of white supremacists in Charlottesville, Virginia, in 2017 is an example of

a group of people being emboldened by their own president to proclaim outwardly what had previously been kept quiet.[5] The alt-right, white nationalist groups, and men's rights groups have been emboldened to strike out with their hate and their racism and misogyny. The dehumanization of immigrants that has gone on in the US is yet another example. The fact that putting children in cages and separating them from their parents was lauded in some quarters shows the depth of the dehumanization. As the philosopher Charles Taylor said when he changed his mind about banning the Muslim niqab in Quebec, "the proposal to restrict the rights of certain classes of citizens has had a side effect of stigmatization and violence."[6] Singling out a class of people like sex workers for shame and stigma, or Muslims for their dress and cultural practices, enables more stigma and can incite violence.

Bad Girl Stigma

Bad girl or "whore stigma," a term coined by Gail Pheterson in 1996, refers to the dehumanization of some women on the basis of their sexual activity, not all of whom actually sell sex. As Pheterson writes, these "branded women, be they paid sex workers or women merely accused of prostitution or women stigmatized as whores due to their work, color, class, sexuality, history of abuse, ethnic or marital or simply gender status"[7] are subject to stereotypes, violence, and humiliation, all as part of "sexist instruments of social control."[8] Whore stigma and slut-shaming, as we saw in the last chapter, legitimize violence against some women by contrasting women on the basis of their sexual status and leads to the control of all women.

Pheterson has shown "how social constructions of sex workers as 'bad,' 'deviant,' and 'dangerous' naturalizes their 'difference' from 'good women,' whose sexuality does not transgress prescribed cultural norms for appropriate female behavior."[9] But the whore stigma "can be used against any particular woman (or groups of women) who serves to model or challenge male entitlement."[10] And as Fox also pointed out in her discussion of the control of good girls, women who transgress face some of the worst punishments devised by mankind. So the counterpoint to whore stigma is the control of the "good" girls: "parents are socialized to protect their daughter's reputation even at the expense of her safety, development or personal liberty."[11] Good girl privilege and bad girl stigma, therefore, are closely intertwined.

In layperson terms, wives are the mothers of your children; mistresses are for sex. Good girls are marriage material; bad girls are not. Bad girls are discounted and are not to be trusted. Trump lawyer Rudy Giuliani is guilty of whore stigma when trying to discredit Stormy Daniels because of her (sex work) profession: "She has no reputation to be damaged ... If you're going to sell your body for money you just don't have a reputation. The business you're in entitles you to no degree of giving your credibility any weight."[12] You are not to be believed no matter what the issue, and you don't deserve respect. This obviously has dangerous consequences for bad girls and for anyone judged as "bad" because of who they sleep with or what they do for a living.

The former executive director of a sex work advocacy organization in Halifax has seen the worst of whore stigma from aggressors and the general public. A local man with a history of violence, pled guilty to the murder of a sex worker. One of his previous victims was a client of the organization:

> He picked up [the sex worker] and took her out to kind of like a quarry and she got out of the car, and he just started beating the crap out of her. He stripped her off, she was duct-taped, and she was in the trunk of his car, and so she remembered that her boyfriend had taught her about the inside of the trunks where you can pull the lever if you're inside the trunk and it pops open, the car was going, she got out of the car, moving car. Now think of it ... She's naked, duct-taped, on the side of a road, a car drives by, slows down, sees her and keeps on driving, doesn't call 911. So that just number one also goes to show you how much some people give a rat's ass in society in general.

She says the worst thing about the case is that another victim had already identified him after a previous violent incident but the authorities chose not to pursue charges. He then went on to murder a sex worker before finally being caught.

What could a person have possibly done (even in our victim-blaming world) to be so revolting to other people that they can be killed with impunity, that they can have their humanity be disregarded, that someone wouldn't call 911 to help them? Why are some people so disgusted by the idea of the whore and why do "whores" lose their right to respect and dignity? Put bluntly, whores (and women perceived as whores) must be punished.

Origins of Whore Stigma

The stigma against bad girls is rooted in the Madonna/whore dichotomy, which in turn comes from our sexual double standard. Sex for men is natural. Sex for women is suspect. What is it about sex that supposedly "sullies" or dirties women and makes us "damaged goods"? What is it about sex that implies such shame, disgrace, and ruin? Biologically, women are "penetrated," and this might be seen as a violation by some or domination by others. Mottier reports that in ancient Greece, penetration was *the* sexual act and a marker of Greek men's masculinity. It didn't matter who was penetrated (woman, boy, or slave) as long as the citizen male did the penetrating. "The ancients adopted a phallocentric notion of sex, defined exclusively as penetration … Men were encouraged to use penetrative sex for domination and control of the submissive partner. Sex reflected social and political relations of power, since men performed their social status as citizens in the arenas of war, politics, and sex."[13] Hopefully, our norms about sexuality have changed somewhat since the ancient Greeks, but the biology of sex and reproduction cannot be ignored.

As Susan Brownmiller wrote in 1975, "Man's structural capacity to rape and women's corresponding structural vulnerability is as basic to the physiology of both our sexes as the primal act of sex itself. Had it not been for this accident of biology, an accommodation requiring the locking together of two separate parts, penis into vagina, there would be neither copulation nor rape as we know it."[14] This fluke of biology also means that in terms of reproduction women always know they are the mothers of their children; fathers have not had that confidence until the rise of paternity testing in the last twenty-five years. This probably accounts for the long history of men controlling women's sexuality so they could control their reproduction.[15] As Brownmiller writes, women chose "protective mating" over an "open season of rape"[16] and their protectors assumed "the burden of fighting off all other potential attackers"[17] so their rights to their biological offspring could be assured. But the price of this arrangement for women was steep. Once men knew their role in reproduction and desired to pass on inheritance to their biological offspring, men began to control women's sexuality in a variety of coercive (chastity belts/seclusion/genital mutilation) and more subtle ways (socialization and religion). "The historic price of woman's protection by man against man was the imposition of chastity and monogamy. A crime committed against her body became a crime against the male estate."[18]

Christine Milrod, a researcher and sex therapist interviewed for the film, concurs, claiming that whore stigma comes from the same two sources:

> I think one source is obviously religion and I think religion has earlier roots in the ancestral evolutionary environment where ... we really have a biological environment where the male dominates. And I think in terms of controlling for errant offspring, I think that the male has always had a need to dominate and control women's sexuality, much more so than his own obviously ... And then I think that has translated to something cultural because when human beings have evolved into *Homo sapiens*, we've had to have some form of psychological mechanism to keep women in their place and religion has served as an excellent purpose for that.

Biology, evolution, and religion make for a potent cocktail of whore stigma. The idea of sex apart from love, marriage, and monogamy is difficult for many people to accept, especially if they belong to any major religion. There are still restrictions on sexual activity within most religious organizations, and the stigma against women's sexual activity in particular is very deep seated, as Milrod states. From the Old Testament to the New, we see the damaging ideas of whore stigma embedded within the Bible. "Like her Babylonian sister, a married woman within the Hebrew culture who was victimized by rape was considered culpable, adulterous and irrevocably defiled."[19] As Brownmiller points out, it is interesting that the Ten Commandments prohibit committing adultery and coveting your neighbour's wife, but do not state, "Thou shalt not rape."[20]

The power of sexuality has always seemed to worry church fathers (see St Augustine) and has always been seen as a force that needs to be controlled, especially women's sexual energies. The downfall of Adam and Eve is a central tenet of all Judeo-Christian religions. Eve is the fallen woman who is tempted by the snake in the tree of knowledge and then lures Adam to eat the apple as well. For her sin, Eve is cursed with the pain of childbirth. In this tradition, "desire belongs to the world of the fallen, not within the realm of the sacred."[21] There is no Eve-worship, as Bibi Bakare-Yusef writes; rather, her sins "must be masked by the veneration of the Virgin Mary. In order to continue to sustain the myth of reproduction without erotic desire or encounter, it is necessary to build a case for Mary's miraculous conception, free of coitus."[22] Patriarchy, she writes, is "hard-wired into Christianity."[23] The mother of Jesus is called the Virgin Mary and it is an important belief in the Christian church that Mary was a virgin when she conceived Jesus and thus without sin. We can probably date the negative reinterpretation of the Madonna/whore dichotomy to Mother Mary and Mary Magdalene (one of Jesus's followers) who may or may not have been a prostitute.

The Christian concept of original sin also leads to problems for women. The idea is that we are born sinful, full of shame, guilt and blame, and must be redeemed. As Kim Anderson argues, Christianity had a profoundly destructive effect on Indigenous women. For example, "Judeo-Christian culture saw menstruation not as a manifestation of female power, but as a manifestation of female sin, contamination and inferiority"[24] and women's "spiritual identity was limited to the troublesome role of Eve or the impossible role of the Virgin Mary."[25] Both of these ideas, she writes, have had a very negative impact on how Indigenous women were treated by men in their communities after colonization. Whore stigma, then, partly comes from religion, particularly from the Judeo-Christian tradition, though stigma against sex and female sexuality is also found in Buddhism, Hinduism, and Confucianism.[26] But stigma against female sexuality in general is completely intertwined with stigma against the actual whore.

History of Sex Work

Prostitution has been called the world's oldest profession for a reason: it's been around since humans started keeping records and we've had anything to exchange. There have been accounts of prostitution since the earliest recorded history across the globe. Laurie Shrage, a professor of philosophy at Florida International University in Miami, has researched prostitution historically and cross-culturally and has determined that

> sex work isn't the same everywhere. And it's not the same if you look historically, if you look back, in the Middle Ages or you look in other societies. But it's very much, like all practices, defined by the values and assumptions and customs in any particular place it occurs. And so I don't think we can make these broad universal claims that pros- titution is always degrading to women or always involves the subjec- tion or subjugation of women ... I think that we have to really look at the unique circumstances ... I think we have to look at the cultural and historical context and then make judgments about that practice in its historical context and its cultural context.

Sexuality itself was also not always shamed and stigmatized because it was related to fertility. Once men realized their role in reproduction, how- ever, and once there was surplus to be inherited from one generation to another, it became increasingly important for men to know who their biological children were, as stated above. And the only way to ensure that their children were their own was to control "their" women's sexuality. As Catherine Hakim states:

> In ancient times, prostitution was not stigmatized and sexuality was not stigmatized. On the contrary, it was actually applauded ... and admired because sexuality implied fertility which was necessary for survival. However, men eventually realized their biological role as fathers and wanted to be sure that their inheritance was only available to their own biological children and it was really about knowing who their children were that they ended up introducing controls on women's sexuality and the controls were really about distinguishing

between indoor women and outdoor women, veiled and unveiled. [Gerda] Lerner describes this process in Mesopotamia very clearly and again there's no stigma attached to sexuality or prostitution. It's just simply that the indoors private veiled women are the ones you can be sure their children are your children as well, and that created the distinction between virgin and whore, mother and whore, that's lasted throughout history.

Prostitution has existed for a long time, tolerated to some extent in most cultures. The earliest mentions of women and boys engaged in prostitution date back to at least 2400 BC. In Greece, by the fifth century BC, some women, called *hetaera*, or courtesans, were educated, literary women with a great deal of freedom. As Mottier points out, *hetairai* "enjoyed a much greater degree of autonomy than women from citizen families and some of them achieved great wealth and public stature."[27] At the same time in ancient Greece where we see the creation of inheritance laws we also see the rise of laws against adultery for women and the veiling of some women. Veiled women were wives of citizens and the veil was a visual way to distinguish between women. Unveiled women were not controlled in the same way and had more freedom of movement but over time became associated with prostitution, concubinage, and courtesans. It was a class marker, according to Mona Eltahawy.[28] Says Hakim,

> What Lerner is saying is simply that they were kept separate, there was no stigma at that time. The stigma is recent. She was simply saying there had to be a sharp division, veiled and unveiled women. Indoors and outdoors women. Women, hetaera in Greece were not stigmatized ... They were admired people, they were not stigmatized in that way. But there was a separation and that was the thing, there had to be separation between the women whose children could be definitely yours and the women who you would never know who the father was. That's not the same as stigmatizing and it's a European puritan thing, a North American puritan thing, the stigma.

On a recent trip to China, there was a sex museum in every city I visited with statues, pictures, and tapestries detailing the history of prostitution.

Evidence of Chinese brothels goes back to as early as 600 BC. The worship of the phallus and acceptance of prostitution as a fact of life seemed clear. Excavations at Pompeii, Italy, have uncovered brothels that had both male and female sex workers (from the first century AD before the eruption of Mount Vesuvius) with pricing of sexual acts listed, sandals with "follow me" imprints, and a variety of erotic art, graffiti, and frescoes on the walls of residences. Worldwide, there is evidence of prostitution, and as in China, in ancient Rome and Medieval Europe it was generally tolerated. Again, in the words of Shrage:

> When I first started doing some research about sex work historically, I came across writings by historians working in the Middle Ages who mentioned a practice in certain European towns where sex workers, or prostitutes, public women often had an initial career as prostitutes, but that their customers would essentially provide them with a dowry so they could be married, so that they would often be seen, after a career of sex work, they had sort of paid their dues to society and therefore were eligible to be married and they were often sought after, I don't know, not by maybe all men, but some class of men saw women who had worked as public prostitutes, as desirable as wives.

The Hulu series *Harlots* attempts to show what prostitution might have been like for women in eighteenth-century England when there were few opportunities for women to work outside the home and when their money, if the family had any, was legally the father's and given to the sons not the daughters. When women married, their money was transferred to their husbands. The producers of the series (mostly female writers and producers) claim that they want to show the women through the female gaze rather than the male gaze presented in most current media. What was it like for women, from women's own point of view? The creators of the series did extensive research into the lives of London prostitutes, including *Harris's List of Covent Garden Ladies* (1757–95), a list of the appearances and sexual specialties of between 120 and 190 prostitutes. The book worked in much the same way as the internet does today, allowing women to advertise their services to the wider public. The point of the series, according to the producers, other than to entertain, is to show the variety of workers and their circumstances and to show their resilience and ability to overcome bad circumstances. While *Harlots* doesn't glamorize prostitution, it does show how women coped without financial resources and shows the strength of poor and working-class women with nothing but their sexual skills and emotional labour to sustain them. From higher-end brothel workers, to girls working in back alleys, to the women who became courtesans and mistresses to kings, we see in a historical context what is still true today: there are enormous differences between women who sell sex and not all the experiences are exploitative and inherently bad.[29]

Prostitution itself wasn't illegal in Canada or even considered too problematic until the moral panic about the "white slave trade" (the first accounts of what we would now call sex trafficking) began to appear. In this context, middle-class white women feared for the virtue of their working-class, fallen sisters. In Toronto in 1867, brothels were discreetly referred to as "disorderly houses" by local newspapers but even then the women working in the brothels were treated differently and worse than the men who frequented them. The women were fined or sent to jail for thirty days to six months while their clients were discharged with no fine and no jail time.[30] As Constance Backhouse has written,

> Prostitution law in nineteenth century Canada was laced with discriminatory intent and impact. Each of the three legal approaches – regulation, prohibition and rehabilitation – featured discrimination on the basis of class, race and ethnic origin. Sex discrimination, however, was even more prominent as each set of laws – whether by design or through application – created legal impediments for women which did not exist for men.[31]

In terms of prostitution, the sexuality of nonwhite women was also seen to be in need of control by the dominant culture and crucial to this was the construction of the "'squaw': the dominantly held belief in the inherent sexual availability and, thus, violability of Indigenous women and girls."[32] An amendment to the Indian Act of 1876 "created a distinct legal category for Indian women charged with prostitution"[33] which in effect codified the distinction between Indigenous women and white women. "The discriminatory cast of prostitution law is clearly evident in its special treatment of native Indian women ... Legal discrimination against [them] ... was even more deep-rooted, in that separate legislation was enacted to cover their activities."[34] This separate legislation meant that "Indigenous women could be forced out of towns ... Many early settler communities located in the country's western provinces saw Indigenous women as causes of 'vice' and threats to morality and restricted them from free access to such settlement."[35] Indigenous women were sexualized and dehumanized as "savages" and "inferior Others."[36] It became normalized to justify the sexual violation of some women as "just whores," either because they lost or never had the protections of the good girls. As Robyn Maynard states, this dehumanization also led to the idea that Black women were essentially rapeable, like sex workers and Indigenous women.

> The purportedly "natural" depravity of Black women did more than degrade their social status and value in the eyes of white society. It not only made them "rapeable" in the eyes of the law, but it rendered them criminal as well. Black women's sexuality was represented as a threat, and those deemed to be exercising their sexuality outside of established social norms were deemed criminal. Though selling sexual services for money resulted in no measurable harm and likely complemented Black women's income in an era of extreme economic deprivation, involvement in the sex trade was widely regarded as a public danger, purportedly responsible for the degradation of society.[37]

In England, the Contagious Diseases Acts (1864, 1866, and 1869) "imposed police-enforced vaginal examinations and registration on working-class women suspected of being prostitutes"[38] and this so enraged middle-class women that they mobilized to have the Acts reversed. Josephine Butler's campaign against the Acts led to their repeal but, as Pheterson argues, her antiprostitution and antitrafficking efforts backfired.

> The [Criminal Law Amendment] Act granted police greater control over poor working-class women and children ... The reformers lost more and more power to the purists until the abolitionist movement strayed entirely from its original intent. Preservation of female liberty

had been twisted into a drive for male chastity, male protection and control of women and state restriction of working women's social and sexual behavior.[39]

And in the United States, Melissa Ditmore, a journalist and sex work activist interviewed for the film, references the Mann Act of 1910 as one of the first attempts to control the "white slave trade," by controlling women's movement and sexual freedom, not the mobility or conduct of men:

> While people say that they [antitrafficking regulations] are implemented to protect women, the people who are most likely to be arrested in the name of protecting them, are women. For example, in the United States with the provision of the Mann Act against white slavery passed in 1910, the people who were most frequently arrested were women. They were charged with conspiracy to violate the Mann Act. This meant buying ... a train ticket across a state line to go see a man with whom they were romantically involved. Many of these women, when these legal tangles were sorted, married the man they were going to meet ... It may be that these laws passed in the name of protecting women are not intended to protect them, that this is an ostensible reason but it's really to limit women's opportunities, even sexual opportunities.

So, if at one time, prostitution was tolerated and women were not as stigmatized as they are now what happened? Whether rooted in biology or culture, fear of women's sexuality is engrained in our culture and since the early Victorian era, women's sexuality has been seen as something to control and contain.

History of Good Girl Privilege

Most women were constrained by at least two principles in the Victorian era: "compulsory virtue" for good girls and the cult of domesticity. Compulsory virtue meant having to be virtuous and appear virtuous, thereby limiting women's actions, freedom of choice, and behaviour. Jean-Jacques

Rousseau said it definitively in *Emile* when describing why women need to be constrained: women, by their good (or bad) behaviour, give men the confidence to know (or not) if their child is their own. The ideal education for girls (unlike Emile) will ensure their compliance in thought, manners, and behaviours so they will bend to the will of their husbands and be ideal helpmates. In the film *The Age of Innocence* Countess Olenska (Michelle Pfeiffer) is trapped and vilified because even though she has not had an affair with Newland Archer (Daniel Day-Lewis), everyone thinks she has and so she must be shunned. Not only does she have to be virtuous to be someone worthy of support, she must appear virtuous. There are no consequences for Newland Archer, except a loveless respectable marriage.[40]

The second principle illustrating what women were valued for in the nineteenth century is now called the cult of true womanhood or cult of domesticity.[41] The Victorian era considered the ideal woman to be the "saintly, sexless wife-mother"[42] in contrast to the "flesh-bound materiality of men."[43] The insistence on purity for women came from men *and* women. As Susan B. Anthony wrote to reassure possible supporters of women's suffrage, "women will, by voting, lose nothing of man's courteous, chivalric attention and respect."[44] In other words, women could still be good girls and be treated well by men. So even suffragettes themselves assumed a sexual Manicheanism; a fundamental dualism between men and women. It was "so deeply entrenched that the majority of suffragists could not and did not consider the manner in which this image served to reinforce male dominance."[45]

The ideal of women's purity and true womanhood was race and class-based, as "whiteness … confers a broad range of privileges, including sexual respectability."[46] As Mottier argues, "working-class girls and racial 'others' were often portrayed as more sexually available or even insatiable … while prostitutes were commonly depicted as hypersexual beings with rotten, corrupted bodies."[47] In terms of Indigenous women, as Kim Anderson writes, "In contrast to the Euro-Western model of the 'angel in the home,' Native women have always had to work … and yet the ongoing poverty experienced by Indigenous women is evidence of a profound loss in economic equity related to the colonial policies."[48] The ideals, however, affected all women and impacted how they were judged and perceived (see Sojourner

Truth's rebuttal to this ideal in her "Ain't I a Woman" speech as mentioned in chapter 2). Women were valued in relation to their relative "piety, purity, submissiveness and domesticity."[49] As Robyn Maynard argues, this created an impossible situation for African American women in the 1800s. "After slavery's abolition, while the mere suggestion of the rape of a white woman by a Black man led to widespread outcry and political action, the rape of a Black woman elicited no public outrage. If white womanhood represented the idealized female subject, then Black women were cast outside of this formulation entirely, as less than woman and, indeed, less than human."[50]

In Africa itself during the Victorian era, Sylvia Tamale argues that "colonialist constructions of Africans as profligate and hypersexual led to the intensified repression and surveillance of African women's sexuality in particular. Colonialists worked hand in hand with African patriarchs to develop inflexible customary laws that evolved into new structures and forms of domination."[51] After adopting Christianity, she writes a "new script, steeped in the Victorian moralistic, anti-sexual and body shame edict was inscribed on the bodies of African women and with it an elaborate system of control."[52]

In similar terms, KelleyAnne Malinen discusses the history of sexual assault in Canada and who was considered "rapeable." She argues that "enslaved, racialized and poor women" have historically had their experiences discounted because of a discourse of "legitimate and illegitimate victims."[53] Misogyny and racism were deeply entwined with sexual violence and "proper white women" had more protection than any others.[54] As she writes, "Those with more social power are more likely to be safe from sexual violence and sexual stigmatization."[55] And the good girls know it.

In exchange for good (white) girls' purity and submissiveness, women were thought to be marriageable. It was rare for women to be financially independent of men and so the purpose of a girl's life was to attract a husband. (Most of Jane Austen's books deal with this very dilemma). In a time period where women's work outside the home was limited to backbreaking factory work or domestic work, it's not surprising that many women wanted the security of marriage to a man who would provide for them. Factory work didn't pay a living wage and so many of those women had to supplement with sex work. The economic power wielded by men had other consequences as well. Without education and jobs, women couldn't provide for themselves; without adequate birth control, women couldn't prevent unwanted pregnancies. The stigma of illegitimate children and the harsh treatment of "fallen women" all led to the social pressures to be a good girl, or else. The conflict between this cult of true womanhood and the realities of women's lives in the 1800s are understood by some historians as the direct cause of "hysteria" amongst women. Women became invalids in order to be consistent with cultural stereotypes of how they should behave.[56]

Good Girl Privilege and Moral Righteousness

It should come as no surprise that European settlers brought with them their Protestant prudishness and brutal treatment of sex outside marriage.[57] The Puritan work ethic upon which both the US and Canada were built promoted the dangers of the sins of pride, laziness, and social climbing, and we see in the nineteenth century an increasingly negative and intolerant view of sexuality. Men were being urged to control their sexuality. Doctors began warning about the dangers of masturbation. Sexuality was seen as a force to be controlled, and pleasure itself became something sinful whether it was dancing, drinking, gambling, or having sex. So while the control of everyone's behaviour was attempted to a certain extent, the restraints on women took on even greater emphasis. As Ditmore states, "the people who are really targeted for arrest, and for moral campaigns to say you shouldn't be doing this, are women. It is about sexual autonomy, sexual morality, and the idea that women perhaps should not be granting men this sexual access."

There were many linkages between antiwhite slave trade, temperance, suffrage, and slavery abolitionist movements, many of whose membership overlapped.[58] Activists linked men's abuse of alcohol to the abuse of women by men, and suffragettes hoped that by getting the vote, women would be able to influence public policy on a number of fronts including health, education, and the outlawing of alcohol and brothels. They were up against millennia of discrimination as the classic words of antisuffrage Quebec MP Jean-Joseph Denis in 1918 suggest: "I say that the Holy Scripture, theology, ancient philosophy, Christian philosophy, history, anatomy, physiology, political economy and feminine psychology all seem to indicate that the place of women in this world is not amid the strife of the political arena, but in her home."[59]

White middle-class suffragettes were on a mission and most did not have a problem working with people with antiwomen religious agendas if they would support women's right to vote and to outlaw prostitution. Says Melissa Ditmore,

> There is a long history of particular feminists working with religious figures to save women. And these are people who have pretty much said we will set aside our differences on female bodily autonomy, about other issues, about marriage, about domestic violence, about reproductive rights, reproductive justice, matters addressing abortion, access to birth control, whether birth control should exist, whether people should have access to condoms, or use condoms ever, in order to rescue prostitutes who are rescue-able and punish prostitutes who are not. And this goes back to the start of the Salvation Army in the UK in the Victorian era, it goes back to rehabilitation efforts in Victorian England, in the US, and I presume in Canada.

Moral righteousness (and moral regulation) was a foundational principle of all these movements. If you see prostitution or alcohol as morally reprehensible, you will not be interested in just promoting abstinence or temperance, you will want to "cleanse the land of the sin of drinking."[60] You will not have tolerance for the idea that one person's sin is a pleasure to others because there is no tolerance in these movements. Antislavery activists, quite rightly, believed that slavery was a sin and irredeemable, and, therefore, they did not believe in reforming the system of slavery – the whole system had to be denounced and abolished. Many nineteenth century (slavery) abolitionists were also very religious and believed that their cause was "God's will revealed,"[61] meaning that they were doing God's work by opposing slavery. Antiprostitution activists in the past and present make the same basic argument. Prostitution is violence against women; it can't be redeemed or reformed, therefore it has to be eradicated, even if it means restricting women's autonomy and freedom.

The overt control of working-class and racialized women continued into the twentieth century. It wasn't just actual prostitutes who were targeted for being "fallen women." Any young woman, aged sixteen to thirty-five, who was pregnant and unwed or just "unmanageable or incorrigible" according to her father could be imprisoned for up to nine months for "morality offences."[62] These young women were often poor and uneducated and so it was much more difficult for them to hide their pregnancies or fight against the system. "The burden rested upon the female, whose only recourse was to prove that she was not 'unmanageable' or 'incorrigible' – and few were successful in doing so."[63] So while, or perhaps because, some women were becoming more educated and working outside the home during the early 1900s, the state found it more and more necessary to try to control women's sexuality and reproduction in a way it hadn't done before.

Given it's just been one hundred years since some (middle-class, white) women got the vote in Canada, and less than that for those same women to be considered persons under the law, it is not surprising that we still struggle with aspects of male domination, particularly around sexuality and prostitution. And as Backhouse[64] reports, the reasons for women's participation in prostitution have never been fully addressed. "The failure of the rehabilitation policy was due to the limited nature of its aims. It was practically useless to attempt to reform prostitutes without simultaneously altering the various factors which drove them to prostitution – poverty, restricted employment options, sexual victimization of young women inside their homes and in society generally, lack of access to birth control and abortion, and the all-pervasive sexual double standard."[65]

Social change usually takes a long, long time. It wasn't until 1884 that married women could own their own property and not until 1925 could women divorce on the same grounds as men. We wouldn't have no-fault divorce in Canada until 1969, when contraception was finally decriminalized as well, and it wasn't until 1983 – one hundred years after the Married Women's Property Act was proclaimed – that the crime of rape finally included sexual assault within marriage. Many overt discriminations have been declared illegal and there have been vast changes in the status of women in the past fifty years, but it is not surprising that more subtle, arguably more dangerous, oppressions are still with us.

State Regulation of Sexuality

One of the hardest battles for women and sexual minorities over the past 100 years has been over the state regulation of sexuality. There doesn't appear to be much that escaped the notice of government censors around sex. Whether through obscenity charges, adultery laws or the criminalization of homosexuality and birth control, the regulation of sexuality has had negative effects on many people. Distributing information about birth control brought charges of obscenity against activist (and reputed eugenicist) Margaret Sanger, and her clinic was raided and shut down by the authorities because it was such a threat to the social order. The idea that women could control how many children to have or even if they wanted any at all was seen to go against nature, the Bible, and God's plan for women's punishment in childbirth. "Abortion and contraception were wrong … because they permitted women to escape just punishment … for their sexual sins."[66] It was too radical for many feminists at the time who were focused on the issue of suffrage and worried about their own respectability.

The Society for the Suppression of Vice in New York arrested Mae West in 1927 for writing and starring in a play called *Sex*, and she was found guilty of obscenity.[67] The idea of people watching or enjoying "obscenity" was thought to lead to a breakdown of society. Hundreds of people lined up to see West on Broadway before the show was closed down. Authorities apparently believed that people must be protected from themselves. So it's not that long ago that society was attempting to overtly control ideas and behaviours some members of society found obscene.

The history of adultery laws is also interesting in regards to the regulation of sexuality. Twenty-one states in the US still consider adultery a criminal offence and have not removed those laws from their books. They are rarely enforced, likely because prosecutors know these laws would be vulnerable to a constitutional challenge, but when they are used it is invariably a way to control a woman's or sexual minorities' rights. It is about punishing women for their sexuality outside marriage or outside their race: "state-sanctioned slut-shaming" as Sarah Laskow has called it.[68]

Arguably, the most extensive attempts to regulate sexuality in Canada were laws against homosexuality. A gay man, Everett Klippert, was sentenced to life in prison in 1967 for having sex with other consenting men and getting caught several times. After his repeated recidivism, he was jailed indefinitely. The justice minister at the time, Pierre Trudeau, thought this was so egregious that when he was prime minister he famously proclaimed that "the state has no business in the bedrooms of the nation" and decriminalized homosexuality, contraception, and adultery in 1969. It would take until 1988 before abortion was removed from the Criminal Code of Canada. Antisodomy laws were not struck down as unconstitutional in the United States until *Laurence vs Texas* in 2003. Same sex marriage was legalized in Canada in 2005 and in 2015 under federal US laws.

Western societies have liberalized so much, and yet … Since the sexual revolution of the 1960s, sex worker rights groups have attempted to use the liberalization of sex laws in their favour to advocate for the decriminalization of sex work. As Melinda Chateauvert and Laurie Shrage have argued, it hasn't worked, no matter how they have tried to reframe the issues and make connections with other social movements. First, sex worker groups made the connection between the legalization of abortion and the issue of privacy rights. Says Shrage:

> In the '70s right after *Roe v Wade*, a number of … sex worker rights groups started to approach women's rights groups on the assumption that the legalization of abortion in the US would lead to greater respect for privacy rights and essentially the protection of what adults do in the bedroom, and so they saw a connection between *Roe v Wade* and the decriminalization of abortion and potentially the decriminalization of prostitution. And when they approached many feminist groups, women's rights groups, they were often of course rebuffed and turned away.

The second push for the decriminalization of prostitution, Shrage argues, came about when sex worker groups then attempted to reframe their issues as workers' rights and as union issues:

> Having been rebuffed by women's rights activists … they decided to try to make alliances with other groups. This was also a time … that some of the clubs that had exotic or erotic dancing were trying to unionize as part of the legal sex industry … and work with different

labour unions so a number of sex worker rights groups began promoting their issues in terms of workers' rights. And if you remember the attempt to unionize the Lusty Lady in San Francisco, they had this big banner, "workers of the world unite," and they were appealing to all the kind of labour rhetoric ... So I looked at how they re-framed their issues from issues of women trying to promote ... control of their own body issues and privacy to the issues of the right of people to work and make a living. But that didn't go very far.

The third (unsuccessful) attempt at taking their issues mainstream and getting attention to the problems of criminalization was their bid to form an alliance with the LGBTQ+ movement. Shrage again:

And so in the '90s with the LGBT movement, you had a beginning of a different kind of alliance, and sex workers saw that with gays and lesbians gaining their right to diverse sexualities, and with potentially at that time the dismantling of laws that ... criminalized sodomy which eventually happens in the United States with *Lawrence versus Texas* in 2003, sex workers who were promoting decriminalization see yet another opening for decriminalizing prostitution. So first you have *Roe v Wade* and even before *Roe v Wade*, you had the decriminalization of contraceptive devices and you had in the United States the decriminalization of adultery, all of these moments, political legal moments, gave sex workers who had been promoting decriminalization, the idea that at some point, they would ... move forward decriminalizing prostitution. At each decade they've reframed their issues, or they've reframed the way they've pushed for the decriminalization ... but the question I want to ask is why have ... they made so little progress?

Part of the answer is that sex work is still criminalized in most parts of the world and denigrated by many people, so it is very difficult to "come out" as a sex worker, as Lucy found out. There are few people willing to take a stand because of the negative consequences, including arrest, though of course there have been sex workers who have allowed their stories to be told.[69] The clients of sex workers are also stigmatized and vilified so they're reluctant to come out too. The LGBTQ+ movement mobilized a critical mass of gay people (and their families and friends) and were able to reframe their sexual identities as not a choice or lifestyle issue but as a biological "Born This Way" reality. The LGBTQ+ community, though still struggling in many ways, has arrived at a level of acceptance in the West that sex workers have just not been able to achieve. Says Shrage to this point:

> One of the things the gay and lesbian movement had going for it was the issue of coming out and of course, there are great risks in coming out as a person with a stigmatized sexuality. They could lose their job and ... when we still had anti-sodomy laws they could of course be arrested. But it ... created a lot of political momentum and engaged I think the public with the issues of gays and lesbians ... I think for many sex workers to come out it would put their livelihoods at risk. They're much more [vulnerable]. I think it would be [easier] for them to be targeted.

But a bigger part of the answer, I would argue, is that on the issues of abortion, contraception, violence against women, and gay rights feminists came together in basic agreement on the issues. It was only on the subjects of prostitution and pornography that feminists were divided, ideologically, and some were fundamentally opposed to what the sex workers wanted. Even today, the US women's organization NOW, the National Organization of Women, is divided between the national office that advocates (and insists on local support) for the Nordic model (where the selling of sex is decriminalized but the purchase of sex is not) and some of the state and local chapters who are advocating for full decriminalization. The dispute threatens to divide the fifty-year-old organization politically and ideologically.[70]

Consequences of Whore Stigma

Catherine Hakim believes there is ongoing stigma against sex workers, "because men want to have sexual access to women at the lowest possible cost and on terms most favorable to them. And so, women who do sell sexual services are labeled as incompetent, drug addicts, and people you really don't want to know. As well as being immoral of course." The consequences go way beyond being judged immoral. Sex workers are subject to violence because of the idea that rape is just part of the job, because sex workers cannot refuse sexual activity. Through this lens, sex workers become seen as "rapeable." Rather than see rape as the sexualized violence that it is, many people dismiss violence against sex workers and blame sex workers themselves for these incidents, contributing to the whorephobia in society today.

This damaging perspective rests on the belief that a client purchases the right to do anything he wishes to a sex worker. In this way, a sex worker cannot *not* consent and therefore cannot be raped. One columnist at the *Chicago Sun-Times* in 2015 stated that to claim sex workers can be raped is to degrade the experience of "real" sexual assault victims – theft of services, at best, but not rape, even when the assault was at gunpoint.[71] A tweet at the time of the article put this widespread view succinctly: "Rape a whore? Isn't that just shoplifting?" Rape for sex workers, then, is seen as a hazard of the job and not a serious concern. If women cannot refuse sexual activity because they are sex workers then they are, of course, vulnerable to abuse and assault because clients know they can get away with it.

The idea that sex workers can't be raped is a dangerous threat to both sex workers and women in general which parallels the idea that married women can't be raped. As Melissa Ditmore says, "we used to think wives couldn't be raped either. But what you've got there is a socially sanctioned sexual relationship [and therefore presumed right of access] in a marriage. So much so that in some places sexual access is so expected to be granted that marital rape is not a crime in some places. So it is about, on some level, control of sexuality." Given that Canada only made marital rape illegal in 1983, it is not surprising that we still blame sex workers when they are sexually victimized because the exchange of money is still seen as having granted a right of access.

There are many examples of sex workers' claims of rape and assault being dismissed because of their occupation.[72] The belief that sex workers "ask for it" or that violence is part of the job, dehumanizes them and contributes to their abuse. Prohibitionists insist that violence against women is why prostitution must be eradicated, but, as sex workers argue, you can only see violence as an inherent part of the job if you believe that sex is inherently violent. Instead, the women I interviewed argue that it is the stigma and criminalization of sex work that makes sex workers more vulnerable to violence. Notably, the violent aggressors who target sex workers are not interested in exchanging sex for money but in acting out their violence and hatred of women.

Lucy, unfortunately, has had personal experience with this misogyny and whorephobia. When she became a sex worker activist (before she shut down her activist and escort websites completely), a man discovered her profile online and started harassing her. He was not a client and they had never met, but he objected strongly to what she was doing for work and as an activist. He found out where she lived, stalked her, and set a small fire in her garage. She managed to get a restraining order against him. In eighteen years as a sex worker, Lucy had never had a bad experience with a client, but for the first time she experienced the dangers of a man seemingly filled with hatred for her, trying to control and threaten her.

It was a very overwhelming experience for me, and I had a lot of friends telling me that they thought I should be doing this, and they thought I should be doing that, and, whatever, you know with putting security systems and all of that in my house, and I'm like, "that's not how I want to live. And that's not going to protect me. If he wants to kill me, he's going to kill me. And that's the reality of it." And as scary as that is to admit, it's still the fucking reality of it.

Fifty years after the sexual revolution we are still dealing with whore-phobia and the sexual double standard between men and women; the consequences of which are epitomized in the bad treatment of sex workers. The second part of this book explores the debates about sex work and the question of whether to continue to stigmatize or try to normalize sex work. What is the best strategy for ending the oppression of sex workers and someday ending the good girl/bad girl binary? For ending whore stigma? Prohibitionists and conservatives want to continue the stigma of prostitution so that women won't sell and men won't buy or at least will be discouraged from doing so. If the stigma was removed and prostitution was normalized, prohibitionists argue, more men would think it's okay to buy the bodies of women. Sex workers and their allies believe that we should stop stigmatizing sex work, sex workers and their clients, as difficult as that is going to be. There is no question that men need to be held accountable for their treatment of women (in all occupations), but what happens when sexual and whore stigma is continually reinforced?

The problems of sex work can be summarized by prohibitionists in one of two main ways: prostitution is exploitative because of the monetary transaction, and it's harmful because of men's violence. I will argue that the third problematic aspect of sex work, which is not as openly acknowledged by prohibitionists but is most common in person-on-the-street interviews, and underlies the prohibitionist critique, is the idea that sex work is degrading, disgusting, or sinful (because of the sex aspect presumably).[73] These three elements will be explored in the next three chapters along with the overarching question of whether or not the prohibitionist goal of eradicating sex work can eliminate slut-shaming and whore stigma.

PART TWO

The "Bad Girl" Problem

Chapter Four

The Money Problem – Is Sex Work Work?

"When I was in college in the Bronx, I volunteered at the
Legal Aid Society and I would watch the prostituted women
be arraigned at night court once a month and I would look
into the faces of these women and I knew ... that I was looking at some of the most broken human beings on the planet."
– Sylvia

"On a scale from 1 to 10, if murder is the worst thing you
can do to your fellow human being, giving them an orgasm
has got to be, like, way up to the top."
– Norma Jean A.

Can the worldviews expressed in these two interview quotes ever be rec-
onciled? The first is from the former executive director of a major antitrafficking organization in the United States who believes prostitution is
inherently violence against women. The second quote is from a well-
known sex work activist who believes that sex work is work and can be en-
joyable for both the client and the provider. The former believes that no
woman will be free until prostitution is eliminated, and the latter equally
firmly believes that no woman will be free until sex workers are able to
work without stigma and shame. The coexistence of these opposing views
vividly illustrates why agreement about what to do about sex work law and

policy has not happened in North America or Europe[1] in the way it has with women's reproductive rights and LGBTQ+ rights, as mentioned in the previous chapter.

Unfortunately, there is a fundamental and perhaps irreconcilable split between prohibitionist feminists and sex worker activists and scholars. On the one hand, if you believe that prostitution is violence against women and is intrinsically harmful, no amount of legal reform can remove the damage. Similarly, if you believe that women have the right to choose to be sex workers then antiprostitution laws are arguably oppressive. The prohibitionists are trying to eradicate sex work and end the demand for it by *maintaining* the stigma (and actually *increasing* stigma, particularly now for clients), while sex work activists and their allies are trying to make sex work safer by *removing* the stigma. Both groups see it as a human rights issue but with diametrically opposed understandings of the problem and therefore of solutions. While the two camps agree on at least three important issues (the sellers of sex should not be criminalized, trafficking is a crime, and children cannot choose to sell sex), they fundamentally disagree on whether male clients should be criminalized and whether prostitution can ever be a work choice.

This chapter will look at the idea of sex work as exploitative from an economic point of view, examine the idea that consent cannot be bought, and show how the women I interviewed were able to challenge these perceptions. The philosophical debates around sex work as work will be outlined as well as the issues of class, capitalism, low wage work, stigma, and "dirty work" to show how choice and agency are manifested for the women interviewed. What, if anything, is wrong with selling sex if there is no violence being perpetrated? If a woman truly chooses? Can people buy and sell sex with respect and dignity? Can sex work ever really be work?

Prohibitionist Arguments against Sex Work as Work

Antiprostitution groups, law enforcement, and religious groups in Canada and the US clearly say no to the idea that prostitution can ever be legitimate work. In fact, prohibitionists refuse to use the term sex work at all. As Sylvia, the former executive director of a large antitrafficking organization in the

US states, "I don't believe that human sexuality is work. I don't believe that every aspect of being a human being can be reduced to labour, to work. I think human sexuality is that part of ourselves, that part of being human that should not be for sale, should not be turned into a commodity that can be bought or sold, so on that front we don't recognize sex as work so we don't call anyone a sex worker."

The term sex work is offensive to antiprostitution activists because it signals women's choice to be victimized, and they refuse to use it.

> We know that that term [sex work] comes out of the sex industry, that wants to constantly normalize prostitution – get us to accept prostitution – and that leads me to [question] why would there be people who might call themselves feminists or human rights people, why would they support prostitution? There's been a real concerted effort to get our culture to accept commercial sexual exploitation as the norm, as liberating even, and you have to understand the sex industry has a huge personal, political and profit-based interest in doing that. (Sylvia)

So antiprostitution activists call sex workers "prostituted women" to indicate that they have not chosen to be used and abused by men and to signal that they can't consent to their victimization. "First of all, we understand that prostitution is a function of lack of choice. All of us understand very logically that prostitution is a function of inequality. That it comes out of negative social conditions. And so you have racism, poverty, gender inequality, pimps, you have a whole confluence of forces that push women into prostitution. Most of us understand full well that prostitution does not stem from choice" (Sylvia).

In this view, prostituted women cannot consent to selling sex because they cannot consent to their own exploitation. As Julie Bindel, a prominent UK prohibitionist puts it, "If 'consent' has to be bought, it is not consent."[2] Trisha Baptie, a self-described Canadian prostitution survivor, contends the same: "Men who purchase sex are paying to rape women. I don't think you can buy consent. Consent has to be freely given and it has to be a mutual relationship that benefits both parties. At best what men buy is complacency."[3] As Ash Denham proclaimed, "The exchange of money does not buy consensual sex. As one survivor put it: 'They do not buy our consent, they buy our silence.'"[4]

Furthermore, prohibitionists believe that selling sex is actually selling bodies, not simply a sexual service. "The buying of human flesh in my view is a human rights violation. I believe truly in the Swedish model which is that that is pure victimization of a person," says Claire, the executive director of an antitrafficking and child exploitation group in Canada. And prostitution includes any sexual activity where anything is exchanged or transacted. Says Sylvia, "I mean we've always defined prostitution as including and not limited to just the exchange of money. Trading sex for anything, so none of that is new. Yes, any time a human being is having sex for any reason other than it's what they want, if they are having sex because they need something that includes being prostituted." That's because, in this view, prostitution gives the buyer control over the seller (e.g. the seller has to do anything the buyer wants because he is paying for it). Buying sex gives men unfettered access to women's bodies, and because of the exchange of money men treat women like commodities and as nothing more than body parts. Sylvia again:

> Prostitution is really about creating a class of human beings that are going to be available to be used and abused through sex. It's about creating a class of human beings who are not supposed to feel. It's about suppressing the humanity of that person that you've bought. Well, any society that is going to be about respecting the human rights of its citizens … is not going to tolerate anyone being bought and sold for sexual use and abuse.

Therefore, the sex trade is inherently unequal and it should be illegal to traffic in sex just as it is illegal to traffic in body parts. The only solution is to end demand. Antiprostitution activists believe that sex work should be eradicated like child sexual abuse and domestic violence:

> The [organization] takes a very principled position on the issue of prostitution. We see prostitution as violence against women. We see prostitution as standing at odds with any goal of achieving equality

for women and we've all grown up with this idea that we heard that "oh, prostitution always was and always will be." And you really have to look at that for what it is, which is an acceptance of the oppression of women. Prostitution is not inevitable. We can absolutely live in a world free of prostitution and we will live in that world. (Sylvia)

The antiprostitution argument, therefore, is threefold: sexuality in general should not be commodified, the act of paying for sex gives men power over women, and, most problematically, prostitution constitutes an act of violence against women (the first and second arguments will be dealt with in this chapter, violence against women in the next). Consequently, prostitution is an insult to human dignity, violates the dignity of women in particular, and is "incompatible with the principles of respect, justice and equality."[5] This perspective is shared by those advocating for the Nordic model where selling sex is decriminalized but the buying of sex is not. It assumes that the paying customer (usually male) is inherently exploitative and is exercising his power over the sex worker (usually female).

There is not a lot of ambiguity in prohibitionist statements because if you believe prostitution is inherently harmful to women then you also believe that as a practice or institution it can't be reformed. If it can't be reformed, then it must be eradicated. Prohibitionists seem to believe that eradicating prostitution will eradicate the sexual oppression of women or at least stop the oppression from continuing in this overt way. How this will happen is not made clear in their arguments. If men didn't think they could "buy" women, they would "respect" women more, presumably, or at least know it is socially and legally unacceptable to buy sex. Would destigmatizing the sex industry lead only to the destigmatizing of male entitlement? Or would it also help us to eliminate slut-shaming and whore stigma?

Philosophical Debates on Sex Work

Most of the antiprostitution voices quoted above come from political activists, but there have been important philosophical debates about sex work as well. The differences between Carole Pateman and Christine Overall, on the one hand, and Martha Nussbaum and Laurie Shrage, on the other, are illustrative here and show how little has changed theoretically in the philosophy of sex work since the 1990s. The matter just seems to have become more polarized and politicized.

Carole Pateman, writing in 1988, argued that prostitution is the epitome of male entitlement, i.e., an integral part of what she called "the sexual contract" where men buy access to women's bodies. She defends against "contractarian" arguments about prostitution on the grounds that "patriarchal right is explicitly embodied in 'freedom of contract.'"[6] Women are not autonomous and equal to men and therefore it is not a contract between equals: it is a contract between unequals.[7] The fact that most prostitutes are women and most clients are male is not a contingent fact for her because "the problem of prostitution then becomes encapsulated in the question of why men demand that women's bodies are sold as commodities in the capitalist market."[8] A liberal analysis, where a "sexually neutral, universal" prostitution is assumed, is faulty because prostitution is fundamentally gendered; the positions of male and female in prostitution cannot be reversed. While women sell themselves, "sex mastery is the major means through which men affirm their manhood."[9] So, asks Pateman, what is wrong with prostitution? "The law of male sex right is publicly affirmed."[10] Her argument, like that of the prohibitionist activists, is that prostitution is inherently exploitative and an example of the sexual contract; male domination won't end until sexual domination ends.

Christine Overall, writing in 1992, makes several convincing arguments as to how sex work is similar to many other types of work under capitalism, comparing "cooks, secretaries and university professors."[11] She says she wants "to discover what, if anything, makes prostitution worse than other forms of paid labor in capitalist society."[12] In terms of violence, coercion, and nonreciprocity, she gives examples that indicate these problems are not unique to prostitution. However, while she recognizes that choices are always constrained under capitalism, she ultimately concludes that because we live in a male-dominated society, sex work can't be empowering or seen as work. She acknowledges the freedom of individual women to be sex workers but cannot support prostitution as a practice for women as a group. As she writes, "I am not condemning sex workers for doing the work they do. I want to maintain a crucial moral distinction between prostitutes as sex workers and prostitution as a practice and institution."[13] In the end, she sides with Pateman that sex work is not to be encouraged – since the practice is so gendered and we live in a male-dominated world. "Prostitution is a classist, ageist, racist and sexist industry, in which the disadvantaged sell services to those who are more privileged."[14] Though again, she reiterates that lots of industries are exploitative, she insists that the problem with prostitution is how fundamentally gendered it is. What is wrong with prostitution, therefore, is that "women's servicing of men's sexual needs ... construct the buying of sexual services as a benefit for men, and make the reversibility of sex services implausible and sexual equality in the trade unattainable."[15] We can't imagine the reverse – a world where women go to male sex workers so the practice must be condemned. It is not "reversible."[16]

Embedded within Overall's argument, however, is a problem that is not adequately dealt with because of her belief that the relations between men and women in prostitution are essentially immutable. "While the sale of sex helps to define woman, it also condemns her; the purchase of sex also helps to define men, but it does not condemn him."[17] This condemnation or "whore stigma," as we saw in chapter 3, is a fundamental problem for all women and that it is not problematized or seen as an issue in its own right to be overcome (by destigmatizing sex work and sex workers – as opposed to accepting the stigmatization as essential) is a major issue not addressed by antiprostitution activists and scholars. In fact, Overall goes as far as to claim that "prostitutes may actually be 'good girls' in the eyes of capitalist patriarchy: despite the individual strengths some may derive from their work, prostitutes serve certain patriarchal purposes very well."[18] So women who sell sex willingly, in this view, can be seen as collaborators to the patriarchy. Her (perhaps ironic) view of prostitutes as "good girls," however, fundamentally reinforces the good girl/bad girl binary. The question of why any of us are judged by and condemned for our sexual/job status is not addressed or problematized by Overall, nor are any solutions proposed except for continued stigma of both women who sell sex and men who buy.

Laurie Shrage disputes Overall's essentialist arguments by showing that prostitution happens in very different social and historical contexts and that accounts of prostitution "should not seek the universal causes of sex work, and it should not presuppose the universal meaning of sex."[19]

I think their work [Pateman and Overall] up until now on prostitution, has made broader claims about sex work, more universal claims
that I'm willing to make ... They think that any form of prostitution
where most of the [sex workers] are women and most of the clients
are men ... just essentially reproduces very sexist gender relations
that are bad for women and it's kind of the argument that if women
are subordinate in the bedroom, they're going to be subordinate in
society. That sex roles define other social roles.

Shrage points out the problem with this analysis for sex workers themselves. Many feminists, she writes, have failed to mobilize in favour of sex
worker's rights because of their "ambivalence" about prostitution, but in
doing so "feminists have contributed to a climate conducive to their continued degradation."[20] Because of their belief that decriminalization will
lead to more prostitution, some feminists are willing to tolerate the abuse
of some sex working women. Shrage argues that "feminists find it fright-
ening to imagine but we can better protect those who sell sex if we tolerate
commercial sex."[21] The main issue for Shrage is whether the work is voluntary or forced.

We have to distinguish forms of prostitution that take place where
there aren't conditions that we see with trafficking, where people are
not working under slave conditions, where they have a fair amount
of control over the terms of their work, where ... the workers are
adults, adult women, adult men, and you know it's not a perfect job,
as I said earlier, I wouldn't say this is the most glamorous work, but
there are people who would choose this work over other options
they have. It's a service job where you have to cater to a lot of demanding customers.

Martha Nussbaum,[22] taking the "contractarian" side, argues that sex
work is just like other types of work and gives numerous examples of jobs
that have aspects in common with sex work. She describes the similarities
of each in order to show how hypocritical our singling out of sex work
really is. She uses the examples of professors, chicken processing plant
workers, domestics, singers, massage therapists, and "colonoscopy artists"

to show how various types of work involve the body, exploitation, and various degrees of autonomy and choice. As she writes, we all sell our bodies in various ways with varying levels of money, control, and options.[23] Is the prohibition against selling sex, she asks, reasoned or prejudiced? She convincingly argues that it is the *stigma* that is the real problem, not the inherent nature of prostitution. As she writes, the feminist [prohibitionist] critique cannot explain the pervasive stigma against women who sell sex and why "prostitutes are ... held in distain."[24] What prohibitionists don't understand is that "stigma has to be attached to prostitutes" and they have to be separated from "good" women based on the idea "that women are essentially immoral and dangerous" and must be controlled by men to ensure their wives' monogamy.[25] Because women are harmed by stigma, and it is based on a "hysterical fear of women's unfettered sexuality," Nussbaum argues that "the real injury [of stigma] ... is not best handled through legal strictures."[26] It is the stigma, then, that must be addressed in any discussion of sex work because it is not "rational or defensible" and only hurts women more. "In short, sex hierarchy causes stigma, commonly, not through feminist critique, but through a far more questionable set of social meanings, meanings that anyone concerned about justice for women should call into question."[27]

Sex Work as "Dirty Work"

Stigmatized work is not a new concept. The idea of "dirty work" or "abject labour" has a long history in management and psychology scholarship. As far back as 1958, E.C. Hughes described how certain occupations become "tainted." Society, he argued, creates these categories of dirty work and then proceeds to stigmatize the workers who do the work, disowning or disavowing them. Society, having created the work, then wants to protect itself from the work, and it is this marginalization from "polite society" that stigmatizes the workers. The status of occupations can change over time, as some work considered prestigious today – actors, singers, performers, for instance – was once highly stigmatized, as Nussbaum[28] points out in her work, and some occupations can be tainted but still be of relatively high status, like law or politics.

Dirty work is considered disgusting or degrading for some physical, social, or moral reason and hence becomes tainted. Dirty work that has its
basis in the physical includes jobs that deal with garbage or human fluids,
so they are occupations like cleaners, garbage collectors, and morticians.
These taints stigmatize the workers as low status or low income but the
work itself is seen as necessary, not evil.[29] Social taints refer to jobs like
lawyers or politicians whose professions the general public tends to mistrust. They can also include jobs that deal with negative social issues, like
addictions counsellors, or those that necessitate being involved with people
who are stigmatized themselves – police or corrections officers who must
associate with criminals. These jobs, though stigmatized, are also seen to be
necessary for society and so not as stigmatized as the final category. Moral
taints are associated with those jobs that go against some societal norm relating to virtue or are perceived as deceptive in some way, like lawyers,
politicians and used car salesmen, or which violate a religious concept like
sin. These workers are seen as especially tainted because the jobs are not
seen as necessary but as "evil" in the starkest terms.[30] Some occupations
have two or more taints, increasing their stigmatization. Sex workers are
tainted on all three accounts and are therefore triply stigmatized: their work
is rooted in the physical (in the messiness of sex and the body), is perceived
as antifamily (therefore antisocial), and is viewed as deeply immoral.

Stigma hurts sex workers as Cecilia Benoit and her collaborators have
shown.[31] They outline the negative effects of stigma "on the working conditions, personal lives, and health of sex workers"[32] and argue that prostitution stigma is a "fundamental determinant of social inequality for sex
workers."[33] They describe stigma as a "powerful structural mechanism of
social control"[34] at the macro (laws, policies, and media), meso (institutions
like the justice and healthcare systems), and micro (public/individual)
levels.[35] Using examples from India, Russia, Hong Kong, Senegal, and Costa
Rica they show how social stigma negatively impacts sex workers. "Female
sex workers, in particular, are subjected to degrading treatment in public
spaces."[36] In the Philippines, stigma prevented many bar girls from having
family or community support when needed, isolated them to the smaller
community of fellow bar girls, and decreased their self-esteem and self-
worth. The bar girls were looked down on by society at large. They reported
rough treatment and harassment at the social hygiene clinic when getting

smears (why would it hurt, she's so used to it?). They were not allowed into church because they were deemed "fallen women" (in a Roman Catholic country where religion is very important). They were called *pok pok* by passersby (a very foul word for prostitute in Tagalog). They could not tell the very family that profited by their labour what they did for a living. They reported not being believed at the social hygiene clinic when they'd been assaulted, not being told what they were diagnosed with when they got an STI, and not receiving treatment.[37] The impact of societal double standards meant that there were no consequences for male customers, bar owners, or recruiters since women were the criminals and men the victims.

Benoit et al. illustrate how sex worker organizations and individual sex workers have attempted to reframe "the apparent immutability of prostitution stigma"[38] by collective action (unfortunately without success as illustrated also by Shrage in chapter 3). "Reframing techniques include seeing sex work as a routine economic activity and reframing sex work in terms that emphasize its normality and acceptability as a facet of one's social identity."[39] But because, as Nussbaum has argued, whore stigma is based on the irrational fear of and for women's sexuality, and our discomfort and hypocrisy about sex, reframing doesn't work without a recognition of the underlying sexual double standard. "The available evidence indicates that prostitution stigma originates in cultural norms about gender and sexuality," as Benoit et al. put it,[40] and it is those norms that must be challenged.

Sex Work as Intimate Labour

Sex work is, therefore, stigmatized work but Laurie Shrage also believes that much of the problem with people's views of sex work has to do with seeing some work as bad or degrading:

> Providing people human and sexual comfort for a living isn't degrading if it's done under conditions that are respectful and where the interests of all parties are protected. And so it seems to me that people who see this form of work as inherently degrading either have fairly negative attitudes toward certain forms of labour that you know have

traditionally been seen as either as low status or they have degrading attitudes toward human sexuality.

Degradation is clearly a subjective term because it indicates humiliation or shame and people feel differently about what counts as degrading activity. Some people have a comfort with the body and sex and others much less so. Some people have more shame than others about the body, which would make working with bodies more difficult for them. But making a living dealing intimately with the body is not uncommon. Massage therapists need to be comfortable doing bodywork and touching people they don't know. They deal with men and women's incontinence issues through manual, digital stimulation, for instance. So do doctors. Aestheticians doing Brazilian waxes and anal bleaching need to be very comfortable with the body. Personal care workers who look after the sick or elderly have to do very intimate tasks. Nannies exchange money for intimate, caring work. We expect seniors and children to be cared for with love and respect but also for money. Why is it so different with sex? As Nussbaum's work points out, there is much hypocrisy and prudishness surrounding sex work.

People who do intimate labour must be comfortable with the body or accept that what they are doing is just work. An Indigenous and African Nova Scotian sex worker who used to work in Halifax underscores this point when she says that her sex work gave her economic and empowerment opportunities she would never have had otherwise even when she didn't enjoy the work.[41] "In my situation, coming up the way I did, the first time that I could say to a man 'This is what you can do, this is what you can't do, and this is what you're going to pay me to do it' was very empowering to me. Someone who has not experienced what I've experienced might not get it, but it put me in control of my body ... Plus, I had money! I wasn't in a situation where I had to depend on somebody else for stuff."[42] She took a very matter-of-fact attitude towards sex, the body, and men. "So, you gotta jerk them off – no big deal. Although I would always be jerking and gagging at the same time. My sister and I laugh, because we both ended up in the sex trade although neither one of us can stand the smell of semen and both of us are scared of the dark [laughs]."[43]

Intimate labour is generally not problematized except if it's for sexual labour. Sex is a special category for moral reasons and probably biological ones. The arguments against sex work seem to always come back to the "invasion" or "penetration" of female "orifices."[44] Using misogynist language to reduce women to their body parts is one way to dehumanize sex workers, as well as making sex work seem less like work than cleaning up someone else's bodily waste. As Shrage has written, "by insisting on degradation, those who use the metaphors only add to the degradation they presumably oppose."[45] Again, the misogyny of using this kind of language is lost on prohibitionists, as the vivid examples from Juno Mac and Molly Smith show. "It doesn't comfort or uplift sex workers to know that our being likened to toilets, loaves of bread, meat, dogs or robots is all part of a project apparently more important that our dignity. Feminist women ... gleefully reference the 'jizz' we've presumably encountered and our 'orifices' and tell us to stick to 'sucking and fucking'... Sex workers are associated with sex, and to be associated with sex is to be dismissible."[46]

Does the exchange of money inherently degrade a sexual interaction? Is selling sex really like selling your body like it's a body part? The women I interviewed certainly didn't think so. As Maria said,

> The exchange of money does not put me in a subordinate position. The exchange of money allows, gives me a certain amount ... [of power/prestige]. Like for example if you go to a doctor you're going to pay that doctor a large amount of money for their time and because that doctor has skills ... you're going to pay the doctor a lot of money and you respect that doctor for the skills they have. And so I felt very much like a professional, very much like I deserved to get paid what I got paid and they respected me more because they gave me money.

Amanda was adamant about delinking sex for money from violence and degradation. "I just don't understand what is violent about that. I would say that to make that argument [we should also be asking] are people who are working at McDonald's or Burger King, isn't that a form of violence? I mean like they're sweating and they're flipping burgers and it's hot back there, I mean what kind of work is that?" Lucy, too, who has worked in many other jobs, objected to the idea that she can't choose sex work because the monetary transaction makes it violence against women.

I have a hard time understanding why it's okay for me to use my body in any other labour capacity, whether, you know I've worked extensively in the restaurant field and why is it okay for me to in the summer time be behind like two 500 degree stoves and a broiler sweating my ass off and working and getting injured, you know with burning myself on pans and working with knives and having those things going on and having abusive managers and chefs yelling at you if you're not performing up to capacity, and I mean I'm renting my body for that capacity, why don't I have the right to choose to rent my body in whatever way I am comfortable with? I actually feel like I've had more autonomy and a more rewarding experience from an employment labour standpoint being a sex worker than I have in the restaurant business.

Laurie Shrage shares this point of view. "I don't think just because something takes place in a commercial context or in a market context that it's necessarily degraded because of it ... I mean in our society we obtain a lot of services and money exchanges hands, but we don't think it necessarily degrades the service or the human interaction. And I would say the same with sexuality. I don't think there's any reason the exchange of money should inherently degrade the interaction."

Lucy, who has been in and out of sex work for eighteen years, has engaged in sex work for many different reasons but ultimately sees her work as intimate labour:

Some of us gravitate towards like intimate labour and nurturing jobs, that's what we're meant to do, that's me, right there. I love helping make other people feel good in a multitude of ways. But it's also for some of us a sexual outlet. I'm a lifestyle person so it's also about my own personal sexuality, my own exploration of my sexuality in my work. Sometimes it's a short-term thing, I just need some quick money, I'm paying off a debt, I want to go on vacation ... So people get into sex work for specific amounts of time, for specific goals.

Even with a cursory glance of the logic behind the antiprostitution lobby, several problems can be seen. Is there something special about sexuality that means it cannot be transacted in a commercial context? Prohibitionists seem to be making a moral argument about the specialness of sex. Anna believes that "prostitution, the simple act of exchanging sex for money, there's nothing inherently wrong with that. [It's] a moral call, and I certainly am not going to judge the exchange of sex for money ... I'm interested in looking at this as work, which is what it is." Norma Jean Almodovar is even more explicit that shaming people for consensual sexual acts is a moral claim that should not carry public policy weight. "And I understand people have a moral issue with prostitution, they have a moral issue with homosexuality and all that. You know what, it isn't their business and as long as nobody forces them to hire prostitutes or to be a prostitute or to be gay or to engage in a relationship, it just isn't their business to get involved in somebody else's life."

So if we can see sex work as unfairly stigmatized work, often because it involves sex and the body, and if we accept the similarities between sex work and other forms of intimate labour, can we also see sex work as simply an economic transaction?

Sex Work as an Economic Choice

Liberal views of work, like Nussbaum's, usually emphasize the contractual nature of work and individual choice. They tend to frame exchanges of money for labour as an exercise of free choice that shows preference for one job over another and to suggest that all jobs have downsides. Many people work in jobs simply for the money and many jobs are low status or low income. Several of the women interviewed took this view. Says Anna, "When you're exchanging any kind of service for money, you're working. So if you're working, how can you do that in the safest way possible and the healthiest way possible? I think that choices are all constrained by something ... So you work at Starbucks not because you choose to [over much better work] but because they had a job opening and you needed to pay your rent." Amanda was also clear that sex work takes different forms and like all jobs has its pros and cons:

And so I would argue that prostitution can be a very compassionate, loving profession and anyone who doesn't like having sex for money shouldn't do it. But those of us who like having sex for money are capable, we're actual women, we're not like little infantile children, you know, we have a voice, we have opinions, we have different experiences from one another. Some days we love our work, some days we don't feel like going in to work. Sometimes you get burnt out and you need to take a break. You have to really know yourself.

Christine Milrod takes a very straight forward, liberal approach to women selling sex. "My response would be that these women feel that they are being paid adequately for a service that they wish to perform and not only that, they are the ones setting the price. If a woman feels that access to her sexual techniques and her sexual behavior and practice is worth $500 an hour, then that's what she feels it's worth. And it's her right to put a price on that."

Socialist feminists like Pateman and Overall tend to view most work as exploitative and are wary of any transactions involving sex, including marriage, as we will see below. They are more critical of the idea of "choice" about work given how limited employee choices actually are. Amanda outlined a classic socialist feminist viewpoint but criticized its selective application:

What they [antiprostitution activists] are saying and what I kind of understand in terms of what they're saying, is that our patriarchal, capitalist system structures the relationship between a prostitute and a client such that the prostitute is never capable of having agency, having desire, being a real human being. And if you're going to say patriarchy and capitalism well, you can't just apply it to prostitutes and clients. You have to apply it to the guy flipping a burger and standing at the cash register and the person buying the burger. What's that interaction about? You know capitalism and patriarchy don't just apply to one small segment of the population. If you're going to use the argument you really have to carry it to its full extent.

Friedrich Engels was one of the first theorists to compare prostitution to marriage under capitalism: "marriage among the upper classes was always a marriage of 'convenience' and often of a crass form of prostitution."[47] Where a wife contracts with just one man – her husband who promised to support her in exchange for her faithfulness and legitimate children – a prostitute contracts with many. And Engels is much more critical of the situation of the wife. A wife "differs from the ordinary courtesan only in that she does not hire out her body, like a wage worker, on piecework, but sells it into slavery once and for all."[48] He also recognized the sexual double standard between men and women. "What for women is a crime [adultery and sex outside marriage] is ... considered a slight moral blemish" in a man[49] so the idea of sex as an economic transaction has been around for a long time, as has the sexual double standard.

Engels recognized that capitalism made all things into commodities including sexuality and believed that prostitution would not end until the "the link between marriage and property" was severed.[50] Only when these social, moral, and economic factors disappear will a girl, as Engels called her, be able to give "herself completely to the man she loves"[51] without fear of consequences. And only when people can freely dispose of their "persons, actions and possessions"[52] will they be able to freely contract on any basis, on an equal footing. Only then will we have "a generation of men who never in their lives have known what it is to buy a woman's surrender with money ... and "a generation of women who have never known what it is to give themselves [*sic*] to a man from any other consideration than real love."[53] It seems almost quaint in this day and age.

If we look at the history of marriage or have watched any version of *The Housewives of Beverly Hills* it is hard not to see the connection between money and sex, so Engels's and Sylvia's belief that all transactional relationships mean women are being "prostituted" might be considered a bit naïve. As Melissa Ditmore states:

> If one were to look at financial relationships and sexual relationships and where they intersect, you really, really want to start dissecting that. The sex industry is just the beginning and the most obvious. Or perhaps, for some people, the least obvious. Financial considerations are an aspect of marriage, in the law. It is not only the sex industry that combines sex and money, but also family life. And certainly marriage law and estate law address this in much more depth than law about the sex industry ... But if you really wanted to disentangle sex and money, you have a much bigger job than just the sex industry.

There are many factors that impact work choices – family expectations, financial needs, education, values, and general life circumstances. Benoit et al. argue that the sex workers in their study got into sex work for three (sometimes overlapping) reasons: "critical life events, desire or need for money and personal appeal of the work."[54] This was no different with the women I interviewed. Anna is the thirty-year-old political strategist who worked on the streets of the Downtown Eastside of Vancouver when she was going to college and then as an online escort. She currently volunteers with a sex worker rights organization and runs media workshops for sex work activists. Anna has experienced the "good" (online escorting) and "bad" (street-level, survival sex) of sex work. This background shapes her perception of sex work as just a job, not to be celebrated or disparaged but to be seen as a labour rights issue. "I did prostitution again the second time and it was actually a good experience. It's the kind of experience that you know most people talk about in terms of job satisfaction: easy work, good money, great hours."

Anna feels very strongly that sex work is marginalized and stigmatized because it is illegal and not seen as real work. "I don't have complaints with prostitution as a concept inherently, exchanging sex for money can be a great way to make money but there's a lot of things about the way our society has itself set up that make it a lot more dangerous, a lot more problematic and a lot more harmful to people than it needs to be." She acknowledges that there are downsides to sex work but believes that it is no worse than other work. "I think that more people doing various kinds of sex work, of all parts of the industry, really do see it as a job. And you know just like most people don't really like their Starbucks job where they're making the crazy mocha latte with the foam and the picky customer who returns it cause it wasn't double whipped or whatever." Anna was the most insistent that sex work is a job like any other and that the health and safety concerns of the workers outweigh any moral issues about the work.

The fact that sex workers are motivated by money should not come as a surprise. Sex work is lucrative for many women, and it is one of the few job categories where women make more than men. Mears and Connell "identify three such occupations: fashion modeling, porn acting, and stripping, each with wage gaps that remunerate women between 200–1,000 percent more than men."[55] While this fact can be criticized for what it says about how society values women's labour and bodies (however much we might wish it to be otherwise), the reality is that women make very good money doing erotic labour of all kinds, most perfectly legal.[56] In the case of sex work, women are actually exchanging higher income for lower status and stigma because of its illegality.[57] How is that different from other workers making an "informed 'rational choice' ... rather than a 'free choice' which is available to few individuals in a society that is structured hierarchically by race, sex and class?"[58] As Benoit et al. state,

> we need to think about sex work as involving a continuum of occupational experiences, ranging in degree of empowerment/choice to oppression/exploitation. Utilizing an occupational framework that makes use of language similar to that used when discussing other types of labor in late modern capitalist societies (i.e., services, emphasis on sex "work") begins the task of normalizing this type of labor and drawing similarities with other forms of employment, particularly low-prestige and low-income front-line service work.[59]

In other words, choices are always made within constraints of one sort or another, and we do not live in a utopia where everyone has the education, freedom, and ability to become doctors or pilots or whatever other job they might think desirable. Women make choices to do work that others think problematic because they believe it is the best way for them to live at that moment and it offers them the best way to provide for themselves financially. As Lucy states,

> to say that someone is a bad person for making a certain choice in their life when they're only trying to do the best that they can ... it just doesn't help I think women when we criticize each other in that manner ... [whether] you're speaking about some of the workers who are in the position of getting involved in prostitution because they don't have any other job opportunities ... [or] whether they're a caregiver for a family member, they have a special needs child, they have education that they're trying to complete, this affords them the time to be able to take care of those things, and when you're getting in the way for them to be able to make money, you're harming the

workers. Okay? You're harming them by restricting their ability to
do their work.

As many studies of sex work show, sex workers have a variety of working
experiences.[60] Many workers prefer sex work to minimum wage jobs.[61]
Some workers do not enjoy sex work and wish to do other things but cannot find work at the same income.[62] Some dislike their clients; some think
of them as friends.[63] Regardless of how many studies are done on sex worker
preferences, however, the exploitation narrative continues unabated. Beloso
argues that this is because class has been written out of feminists' accounts
of sex work.[64] We fail to see sex workers as labourers and sex as a product
of their labour, so we are left with only the lens of exploitation. "Instead,
feminists tend to conflate the two, everywhere seeing prostitutes as victims
who always happen to be women (or girls) but never workers."[65]

"Bourgeois consciousness," in the words of Brewis and Linstead, is also
notoriously unwilling or unable to see that sex work may genuinely be
preferable for an individual to working at McDonalds or a slaughterhouse,
in their example.[66] And, as Beloso states, "the feminist who sees only victims
everywhere she or he looks at prostitution misses entirely the ingenuity and
agency of the human being who chooses to work in the sex industry rather
than, say the sweatshop industry ... because the wages and working conditions are, to his or her mind, better."[67]

All of the women I interviewed said good pay and flexible hours made
sex work a choice for them. And sex work is a lucrative way to make a living
for women with and without other job skills. A minimum wage worker
might make $15 an hour; a professional maybe $50. An escort like Lucy
with a two-hour minimum makes $200 an hour. A high-end escort like
the one Eliot Spitzer went to makes ten times that amount. It makes sense
then that some women would choose sex work over other options. As
Almodovar states,

Why can't you earn a living doing something you like? If I like giving
pleasure and I make good money at it, why do they have to get in my
face and say "you're being exploited"? Excuse me, I'm an intelligent
human being and I say bullshit. I am not being exploited. This man
is paying me for my time, he's paying me, he's compensating me for

something that I could otherwise legally give away to thousands of men for free and nobody wants to throw me in jail.

Her comments highlight another hypocrisy about sex work: criminalizing sex between consenting adults because of the belief that women are inherently victims. The rise in sugar dating for university students trying to pay off debt and pay their way through school is another example of the exchange of sex for money. While sugar babies want to distance themselves from prostitution, they are trading their sexuality and company for money or presents, just as escorts do. In the 2018 Canadian film *The New Romantic* the main character debates with her best friend whether what she is doing (exchanging sex for an expensive scooter and jewellery) makes her a "hooker" (her words, not mine) but is reassured that because she has a "relationship" with the older, richer man, it's not prostitution.[68] Perhaps if we didn't have such a stigma against the exchange of sex for money and contempt for women who are "gold-diggers" we wouldn't need to distance ourselves from other women who *are* "hookers." Stigma and class encourage white, middle-class young women to distance themselves from what they are doing and further stigmatizes actual sex workers. Proclaiming "I am not a prostitute," just like "I am not a slut," reinforces the idea that it is bad to be one.

But the bigger point is Almodovar's question: If you can do something for free, she asks, why can't you do it for money? We can use Tinder and Grindr and have sex for free with whomever we want. We can have children and give them up for adoption. We can donate our kidneys and our eggs and sperm, and be surrogates for others, but we can't do any of these things for money (at least in Canada) because it supposedly taints the interaction and makes it open to abuse.[69]

But why isn't the (regulated) market an appropriate model for the selling and buying of sex? The arguments against paid egg donation and surrogacy are relevant here because they are also about "protecting" women and not adding to their exploitation. Women are seen to be unable to make decisions that might be in their best (economic) interests because they will be vulnerable to exploitation. Although it sounds counter-intuitive to me, Francoise Baylis, a prominent bioethicist at Dalhousie University, argues that eggs, surrogate services, and breast milk "should be gifted, to protect the donor's autonomy."[70] By this she means that "consent and autonomous decision making can be compromised when money is on the table." She makes a distinction between the exploitation of women (not being paid enough) and coercion (paid *too* much) so it is an incentive, presumably, for them to sell their eggs or surrogacy services.[71] As she notes, "the federal government aims to defend and promote the current altruistic system" by clarifying what expenses can be reimbursed to surrogates without actually paying them. This, she says, "allows the woman to give the gift of the ultimate gift of life" without compromising her autonomy.[72]

But maybe her autonomy is being compromised by not being able to exercise rights over her own body. Why does women's labour always have to be free: free eggs, free surrogacy, free sex, free milk? A recent debate about the regulation of and payment for women's breast milk led to the conclusion from the Canadian advocate that basically women should do all this labour out of the goodness of our hearts – "the Canadian way" as Baylis puts it.[73] The American woman was much more practical about the labour involved in women pumping milk for other women. It completely discounts, as she said, the work and time involved.[74] Until capitalism is eliminated this makes no sense at all and discriminates against women using the few advantages they have vis-à-vis men. Further, the arguments made by antisurrogacy and antiprostitution activists that no one has a right to children or sex is true legally, but both desires are strong drivers and if there are willing women and men and they choose to exchange their labour for money what is it but paternalism to say they have to do it for free?

Other consequences for poor people are more life threatening. In the documentary *Tales from the Organ Trade*, Canadian director Ric Esther Bienstock shows the shocking conditions of kidney donors in nonregulated systems and argues that because donors are always poor, we need to come up with an ethical and safe model for their compensation.[75] Like the sex trade, making the organ trade illegal has not eradicated it. Organ donations are happening, she says, whether we want them to or not, and so how do we make it as safe as possible? Most of the donors are poor and they're donating their kidneys in very unsafe and unsanitary conditions but because we can't accept organ donating for money, politically, we let it continue unsafely and with rampant exploitation. There are many legal and moral dilemmas with exchanging money for organs, eggs, surrogacy, and intimate labour, of course, but public policy makers also need to be concerned with people's safety, economic well being and autonomy.

Apart from moral arguments about sex, the idea that women can't consent to selling sex is also problematic. What is it about taking payment for sexual services that eliminates consent, when taking money for other services like personal care work or aesthetics does not? Does the massage therapist who takes money for a massage lack the same ability to consent? She wouldn't give the massage, probably, unless she was paid but how does consent work in this case and not in the case of exchanging a sexual service for money? I probably wouldn't teach if I wasn't paid, though I'd do my research for free, so does that mean I lack consent when I exchange my teaching for money? And if prohibitionists really just mean "consent for sex is not consent" then what about all other exchanges or transactions of a sexual nature? Exotic dancing and pornography aren't illegal but do the dancers and the porn actors lose their ability to consent because they are paid?

The only way we're going to truly know if women and men would "freely choose" sex work is if there was total economic well-being and equality between the sexes and between the First and Third Worlds. It would mean the end of capitalism as we know it because many people work at jobs they don't like just for money. It is particularly a catch-22 for sex workers in the Global South. A graphic comic called *Threadbare: Clothes, Sex and Trafficking* details the bleak choice between sex work and sweatshops.[76] Women leave garment work for sex work for better money but are rescued by antitrafficking activists and are put back into garment factories, trading the better-paid sex work, with its illegality and social stigma, for poorly paid work in sweatshops. The comic is a commentary on well-meaning nonprofits who want to criminalize the only (better) option the women have. It becomes a vicious circle.

Prohibitionists want to criminalize men buying sex because of the vulnerability of some women working in the sex trade. But the women I interviewed rejected the idea of trying to eliminate an entire industry because of bad players. As Anna says, "I just don't think that's a useful way to look at it. I don't think we look at other industries and say do we make rules for the happy construction worker and the unhappy construction worker? We make rules that make sense for construction workers, right? So I think, by

the same token, we want to be able to try and figure out what can go wrong
and how we protect against it."

This echoes the sentiments of many sex workers. As Ruth Morgan
Thomas, a former sex worker who is now the coordinator of the Global
Network of Sex Work Projects (GNSWP), says, "I come from a coal mining
family in Wales ... Lots of miners died. They didn't stop coal mining; they
made coal mining safer with better labour legislations."[77] Making work
safer means ensuring there are health and safety regulations, that women
can go to the police with assault claims, that they don't have to worry
about the police assaulting them, and that they have working conditions
that are respected.

Anna was more sceptical than the other women that sex work should
be valued in and of itself because she sees it mostly as a job that people do
for money. But all the other women interviewed for the film took a far more
positive view. They thought there was a value to sex work, other than just
money for them and sex for the clients, and that they themselves were empowered by it.

The Value of Sex Work

What is the value of sex work? To many people, including myself before I
met Lucy, this is an incomprehensible question. There is no value in sex
work outside the benefits to individual men having sex with desperate
women or perhaps to men (as a group) who benefit collectively from
women's disempowerment. There is no value in sex work because to most
people sex work is illegal and immoral. It is considered an inevitable but
regrettable part of society that most people would rather not think about
and generally only do think about when it shows up in their neighbour-
hood and a NIMBY petition starts to circulate. Polite society would prefer
that it just didn't exist. But it does exist, and public policy hasn't caught up
with more liberal sexual mores. There are internet adultery websites and
sugar-dating websites, and dating sites for just about any fetish you can
think of, which are all perfectly legal between consenting adults. We fixate
on the exchange of sex for money, and we conveniently ignore pornography, stripping, and all the ways transactional sex occurs in society which

are not illegal. It also ignores the goods of sex, which, as I will elaborate in more detail in chapter 6, should be as much of a concern to women as to men. As Lucy states, being sex-positive is important for all people. "Right now, there's a lot of, I think that there's so many people that have to hide who they are as a person because of just the general attitudes of society that we have about sex and it being bad and so, so I want it to be positive. I think when you embrace your sexuality that good things come from it and that it creates a more positive society when people are allowed to do that."

Are there ways, then, to view sex work other than as exploitative? And rather than reinforce patriarchy, does the ban on prostitution patronize and control women, taking away women's freedom and autonomy? This is the argument of Catherine Hakim, a British social scientist who has developed the theory of erotic capital:

> Erotic capital is a combination of physical and social attractiveness which has social benefits and economic value both for men and for women who chose to exploit their attractiveness ... And so we have overlooked the fact that it's not only human capital, and social capital, who you know rather than what you know, that are helpful and valuable in getting ahead and success in life, but erotic capital also has enormous value in helping people get ahead.

As economists often write, the question is not why women sell sex but why more women do not, given how lucrative it is.[78] And though more and more women have access to the same economic capital as men, and no one is arguing that erotic capital is women's only source of power, Christine Milrod's research shows us that there are very many women who enthusiastically exchange their erotic capital for men's economic capital.

> You can go on the web and see how many women have invested enormous amounts in their appearance, they have invested significantly in maintaining, how shall we say, very elaborate websites, they go on tours, they have fan clubs. I think somebody who doesn't want to do or perform sex work wouldn't go to that extent if they really didn't want to do it. And we're not just talking about one or two providers, we're talking about the fact that there is a whole industry of providers

who operate independently and travel from city to city, where they
have a fan base, they announce on discussion boards that they will
be coming to that city and they charge maybe $600 an hour, $1000
an hour and that's just to talk to them. That's not ... to have sex.

As Milrod, who has done research on clients and providers, also says
about the escorts in her research, "These women were not doing this to survive, they were doing this to make extra money and possibly to combine
business with pleasure. And I think that's the hardest part for people to understand." All the women interviewed for the film claimed they had choices
and they chose sex work for financial and lifestyle reasons. Benoit et al.
found that a quarter of their sample of Canadian sex workers had reported
the attraction of the work itself as a key reason for getting into sex work.[79]
"Thus a substantial minority of participants in this study said sex work
appealed to them largely because of the job's intrinsic qualities, including
opportunities for sexual and personal exploration, sexual gratification and
expression of sexuality and gender identity. These motivations were often
expressed in conjunction with economic need and desire, and were more
strongly connected with independent indoor work."[80]

Pro- and antiprostitution activists all have the same goal of emanci-
pating women from oppressive conditions, but how do we get there? Will
we do that by controlling women's sexuality or by freeing it? Are sex workers
the most oppressed people on the planet, as Sylvia's quote at the beginning
of this chapter indicated, or are they amongst the most liberated women,
as Norma Jean's quote suggests? No one is arguing that there aren't bad aspects of sex work or that it isn't stratified by race, class, and gender identity,
but is there something inherently problematic about buying sex, as prohibitionists claim? Is prostitution really a "form of male abuse" and "paid
rape"? The next chapter looks at the buyers of sex, their motivations and
some of the reasons we might want to normalize people buying sex (even
if those buyers are mostly male) if it normalizes and destigmatizes the people selling (mainly female) who are impacted most of all.

Chapter Five

The Male Problem – Is Sex Work Violence against Women?

I was writing the very first draft of this chapter when news broke that 104 men were arrested in North York, Ontario, on charges that they attempted to buy sex from girls who they thought were between the ages of thirteen and sixteen.[1] As part of a sting operation, Toronto police put ads online for sexual services. Over four years, hundreds of men responded to the initial ad. Most stopped communicating when the "girl" said she was underage. Eighty-five men who showed up and were arrested thought she was sixteen or under. Nineteen men came to the hotel room expecting to have sex with a thirteen-year-old. As a friend of mine said on Facebook, "I hope they all rot in hell."

It's hard to write anything positive about the male clients of female sex workers without seeming to be justifying their bad behaviour or condoning sex with teenagers. Efforts to explain the desire to have sex for money (that does not involve the desire for domination and violence) seem feeble when juxtaposed with the gut-wrenching idea of men having sex with children. We don't have to go very far to find examples of stigma, abuse, and exploitation within adult prostitution by police, clients, and society in general.[2] And when I worked in the Philippines and went into little casas or shantytown brothels and saw the conditions that the girls and young women lived and worked in, it was impossible not to ask, as one of my male colleagues did, "What kind of man could come in here?"[3]

What kind of man, indeed? The kind of man who, according to antiprostitution activists, routinely abuses and exploits women. And of course, this is the main reason that antiprostitution activists are against men buying sex – because they see all men who buy sex as inherently violent and exploitative, or as people who think they are entitled to the bodies of women. Leaving aside for a moment the fact that women do go to escorts and become sex tourists and that men also sell sex, although mainly to other men, this chapter will concentrate on the cisgender male clients of adult cisgender female sex workers. It is the most common scenario and the one most fraught with problems for those who have a problem with paid sex. The perceived power imbalances and the biological differences between men and women mean that the female sex worker and the male client will be the harder case to justify.

Prohibitionist Arguments against Sex Work Because It's Violence against Women

Antiprostitution groups very clearly see sex work as violence against women. As Claire, the executive director of an antitrafficking group in Canada, says, "There's no safety in sex work. You could be selling yourself to a deviant and you just don't know until it's too late." Here, she is referring to serial killers like Robert Pickton of Canada and Gary Ridgway of the United States who are infamous for murdering dozens of women they thought or knew were sex workers. Prohibitionists, like Claire, don't distinguish between "predators" and "normal" clients so they want to criminalize all johns, pimps, and traffickers and are very much against the decriminalization of the entire industry. As Sylvia explains,

> We actually want the demand, which is the men, to be discouraged from buying. Men need to get the strong and unequivocal message that it's not okay to buy sex. And so we don't want the men decriminalized, we want the criminal penalties to flow to the buyers and the traffickers and we want the women to be given an exit strategy. So we don't want the legalization of prostitution, but we do want the women not to be treated as criminals and to be given the services they need to get out.

Because of their assumption that all women in the industry want to leave sex work (except for the outlier "happy hooker" type who is the exception),[4] antiprostitution activists focus on the male clients as the criminals and insist that men must stop abusing women in this way. They believe that prostitution is the world's oldest oppression (a play on the notion that it is the oldest profession) and like sexual assault, domestic violence and child sexual abuse, it must be eradicated. According to Sylvia, without male privilege there would be no prostitution. "If women and girls had equality, you would not have for instance male privilege which allows men to grow up with a sense of entitlement to the bodies of women and girls."

Prohibitionists are concerned mainly with cisgender women and girls, even though they claim that anyone theoretically can be prostituted. As Melissa Ditmore says, however, antiprostitution activism is fundamentally gendered in terms of the focus on cisgender women, not male or transgender sex workers, even though transgender sex workers of colour are subject to some of the worst violence. "There's an aspect here about gender that can be a bit unsettling. No one talks about male prostitution the same way and actually transgender sex workers suffer perhaps the highest rates of violence of any sex workers." As Ditmore says, being transgender puts women at even greater risk of violence and stigma. "Sex work is doubly problematic for transgender women who are disproportionately targeted by the police for crimes such as loitering. In New York City police still have broad powers to arrest anyone who looks like their idea of a prostitute for what they are wearing, where they are walking or if they're hanging out on a street corner."[5]

Regardless of this reality, antiprostitution activists focus their energies primarily on cisgender men as the clients of cisgender women. They argue that there is no place in a world of equality for prostitution because it gives men a sense of entitlement to women's bodies.[6] "In this highly binary view of sex work (male and transgender sex workers neither fit in nor impinge on the analysis), it is the man who by virtue of his gender has all the power, and the woman, by virtue of hers, who is powerless."[7] The only solution is to end demand. Says Sylvia again, "What we would like to see and what we are encouraging [is] principled male leadership because we know that the problem of sex trafficking, ending sex trafficking is going to take leadership from men, confronting other men about buying women and girls for sex."

The prohibitionists I interviewed believed strongly that the male sex drive had to be controlled, just like any other desire. One made the argument that it was like wanting a Pepsi in the afternoon or wanting to drink

a bottle of wine at night. She'd like to but she wouldn't because she knew
it wasn't good for her. She had to control her bad impulses.

> The adult sex industry leads men [to believe] ... that [their] ... sexual
> impulses must be met. That is the message out there. Whereas, why
> you know? I'd like to drink a bottle of wine every night, I can't. I can't
> satisfy my impulses right but for the male sex drive, it's like messaging
> is ... your needs must be accommodated ... there are no limits, you
> know ... we're going to clean them [women in brothels] all up, they're
> going to have that health certificate, you can walk in and be guaran-
> teed you will not get any nasty disease, she will look pretty, she will
> be clean and you can come in filthy drunk, dirty and diseased ...
> That's misogyny and that message is out there unfortunately to men.

These ideas are convincing to many people because they resonate with
the victim-narrative of prostitution. The idea of adult men desiring sex
with young girls is deeply disturbing and can't easily be argued away by saying that legal prostitution will only involve adult women. Often, antiprostitution activists will point to the erroneous statistic that most sex workers
enter the trade when they are only thirteen years old.[8] No matter how many
scholars attempt to demonstrate that the statistic is wrong or based on
faulty methodology,[9] the idea continues to be accepted in policy and advocacy circles.[10]

Most sex work researchers are careful to state that they are not referring
to child prostitution and that the decriminalization or legalization of prostitution can only be applied to consenting adults (although Steven Bittle
makes some interesting points about the problem of criminalizing clients
of youth sex workers for the youth themselves).[11] Some researchers say that
the age limit should be raised to the legal drinking age in the United States.
Says Laurie Shrage, "We should even think of having minimum age laws
that are higher than those right now for the age of majority so that we might
have minimum age laws of twenty-one, which is the minimum age for
drinking in the United States because this is a very I think difficult industry
for someone who's eighteen to work in. And they often haven't had either
enough sexual experience or work experience to really avoid being ex-

ploited and abused and to understand the consequences of working either in a pornography industry or in prostitution." All of the women I interviewed except Anna were in their early twenties before they got involved in sex work.

The Interviewees' Views of Violence against Sex Workers

The women interviewed did not deny that violence occurs in sex work, though they personally had not faced client violence. Lucy describes why she thinks some men abuse sex workers:

> Some of them do act out by trying to control the worker, okay ... sometimes it's about trying to control the money or the price. They can rob or short a worker. They might negotiate the price down, "oh no, I'd never pay that much for it," whatever ... They also might be difficult during the session, whether it's badgering you into doing things that you don't want to do or trying to like take the condom off or things like that. Not respecting you during a session shows a man trying to get that power back that he feels that he's lost in other ways from his sexual desire towards women. And of course, that can manifest in straight up violence, rape, beatings, murder. I think we all probably, most of us probably know serial killers commonly pick sex workers. And they do that as an outlet for their violent behaviours and their feelings about women. But again, predators seek out the most marginalized and this is why it's important to really think about that when you're talking about sex workers' rights issues.

Lucy has avoided bad dates for the eighteen years she has been in the business, mainly because she screens, gets references, and has a lot of regulars. For first time clients, like the man she met when we filmed her in Las Vegas, she obtains credit card information, phone numbers, and knowledge of where the date works before she sets out to see him in a hotel room in Las Vegas. But she has never actually met him before. Once they meet and have a good experience, as she did with the man in Las Vegas, then there is

a level of trust between them and he can become a regular. If things don't
go well, she can refuse to see him in the future or leave. Here she recounts
how the first date went:

> He was very much a gentleman. It was a first-time client, which I
> don't really have a whole lot of apprehension you know meeting first-
> time clients because I have been doing this long enough. I don't really
> have a lot of anxiety about what I do and [that is] partly because of
> the safety precautions that I take [when] meeting people and my
> screens. You know I showed up and he was such a sweetheart, he's ac-
> tually really like almost an ideal client in certain ways because he had
> candles out, he had bought me … a couple of nice gifts, nothing too
> extravagant. And then as we progressed throughout the evening then
> I got a second little bag that had a little toy in it which was a lot of
> fun and then when I left at the end, he gave me a final gift along with
> my tribute of a little lingerie outfit so he was very thoughtful and he
> had obviously put a lot of thought into our meeting … So it was really
> nice, it was very enjoyable. He was very sweet and I'm sure that we're
> going to see each other again.

Maria, the woman who approached me after a conference presentation,
also felt strongly that prostitution was not violence against women:

> I wouldn't be able to relate to what they were saying based on my
> experience at all. Like I said, I found the men to be very caring, very
> respectful. Men came from all different socio-economic backgrounds,
> not only wealthy men but men that were working class. They still
> were very respectful, they were paying me a large amount of money
> and so this was an investment. I was like an investment for them
> and this was very important for them. In no way did they want to
> harm me, they wanted to honour me. Like I said before, they brought
> me flowers, they brought me gifts, they were, no way did I ever ex-
> perience any violence and so that's just strange for women to say
> that this is violence against women. That's not my personal experi-

ence of sex work. I experienced you know compassion and caring and it was wonderful.

The escorts I met perhaps hadn't encountered violence from clients because they were not street-based workers. There is more violence against outdoor workers because they are more marginalized generally.[12] Working conditions are much better for indoor escorts, and they are safer from violence. A study done by Tamara O'Doherty (interviewed for the film) found that indoor sex workers reported very little violence from clients.

We found that there are many women who can sell sex without experiencing violence. There seem to be very specific conditions, the idea of being in control, the idea of actually being able to set out boundaries for yourself of what you will and will not do, being able to communicate that directly to the client so that both persons' needs and desires are being met. That's often the source for conflict is when people have expectations of one thing going into an encounter and it doesn't turn out that way. So that's basically why I think the independent workers who are part of my project, showed such low violence rates.

This was Anna's experience when she transitioned from street work into online escort work. "I had more control over clients. Nothing bad happened. But it was a night and day difference to be on the street versus escort." Anna was the only one of the women interviewed to have negative experiences with sex work, and those incidents occurred when she worked on the streets. The others had good experiences and if sex work wasn't illegal they'd still be doing it.

However, the main reason given for why sex work is dangerous is an obvious one: women are going to hotel rooms or apartments or into cars with men they don't know. When the date is the first one, there is an unknown to it, even with as much research or data on a person as online escorts can get. Problems arise when, even with all the screening, you are dealing with a violent or abusive man.

Violence against Women in General

A fundamental difference between men and women in relation to their sexuality would be about their level of comfort and safety with a man or woman they've just met. Men, in general, are less likely to worry about their physical safety than women. When I was doing research for this project in Los Angeles, I made contact with a male sex surrogate who was willing to be interviewed about his work. I met him through a female sex surrogate/tantric sex teacher who recommended that I speak to him about his practice. He lived in the hills of Pasadena and he invited me to his home for the interview. I asked a friend to drive me there and she waited in his living room while we talked on his patio overlooking the beautiful LA hills. He seemed surprised that I brought my friend. Neither my female friend nor I thought it was strange. I wasn't about to (nor was my friend going to let me) go to some strange man's home alone. Afterwards, I felt a little foolish for my concerns. But as a woman, I've been so indoctrinated with the idea of protecting myself and avoiding situations where something could go wrong (and it is perhaps an example of my own internalized good girl and self-victim blaming) that it would not have crossed my mind to go to his home alone. The media highlights the worst possible cases and there are incidents where, for example, a female real estate agent showed a home to a man and she was killed;[13] a young woman in Ohio out for a jog, murdered.[14] A woman police officer was killed by a man she had just met in a bar in Halifax.[15] Cab drivers have sexually assaulted multiple women in Halifax.[16] The bad news is everywhere. And sex workers are at risk because, unless they are dealing exclusively with repeat customers who they trust, they are meeting with men they don't know. Even if sex with strange men is not a problem for them, a bad date is.

But there is no guarantee of safety for any woman. Knowing someone does not prevent them from being violent; look at the prevalence of intimate partner violence and date rape. The reason that sex workers are so often the chosen victims of aggressors is that their legal and social status make them easy targets. While it is terrible that sex workers are vulnerable to violence, the statistics on violence against women *generally* are not good. Approximately 18 per cent of American women have been sexually assaulted, one in four women have experienced domestic violence, and 43 per cent of college women have experienced abusive dating behaviours.[17] Twenty per cent of women in the US military have been sexually assaulted by their fellow soldiers, and sexual assault is considered an occupational hazard of military service.[18] While Indigenous women make up only about 4.3 per cent of the Canadian female population, they make up "16% of female homicide cases."[19] The murder rate for Indigenous women in Canada is five and a half to six times that of non-Indigenous women.[20]

The appalling statistics about male violence against women generally and sexual violence in particular may explain why antiprostitution activists believe that destigmatizing sex work will bring more harm to women because it seems to allow more sexual access to women. On the other hand, it may be that because some men have been allowed to abuse women with impunity,[21] the opposite is true. If men knew there were consequences for their violence and bad behaviour, they might think twice about doing it. But that still doesn't explain why people put prostitution in the same category as sexual violence, unless you believe, as Andrea Dworkin did, that most sex is rape.[22] It would seem more helpful to separate out violence and sex and condemn and criminalize actual violence and exploitation.

Although the decriminalization debate will be presented more fully in chapter 7, most researchers and international organizations believe that the criminalization of prostitution makes the work of prostitution more dangerous for women. As Laurie Shrage says, "if the laws against prostitution aim to protect sex workers, they do a terrible job of it ... Incarcerating people for sex work doesn't really protect them and it makes them just simply have to work in ways that are dangerous to avoid arrest. It doesn't protect the public either because then it makes the work go on in a way that you can't regulate it, you can't make it safe."

Even if prohibitionists could agree that not all acts of prostitution are acts of actual violence, they would still have a problem with what they consider is the legitimizing of sexual access to women's bodies. What is the problem for women collectively of men buying sex? How is it a crime against all women? Male privilege means male entitlement and that already is a big problem. Won't giving them more access to women's bodies further the entitlement and privilege? Says Laurie Shrage:

The other [reason to oppose prostitution] is more symbolic ... So, if women submit or are subordinate to men sexually, either as wives or as prostitutes, right, then that's going ... to shape the way women are seen in society. They're going to be seen as essentially sexually available to men all the time or as people who should be sexually available to men all the time. So, it will reinforce the idea in men that men should always have sexual access to women, which, of course, is problematic and so for that reason, they oppose it.

This is where antiprostitution activists have the hardest time seeing the difference between desiring sex (and paying for it if necessary) and dominating women – they are one and the same according to many prohibitionists. According to this argument, men have access to women's bodies because of their greater economic and social power and their ability to exploit poorer women. It's male entitlement that assures men's access to all women's bodies – not just the ones they are getting a service from at that moment in time, but that extends to all women. If one woman can be "sold," the argument goes, then all women can. Anna sees it this way:

It comes down to a feeling that if one woman is willing to stand on the street corner and say "I'm willing to commercialize sex and this is how much I charge" and willing to have people look at them as a sex object and that's okay with that person, and they're going to keep doing that, then any woman including them, including their sister, including their daughter, is someone who other men could potentially look at as someone who could do the same. And I think that makes them profoundly uncomfortable.

But blaming the buyers of sex for male entitlement in general doesn't get at the root of this behaviour.[23] If, as Hakim stated in chapter 3, men want sex for free or as cheaply as they can get it and have created a belief system that women who do sex work are dirty, disgusting, and immoral, then we need to really question our own complicity in this ideology.

If we are thinking about the small subset of men who desire sex with children and the aggressors who want to hurt women, I understand people's desire to just stop men from having sex for money – period. It is certainly simpler to be prohibitionist than put forward a more nuanced view of men's desire to obtain sex for money. Let's just end demand, as the prohibitionist campaigns state. But that is easier said than done (and a long-term goal at best) and it doesn't distinguish between men who do desire to hurt and humiliate women and girls and the majority of men who simply want to have sex and have few or no outlets.

Why Do Men Go to Sex Workers?

According to the General Social Survey, 15 to 18 per cent of American men report having paid for sex, with similar percentages in the United Kingdom, France, and Australia.[24] These numbers are probably low due to under-reporting caused by stigma. The numbers for Spain and Italy, where there is less stigma, are 30–45 per cent and in Thailand and Cambodia are more like 60–80 per cent.[25] Male and transgender female sex workers make up 20–25 per cent of all sex workers and most of their clients are male.[26] So, even though a growing number of women are sex tourists and do go to male escorts,[27] the clientele for all forms of prostitution is still overwhelmingly male. We can all agree that prostitution is a fundamentally gendered practice, as it stands today, even if we may not agree with the essential nature of sex work or its potential reversibility.[28]

Clients of sex workers have only recently begun to be studied because they have been a hard to reach population. It is almost as stigmatized today to be a client of a sex worker as it is to be a sex worker because buying sex represents personal failure and public humiliation, if caught. In on-the-street interviews, the overwhelming response to the question of whether someone would go to a prostitute was "no: only losers have to buy sex."

Just as sex workers are on a spectrum of choice, agency, and exploitation (from those working on the streets for housing and food to high-end escorts making $4,000 per night), the clients of sex workers vary as well. But while for most people the stereotypical sex worker is the so-called "street-walker," the stereotypical male client varies according to your view of sex work. If you believe that sex work is violence against women and inherently degrading, then your stereotype is the violent male predator like Gary Ridgeway or Robert Pickton, who literally preyed on vulnerable street women because they knew they could get away with it. As horrifying as this reality is, this type of perpetrator is the tiny minority, and far more men are in the second category of stereotype – someone who has trouble with women and can't get a date. Men who are virgins or who are very shy around women are the stereotype held by people who think sex work is problematic for moral or ethical reasons but not necessarily violence against women.

Several researchers have looked specifically at male clients and claim they come in all shapes and sizes and have very different motivations. Some are widowed or single and have a very hard time dating. Others are workaholics and don't have time for relationship sex but still want the closeness and intimacy of partnered sex, as opposed to masturbation. Disabled men, obese men, socially awkward men – not all men have equal power and ability to attract women and have intimate relations with them. Some men aren't interested in long-term relationships and some want more variety.[29] Alfred Kinsey's research in the 1940s outlined the same issues: insufficient outlets, sexual acts not available from unpaid partners, the men were disabled or deformed, paid sex is cheaper than a wife, it's better than an emotional affair, fear of rejection, lack of emotional complications, and the desire for sex without relationship responsibilities.[30] Clients have a variety of problems, needs, and desires. Mainly they want sex with adult, consenting women and are unable to have sex with women (or can't get the sex they want) without money changing hands.[31] Other men, who would have no problem getting all the sex they want from willing, unpaid partners choose to have sex with sex workers for other reasons. Charlie Sheen, Hugh Grant, Eliot Spitzer, and many others have lost careers, relationships, and respect by going to sex workers and they probably each had very different reasons why they did.[32] There is a forbidden element to it and, in Sheen's case, as he put it, he didn't pay them for sex, he paid them to go away and not expect a relationship with him – perhaps the height of male entitlement.

Christine Milrod, who has studied both clients and providers using data from the website *The Erotic Review* and has done surveys of more than 600 male clients, reports that the men she has interviewed come in two basic categories:

I've studied motives and I've separated them according to marital status and we see that the [partnered] men are basically paying for sex because they want to know and do things that their unpaid partner won't do and they also want to have more sex because there's a discrepancy in sexual desire so they want to purchase those sexual services. But what we see in single or widowed men, is that some of them say they just have trouble meeting women and that they're not doing well in the dating game so to speak and that it's just easier for them to pay for the sex because it's guaranteed sex.

After eighteen years of selling sex in various venues, Lucy's experiences with men have led her to similar conclusions:

Why do some people buy sex? Certainly probably the number one is ease of negotiation. No multiple dinners, courting, marriage proposals, to get their sexual needs met or even brief emotional or intimacy needs met. It's a physical release … It's also stress relief, just simple stress relief. The idea of building up to a climax and then having a release, it sends endorphins through your system, and it relieves general stress in your life and anxiety. And this is also how you know we'll work stress out by going to the gym and working out. Some people have sex, that's how they work out the stress … We're still a society that very much judges people about their sexual habits and what they're interested in and we still don't know what is normal across the board and so people will sometimes come to a sex worker because it can be a non-judgmental place for you to bare your soul and your fantasies and find acceptance, without judgment.

Milrod's client research also shows how "normal" the men's desires are. Rather than wanting to control women or abuse them, or even wanting very young women, her research shows how "vanilla" men's desires can be: they just want sex with willing, enthusiastic partners.

I found that these men very much liked to consort with women who are pretty much like themselves, maybe ten, fifteen years younger tops. These men don't even want young women … They want women who are sexually uninhibited, who are interested in wanting to have sex, who have cheerful personalities, and who are basically into the sex act just as much as they are and whether that's pretend or not, no one knows, but that's what these men want. I also found that the sexual behaviour that they most often engage in is very "vanilla," it's very normalized behaviours in the context of a heterosexual partnered relationship. In the sense that the top behaviour was penile/vaginal intercourse, followed by fellatio, followed by cunnilingus and followed by deep kissing. So these are very, very traditional behaviours.

These are definitely the stories the escorts tell. Their clients are not perverts and most of them want the girlfriend or porn star experience. They can be needy. They can lack other outlets for physical and emotional contact, and sometimes they just want a hug. Most are middle-aged men with few outlets for sex. Lucy described her date in Las Vegas:

As a lot of my clients are, they tend to be in the maybe mid- to upper thirties up through maybe sixties is my general client age group and this guy is right along with my [age bracket]. I mean I'm going to be forty this year. We were actually conversing about our love of the TV show *MASH* and so we were really giggling about how we watch every episode even though we've seen it ten million times before and we were going over all of this. So he's right in my age bracket. He's a computer IT guy. So I do have a lot of computer IT guys that I end up seeing for some reason.

The women interviewed all talked about their clients in very similar ways: their clients have had no luck with women, they are very shy, they are disabled in some way, they are lonely, they get comfort and happiness from talking and having sex; they become a sugar daddy, they are buying comfort and human contact as well as sex, and they just want to talk. Maria's experiences led her to believe that some men are very insecure about themselves:

You know women have their insecurities, so do men. Men feel like they don't have enough muscles, or that they're overweight. They're not a GQ type, you know model type ... And also men felt insecure if they ... didn't have a lot of money to support a woman and they would talk with me about that and they felt that paying me was less than what it would take to get married and support a wife ... and they felt like they couldn't fulfill those [needs] and so what I did in terms of unconditionally accepting them, they didn't have to do anything like that for me.

The other commonality between researchers and the sex workers was recognition of the importance of an emotional connection and how many men fell in love with the sex workers. According to Milrod many of the men became smitten with the worker:

What I also found was that 40 per cent of these men ended up falling in love with the sexual service providers. They became so-called ATFS, all-time favourite, and the strongest correlation in the entire study was that when these men fell in love with the women, boundaries would be completed blurred and they would start giving money to them aside from the base rate that they would pay for the hourly sexual experience and also tips, exclusive of tips ... I found that they would pay more money and that they would fall in love with them and that they really established relationships with these women that went way beyond the sexual actions.

Lucy, Maria, and Amanda spoke about the importance of the emotional labour of their work and about the intimacy created by the interaction. As Amanda states is wasn't all about sex:

I would say that about 20–25 per cent of my clients, we didn't even have sex. They wanted a conversation, they wanted a hug. That broke my heart. That would break my heart, when people were calling me because they wanted a hug or they were calling me because they haven't had sex with their wives in like ten years and then you get there and they're like you know you're beautiful, you're sexy, but you know that I really just want to have sex with my wife and I don't know how.

As one of the clients said to me, there's "an emotional connection there that a lot of people just don't get. They just want to say, they want to make it black and white and it's not. There's so many different levels to it."

A Client's Story

The one client who agreed to go on camera for the film is a man I'm calling Jim who is a long-time client of Lucy. He is an example of someone who wants both a sexual and an emotional connection. He was in his early forties when I met him, and he is a long-haul trucker and has been one for over twenty years. He was very overweight which he mentioned himself and said that the women he is interested in are not interested in him. "I guess part of it is maybe a little bit of self-image, you know. I am not a really well-built guy, I'm overweight, I've always been overweight my whole life, and, you know I just, the kind of women that I'm attracted to generally, not always but generally, are not attracted to bigger guys." He is on the road for 300 days a year and didn't think it was fair to have a real relationship with someone and wondered if it was even possible for him. He seemed regretful about that and appeared to me to be typical of one of the categories of men Milrod discusses in her study – men who fall in love with their escorts and have all-time favourites. He seemed to really care for Lucy.

> It's hard to meet women and there are a lot of, you know everybody has kind of a thing they're looking for and maybe the kind of person I'm interested in isn't necessarily interested in me. And so I can find somebody like Lucy who I'm attracted to and interested in, who then you know ... there's an illusion to it, you don't necessarily delve too deeply into it but she is willing to spend time with me in exchange for compensation.

He seemed very shy and sweet and said he becomes tongue-tied around women. He can't approach women in bars because all he can think about is what they look like, even though they could be good friends eventually. "My whole life I've really had a really strong sexual attraction to women and so I have a hard time getting past that in just like normal conversation ... walking up to a woman in a bar ... I've really got one thing on my mind, yah she might be somebody I'm really interested in later on but what's drawing me to her initially is her physical appearance and ... it's hard for me to get past that naturally so I don't even try quite often." It's just easier, he said, to pay someone for the illusion of a relationship and hopefully they can both have fun.

Jim has been to the brothels of Nevada and Amsterdam and prefers independent escorts like Lucy. He has never been to Southeast Asia because he worries about his own health and the women's situations:

I've considered both the Philippines and Thailand. They both have, you know, quite a reputation, but the thing is with both of those places you have to deal you know [with] a really high incidence of sexually transmitted diseases, really unsafe sex practices and quite honestly you don't know what you're getting into over there. You know you could end up with somebody who is being taken advantage of or forced to do that. You could end up with somebody who is underage and those are both things you just, you just don't want to get involved.

As a truck driver he sees survival sex workers (disparagingly called "lot lizards") at many truck stops in the United States. He says he doesn't get involved with those sex workers:

They're in a more desperate situation. I don't really want to be somebody who is involved in a situation like that. I don't want to be with somebody who's doing it because they have to do it. I'd rather be involved with somebody who is doing it because they want [to be], they need something and they're also interested in it, where it's not something they're being forced into doing out of desperation. And so if I ever get that vibe from somebody, I just leave the situation; I just walk away.

He was also not going back to Amsterdam because he is interested in the girlfriend experience where there is some illusion of a relationship.

A lot of the women [in Amsterdam window brothels] were surprised when I wanted to make an arrangement for half an hour or an hour or more. They'd be like no, no, fifteen, twenty minutes tops. And I'm like, no, that's not long enough and they're like, no, they would all say I have guys that come in for five, ten minutes on their way home every day. It ... becomes part of their routine or several times a week. Not everybody goes every day, but because it's ... legalized and in the open there it's a very acceptable thing.

Which of course is exactly what antiprostitution activists are worried about – the legalization and normalization of men buying sex on their way home from work every day, as if it's a self-care massage. But whose problem is this? It wasn't for the sex workers in Amsterdam because it's how they make the most money safely. The twenty-five-year-old window brothel worker I interviewed in Amsterdam was from Bulgaria, and she had the same expectations as the women Jim met. As she said through a translator, "This is not a relationship. This is a transaction and I want to do as many transactions as possible to make the most amount of money I can in a shift." Her goal was to work for three years to make enough money to go back to Bulgaria and open up a bed and breakfast. She worked 8 a.m. to 8 p.m., Fridays and Saturdays because she did not want to work at night when the clients would be more apt to be drunk. She charged 50 euros for a quickie and paid 150 euros per day for her rent. Math tells us she would have to do three a day just to break even so of course she wouldn't want men taking their time to chat and socialize.

Jim claimed that "girlfriend experiences" worked for him and for the women he bought sex from.[33] He did not think he was exploiting them and wouldn't be involved if he thought he was. He said he wasn't ashamed of what he was doing and agreed to go on camera because his close friends knew what he did and the only people he'd want to hide it from were his mother and sister.

I think a lot of people are ashamed because they think they're sup-posed to be ashamed. Society's taught them to be ashamed of it. I've always felt that society pushes us into a lot of places we don't neces-sarily want to be or should be, you know, you have to get married, you have to have kids, you have to settle down. You can't do this and you can't do that and … you know, you shouldn't see women who are in the sex workers' trade and I just think … that's wrong.

According to the escorts I met, men like Jim are the majority of their clients. He treats Lucy with respect and seems to genuinely care for her. He claims that he just can't find (or doesn't want) sex the "normal" way. Does this mean he has power over Lucy or is dominating her? Is he abusing her and acting out violence against her? From what I could see, Lucy has the power in that relationship in terms of saying "yes" or "no" to him based on his behaviour towards her. He recognizes that his access to her is limited by her boundaries.

Biology, Socialization or the "Goods of Sex"?

I wouldn't deny that in some cases men do want to dominate sex workers, as is also true in many walks of life, but it may be the case that, on average, men simply desire more sex than women do, for a whole host of biological and social reasons. Biology is an area that most feminists don't want to touch because if something is biological then it is assumed to be natural and therefore immutable. This has generally not been a good thing for women. "Natural" has meant subordinate roles for women going right back to Aristotle's theory of biological determinism – the theory that biology determines psychology, which determines social roles. For women that has been understood to mean that our child bearing bodies lead naturally to social roles within the home. It is an idea that has been with us for thousands of years. So, it is not surprising that biological differences have been rejected by most feminists as the explanation for or justification of women's oppression since Mary Wollstonecraft started theorizing about feminism and the vindication of the rights of women in the late eighteenth century.[34]

That said, it cannot be denied that the average man has approximately twenty times the testosterone of the average woman and that fact has significant impacts on sexual desire.[35] Researchers like Catherine Hakim claim that men think about sex much more than women do, masturbate more, and are much more driven by their sexuality than is the average woman.

This is not to say that some women, like the women I interviewed, can't have the same sex drive as men, but it is more unusual, mostly because of the social factors that inhibit women's desire.[36] Christine Milrod agrees with Hakim's analysis. She is a sex researcher but also counsels trans people who are transitioning. Based on her studies, she believes there is a biological connection between male hormones and sex drive.

> I think there are innate differences and the innate differences I think [are that] men produce twenty times the amount of testosterone as women do, and what's interesting [is] that in my work – because many people say "well how can we perform controlled experiments?" – well I live with these controlled experiments on a daily basis because I have clients who transitioned from female to male, and their sex drive after they are administered testosterone becomes equal to that of male-born individuals, and so they go from 0 to 60, they go [to] masturbating very frequently … and they become much more sexual … So for trans men, yes, there's an extreme rise in sexual desire and focus on sexual thoughts and that I think is the innate difference between men and women; the hormonal difference that you're seeing in you know, the average male and the average female.

Is men's sexuality biologically different from women's or are any differences just due to socialization? There are various points of view of course but surely men's higher levels of testosterone account for some of the differences. For theorists like Catherine Hakim, prostitution is the natural consequence of the male sexual drive. She argues that the problem is the "male sex deficit," that men in general want sex more than women in general do.

> The male sex deficit is the fact that throughout the world men want sex more than women do and this used to be regarded as an out-of-date stereotype, an old-fashioned idea, but … about thirty sex surveys have been carried out in about thirty countries, in Europe, North America, Australia, China, other countries. All of the sex surveys, even those in Scandinavian countries, show that men want sex more

than women do, it's ... across all age groups, across all social classes, all education groups, urban and rural and for men, it becomes a serious problem.

Students in my classes have lively debates about whether men really do have higher sex drives. Says one female student from the filmed class, "it's just easy for us [women] to get sex. I mean guys seem to want it or whatever, I mean they give off the vibe that they want sex all the time so it's really easy to get a guy to admit that he wants to have sex with you and he'll go home with you no problem." Says another young woman, "I work at a bar so I see it firsthand every night that guys walk in and they'll go from girl to girl, that's the thing like, this girl and that girl turned him down, the next thing you know they're at this other table with this girl and literally just looking for a girl. Whereas most girls are together like in groups together, they're just there to dance and have fun whereas the guys in groups are there like being each other's wing man to find girls, and the girls usually go home with their friends and the guys are still trying to find someone."

The students were divided about whether this was biological or social because they realized men are also given much more societal approval for their sex drive and the continuing sexual double standard means women are condemned for behaviour (having multiple sex partners for instance) that would be celebrated in men. Researchers have mixed perspectives too. Milrod, as stated above, thinks it's partly biological; Hakim claimed she was just reporting the data.

I don't know the origin or the source of the male sex drive. I'm a social scientist so I simply report the survey results. And the survey results show that men have a stronger sex drive. Social psychology studies, a whole variety of them in North America, all show exactly the same thing. Men will risk more for sex, they will pay more for sex, they will pursue it more, they fantasize more about it, they masturbate three or four, five times more than women do. Some women say they don't masturbate at all; men, almost invariably all of them, do, even those who have a sexual partner and regularly engage in partnered sex. So the male sex drive is just vastly stronger, more driven than women's and for that reason a lot of women just don't believe it's there ... And those women who sell sexual services are very aware that it's there and that men will pay a great deal of money to have willing partners.

In our on-camera interview Hakim also reports the same findings as Milrod in terms of the differences between heterosexual couples and their mismatched desire for sex.

There is a massive male sexual deficit within couples, a very high proportion of men, around a third or more, we're talking about the problem of a sexual mismatch in desire and sex drive within a couple, and women didn't report this. It was the men who were reporting this. And the second result is that men were saying they wanted more sex than they were getting in a general way and very, very few women reported that. Women who were celibate and said they had no sex in the last year were perfectly happy with that situation, whereas men who had no sex in the last year, were not happy with that situation ... [there] are still substantial differences between men and women which continue even after the sexual revolution.

More controversially, she states that women are getting as much sex as they want either because they have lower sex drives or greater access to men. While this might be true for younger women, as my students' stories point out, older or less physically attractive women face the same dilemma as some men in finding partners. And having a sex partner doesn't mean women are having good sex.[37] There is a reason that middle-aged women are more frequently becoming sex tourists in the Global South. We may never solve the issue of biology versus nurture but, as I will explore in chapter 6, part of the problem is that women often don't have good experiences with sex and therefore are not as interested in having sex or do not know what they may be missing in terms of the goods of sex. As Rowland outlines, this is a specific issue for cisgender heterosexual women having sex with cisgender men and one that lesbians generally don't have.[38] As well, a key part of being a sexual gatekeeper, of being a good girl, is denying yourself sex because of the sexual double standard and good girl/bad girl dichotomy.

Women are not encouraged to be sexual, except in appearance, and are punished for their overt sexuality.

Regardless of whether it's biology or socialization, I understand that some people have little sympathy for men who are unable to have unpaid sex, who may struggle with issues with women, or who may simply want more or different sex than they're getting at home. But we may also undervalue the "goods of sex" when we belittle the importance of access to sexual partners. The goods of sex include intimacy, closeness, and touch. When antiprostitution activists say that people who can't have sex without paying for it are just out of luck, regardless of the circumstances, they may be taking for granted their own abilities to obtain unpaid sexual partners or they may simply be unable to understand why anyone would want to have a lot of sex with multiple partners. Discomfort with minority sexual practices or with nonmonogamy may be at play here, too. Again, some people may have moral problems with premarital sex or adultery, but these practices aren't illegal, at least not currently in North America. It seems hypocritical to make some consensual sexual practices between adults illegal and not others.

Many antiprostitution activists worry about emboldening men if the purchasing of sexual services is not criminalized. If the only reason many men don't go to prostitutes is because doing so is illegal or stigmatized, then what will happen when it becomes legal and normalized? More people will do it. And it will become normal to talk about it as a leisure activity and hence normalize women's inequality, which to many prohibitionists is the only reason why sex work exists. But is criminalizing consensual sexual activity the right strategy? Do we attempt to control men's behaviour in the same way that women's sexuality has been controlled historically or do we put our efforts into freeing women and men from a constricting and prudish sexual double standard? As Jacqueline Comte writes,

> Contrary to abolitionist allegations, the elimination of the sexual oppression of women cannot be done by forcing men to the same repressive sexual norms that presently control the sexuality of women. This would only maintain the sexual repression of women and the stigmatization of those who dare to show a sexuality different from

the one they are allowed. It is only by questioning those norms and by recognizing, for women, an inalienable right to self-determination regarding one's own sexuality that we will be able to get rid of this sexual oppression.[39]

I think Comte's argument poses a fundamental question for feminists. Do we continue to stigmatize certain sexual practices, or do we try to free ourselves from sexual stigma generally? Perhaps legalizing sexual services would create new markets that might include women, the disabled, and other marginalized groups and might lead to a normalizing of sex itself, as Shrage believes:

> If in fact sex work were decriminalized and then regulated, it might change the way we look at sex workers. They might not be seen as women who are so subordinate to men because of course they wouldn't be working in an illegal profession. So part of the reason the work is so degrading, especially right now to women, is they are essentially working illegally and therefore always susceptible to a criminal status. Also, I mean men work in the industry; if the industry were legalized there might be more women who were clients and so the gender relations in the industry might change.

Prohibitionists want the stigma of paid sex to continue and now be placed on the male client but that does not lead to destigmatizing women in the sex trade. As Juline Koken writes, the antiprostitution arguments replicate the good girl/bad girl dichotomy with women who have been forced into prostitution as the innocent good girls and the voluntary sex workers, as the fallen bad girls.[40] What I think Koken means by this is that prohibitionists are still (inadvertently or not) making the distinction between prostituted women who are victims (the good girls) and sex workers who are not (the bad girls) – because sex workers continue to profit by being sex workers and do not see themselves as victims or understand that they are harming other women. As Julie Burchill infamously stated, "when the sex war is won prostitutes should be shot as collaborators for their terrible betrayal of all women."[41] Or as our Filipino partners would say, "we hate prostitution, but we love the women,"[42] meaning we try to love the individual regardless of what she does, but we hate the sin. Are these distinctions something we want to challenge or perpetuate?

Unfortunately, solutions are not as simple as telling men not to buy sex and criminalizing them. The consequences of criminalization are deadly for the workers because the lack of police or labour protection make sex workers easy targets for violence, threats, and coercion. The downside of trying to eliminate sex work by ending demand is that it still hurts those who choose sex work and doesn't do anything to end whore stigma. On the contrary, criminalization and stigmatization continue to make sex work and sex workers unsafe and seen as deviant or immoral in the eyes of the general public. What is it about the sex in sex work that continues to be so problematic after the sexual revolution? The next chapter examines the idea that sex work is degrading for women and is "bad sex."

Chapter Six

The Morality Problem – Is Sex Work Degrading?

As I continued with my research for the film and then this book, the problems I had with sex work (such as the worry about sex workers being exploited monetarily and men's violence and abuse against them) got put into context. Clearly not all johns are violent and not all third-party managers are "pimps."[1] Clearly some women are doing sex work by choice and do not feel exploited by the work. I eventually realized that the main problem I had was not with sex work itself but with sex. I had bought into the continued stigma about sex and its negative effects on women.

In many ways, the main problem with sex work for both left-wing and right-wing critics of prostitution is the problem of sex. As Milrod states, "I think that there are women who have really chosen to do this work and their struggle is not about the work, their struggle is to overcome the stigma of others looking at them and saying you cannot possibly be doing this work and enjoying the work ... It doesn't matter what sort of political stripe you're of, the hardest thing for people to understand is that there are actually women who enjoy sex work and who really enjoy having orgasms with strange men." This chapter will look at the problem of sex for conservatives and radical feminists alike and connect their discomfort with sex to their desire to criminalize what they consider "bad sex." Where conservatives condemn the "bad girls" for this state of affairs, radical feminists condemn the "bad men."

Sex work is thought to be degrading because, according to the sexual double standard and good girl/bad girl binary, sex is degrading to women.

In many discussions of sex work, as I have experienced firsthand, there is a notable focus on anal and oral sex (and "sucking dick" for a living). Using sensational examples of women being forced to give oral sex reinforces the idea that there is something inherently degrading about oral sex. Anal sex is also described crudely and violently in many antipornography and antiprostitution texts, so for many people it reinforces the belief that these acts are somehow deviant and harmful for women.[2] As Trisha Baptie put it at an antiprostitution workshop in Halifax, "We have to remember what we're talking about and what we're talking about is putting their face in somebody's crotch that they don't know for money. Do you really think that's what all of these women want to be doing with their lives?"[3] She might as well have said "gross" and "icky."

Katherine Rowland reports how much more common oral and anal sex are now for women versus even the 1990s.[4] Still, it was not that long ago that certain sex acts like fellatio and anal sex were perceived as acts that only sex workers did. Good women certainly did not. As our Filipino colleagues explained to us, these sex acts could only be done with prostitutes because how could we do "'that' to the mothers of our children"?[5] This is the Madonna/whore dichotomy writ large and made explicit – only bad girls would degrade themselves in such a way. So there is a long history of seeing fellatio as a degrading act and one that respectable women do not engage in. Things have certainly changed. Orenstein and Tanenbaum report how common it now is for girls to provide oral sex for boys, although it is not often reciprocated.[6] It is not surprising that the narrative has changed in terms of the frequency of women performing fellatio given the sexual revolution, but what has not changed is the idea that the act degrades women. In contrast, for instance, there is quite a different narrative for gay men who take pleasure in their ability to perform fellatio and believe that selling sex gives them power over the recipient.[7] As Julian Marlowe argues, "the very act of paying another man for sex could be viewed as submissive [versus the dominance argument of radical feminists], because the client is effectively conceding that his own attractiveness is insufficient to entice the hustler without a cash incentive."[8] Why is this narrative not transferable to or believable for women? Is sex really so different for women?

Prohibitionist Arguments about Sex and "Healthy Sexuality"

The antiprostitution activists I interviewed were adamant in their beliefs that men had to "take back" their sexualities from pornography and return to a "healthy" sexuality. Human sexuality, they believed, has been hijacked by violent pornography and men need to relearn healthy sexuality and take responsibility for their needs and desires without using the bodies of women. As Sylvia put it,

> What I believe is happening in the world is that because the average age of exposure now to pornography is eleven, more and more men's sexuality never gets a chance to be one that is premised on equality, rather than domination and subordination. And so more and more men are trying to have the sex that they're seeing in pornography by going to prostitution. And so that's what I mean when I say men must take their sexuality back from the pornographers and fight for sexuality that's premised on a respect for women and girls and one that is about not exploiting and treating women and girls as [an] object. And having a sexuality that is premised on a healthy sexuality.

Claire, the Canadian executive director, echoed these sentiments:

> You know the porn industry is … don't tell daddy, young cheerleaders, whatever, all messaging around youth and not just about girls, about boys as well, okay, so that messaging is out there. On the internet, they get validation from others when you look at sex tourism on the internet you will see tons of Asian girls, you don't know how old they are, again a messaging, they're young, they're beautiful, they're cheap, the beaches are nice, and they'll do whatever you want in great numbers as long as you've got five bucks. [A]ll that messaging develops layer upon layer on men who are not hearing the opposite which is [that] healthy men don't engage in this because it's wrong.

There is no linkage in the research between increased use of pornography and engaging in prostitution,[9] but I do understand what they're both saying about the sexualization of children and of young men seeing something in pornography and wanting to act that out. I get it. I have nieces and I worry about them. I'm not thrilled to think of them becoming sexually active with boys who have been watching too much porn, who want to pressure them into doing things they don't want to do or aren't ready for or make them feel bad for the way their bodies look. And even if they have a great experience and all goes well, I don't like to think about them getting a reputation or being called names or being harassed for doing something that the boys are doing without consequences.

But I also worry about the use of the term "healthy sexuality" by prohibitionists. Historically, healthy sexuality meant heterosexual, procreative, monogamous, and married sexuality, and to some it still does.[10] Even today, many people believe that sex should be between men and women exclusively, who have some emotional connection and the more monogamous and committed the better. This "valorization of the heterosexual conjugal bond" has created many problems for sexual minorities and women, as Edna Keeble has thoroughly argued.[11] It is "the uncritical acceptance that sex must always be relational (ruling out self-satisfaction), dyadic (ruling out multiple partners), heterosexual (ruling out sexual minorities), and meaningful (ruling out pure carnal pleasure)."[12] The problem with this conception should be obvious: historically homosexuality was seen as deviant, and premarital sex, extramarital sex, and masturbation were considered taboo. What is considered "healthy sexuality" changes historically and culturally and usually contains some element of state control or stigma, as I outlined in chapter 3. Minority sexualities are left out of definitions of "healthy" sexuality, by definition, since they are not in the majority: polyamory, kink, BDSM, swingers all involve either nonmonogamy or a "deviant" lifestyle that "normal" people wouldn't want to be involved in.[13] Designating some acts as normal and some as deviant, given our past history of abusing and criminalizing sexual minorities, would appear to be a problem, if we are dealing solely with consenting adults.

Clearly, prohibitionists are making a moral argument as well as a political one: that sex for money is bad sex and therefore should be criminalized. "John schools," where clients can have their convictions for solicitation overturned by participating in a day's information session, are explicitly designed on this premise. As Ummni Khan argues, they "are built on moralistic understandings of good and bad sex" and offer redemption to clients if they "recommit to coupled, noncommercial normative sexuality."[14] Is this a concept of morality that should be accepted or challenged? Gay sex was seen as bad sex and criminalized (and still is in some countries) and so the distinction between healthy sex that is good and nonhealthy sex that is bad (and should be criminalized) is very problematic.

It is likely that most antiprostitution activists and scholars have absorbed the socialization of society in regards to sexuality since it's very hard to avoid. Anyone invested in being a "good girl" will definitely see sex work as damaging to the psyche. If you think sex without love is degrading and especially that giving others pleasure is degrading then of course selling access to your body or your sexual services will be problematic. If you lack body confidence or are embarrassed by sexual activity, if you think sex is "icky" or "dirty" or the body is "gross" then sex work is clearly not for you. But it is not sex that is the problem. It is our morality about and discomfort around sex that is. If we are prudish about sex, it becomes difficult to imagine people enjoying what we think is wrong or gross or dirty. And that is what I believe the prohibition of selling sex comes down to: people's discomfort with sex in general and women's sexuality in particular.

In just one random issue of the *Globe and Mail* there was an article on controlling sex between residents in nursing homes because we're squeamish about elder sex,[15] three articles and editorials on the repeal of progressive sex education in Ontario because of the fears of social conservatives about promoting sex,[16] one article on the stigma around and hostility towards breastfeeding,[17] and one on the decline in access to abortion in the United States and women even being jailed for trying to self-abort.[18] What do these articles tell us about our continuing struggles around sexuality? Western society is prudish about sexuality, does not want to encourage old or young people to have sex, and there are still people who want to control and punish women for their sexuality.

Where does this prudishness come from? How and why is sex still a morality issue? Suffice it to say that North American society has very conflicted feelings about sexuality despite our liberated times. We are hypersexualized in terms of popular culture and the use of sex to sell everything, and at the same time we are fundamentally antisex in terms of morality and women's pleasure. This conflict was vividly illustrated in the commentary about the 2020 Super Bowl half-time show. Featuring Jennifer Lopez and Shakira in what some called a Latina show of woman power and anti-children-in-cages politics, the show was also called "sleazy and disgusting" because the women wore skimpy clothes and engaged in pole dancing and suggestive dancing and twerking.[19]

Many people still feel shame for their sexual bodies, at the same time as we are inundated with sexual images and pornography. Women are pressured to have sex and have lots of orgasms but shamed at the same time.[20] There is good sex (married, heterosexual, for love or procreation) and there is bad sex (outside monogamy and purely for pleasure), and even with good sex we don't want to hear about it, in public at least. There's a reason the online pornography industry is a billion-dollar business. According to historians, we can partly blame a puritan culture for our discomfort with sexuality. Says Catherine Hakim,

> What you've got in the Western world, particularly Northern Europe and North America, is the puritan culture that is very negative about sexuality, very uncomfortable with sexuality and therefore also very negative about the sale of sexual services. Whereas in the Southern European culture to this day, there's a lot more comfortable feelings and acceptance of sexuality, hedonism, having a good time, and the carnival spirit is clearly part of that. And you don't get the same discomfort around sexuality. People are for example, much more likely to have affairs, much more likely to openly admit that they see prostitutes and regularly go to see them and there's a different attitude towards sexuality and the sale of sexual services.

Puritanism and its related morals are one explanation. But sex and morality are always related in one way or another. Morality means treating others with dignity and respect; it means living by ethical principles; it can mean living with integrity, honesty, and decency. What does sex have to do with it? Can sex outside marriage and procreation be done morally? According to societal mores about monogamy, prostitution is a big problem because of the inherent adultery involved. Many people don't have a problem with single men going to sex workers, but they have a big problem with married men doing the same. My students believed this was one of the biggest problems for the acceptance of prostitution. Says Alison, "I don't

think it's so much the prostitute aspect that bothers people. I think it's ...
the cheating aspect. When you look at Eliot Spitzer, Bill Clinton, and I can't
remember his name but the governor of South Carolina [Mark Sanford],
it was the fact that they were cheating on their wives, and of course you've
got to love that news conference with the wife standing there supporting
her man and it's that I think that bothers us more ... it's the cheating that
bothers people more than the prostitution I think."

After Lucy's date in Las Vegas, I asked her if she thought her new client
was married. Her short answer was, "Didn't talk about it; didn't come up."
She then elaborated:

> But because of his particular attention to detail I suspect that he's
> single. We did not talk about it, but I suspect because he put so much
> effort into the niceties, not to say that some married men don't do
> that also, those types of married men usually really have disjointed
> relationships where they're not really able to engage with their wives
> in that way and so it's an outlet for them to do those nice things that
> they like to do for women as well. But most of the time that indicates
> to me that there might be a lack of a partner at home.

As my students mentioned, the morality question arises with prostitution because it is considered adultery if the man is married. However, the
women I interviewed were not interested in the client's marital status, not
because they are any more immoral than the rest of us but because it simply wasn't relevant to them. In many ways they thought they were helping
marriages stay together. Lucy argued that sex workers "are a pressure valve
and without them marriages would end. We save marriages, not break
them down."

But regardless of your thoughts on adultery, it isn't illegal anymore and
you can go on the internet and take your pick of adultery and sugar-dating
sites. And since the concept of morality has been used historically to control
many people's sexuality, I ask again, should we be policing people's sex lives?
Do we really want to be criminalizing sex between consenting adults?
Hakim, in fact, believes that the concept of "morality is deployed by men
to restrict women's ability to exploit their one major advantage over men

and to humiliate women who do succeed in gaining money or status from sex activities." In other words, they punish the bad girls.

Socialization to Be a "Good Girl"

Somehow Lucy and the other women I interviewed had avoided or overcome this puritan culture, did not have a prudish, antisex upbringing, or had surmounted their socialization to be a good girl. As Hakim says, "I think some women discover just how free they can be once they drop the idea that it's a bad thing to be a bad girl and they realize that actually bad girls have a very good time and they may make a lot of money while they're enjoying themselves."

The escorts interviewed also thought that the *fear* of sex was a big part of why people were so antisex work. Says Norma Jean,

I think that there's a lot of people out there who have hang-ups about sex and that's really what it boils down to. They don't feel good about themselves, and they can't understand how a man or woman could look at them, their own bodies and say I enjoy myself, I enjoy sex, I enjoy being with other people, I enjoy making other people feel good, they cannot handle that kind of thinking. And it's like oh no, no, no, you're evil; you're bad.

Maria thought the same, although, for some people she said, there might be good reason:

I think they're afraid. I think they're afraid of sexual freedom. I think they are repressed themselves, there's just such fear of sexuality and where people are afraid, people have certain ideas about their bodies, their body type, a lot of insecurities, I think it's fear, and I think also there's … been violence out there, there has been rape, there has been molestation and a lot of these people have been damaged and so they automatically think that because they've been damaged, well of course this is going to be a damaging experience for everybody else.

All of the women interviewed were extremely comfortable with their bodies and sexuality. Seeing that comfort changed how I thought about why people might be able to do sex work without harm to the psyche. Unless you have a strong sense of self, including little to no shame or stigma around the body or sex, as Lucy pointed out to me, it will be hard for you to do sex work and not feel the stigma of others. And the stigma is still strong.

I remember showing a rough cut of the film to some friends and one scene showed Lucy laughing about a potential group-sex party, teaching a girlfriend how to have multiple orgasms. My friends, who presumably thought the scene would undermine Lucy's character, immediately responded, "That's gross. Take it out!" When women (and of course men) police other women's sexuality, as Tanenbaum points out,[21] we are telling others what we think about sexuality and particularly what we might think is *deviant* sexuality. As I discovered, as liberal as I might be politically, in terms of sex it turns out I am pretty conservative. In fact, I realized I had been projecting my own ideas of harm or degradation onto others. And maybe, just maybe, so are many people who weigh in against sex work.

When I reread my transcripts recently, I was embarrassed to see that one of my questions to Lucy communicated my own squeamishness about what she was doing from the very beginning. When I interviewed her as she was getting ready for her date in Las Vegas (and the point of the interview was to ask about what she was doing that night and how she had set up the date), I asked her, "So maybe you can just, you know, without going into the gory details, or whatever you're comfortable with, what are you doing tonight? What are you getting ready for?" Gory details? What did I think she was going to say? And when I saw her the next day and asked about her date, I said this, "So last time we saw you, you were getting ready to go out, and we got you into the cab, so what … I mean, not what happened! Cut! I'm going to try that again. I don't want to know what happened!!" and started laughing like an embarrassed ten-year-old. My film editor wanted to keep it in, but I insisted we take it out. I couldn't really be that naïve and nervous about talking about sex, could I? Yes, I could. This debrief also became the climax for the film – no pun intended – because after I asked about the date in general, I then probed tentatively, "okay, and more personal question, when you say that he wants someone who's adventurous and embraces her sexuality, do you get anything out of the experience or is it all about him?" She replied, "I think I had ten or twelve orgasms." She was not kidding, and, as I say in the film, my mind was opened just like that! Because I saw prostitutes solely as victims, it never occurred to me that this was something they could actually get pleasure out of doing. The women I met have done other jobs and chose to be sex workers because they liked doing it. They genuinely enjoyed the work *because* of the sex. As Lucy said when she found out what her "lingerie" job really was, "I was intrigued, I was excited, I was like I love sex and this would be wow I could make money at having sex, this would be great you know."

Women and Sex: Part II

A Canadian newspaper article proclaims, "High sexual desire in women can be totally normal."[22] This might be news to some readers, but it certainly would not be for the women I interviewed. I think they would negatively react to the inherent problematizing of high sexual desire contained within the title. In the article a researcher is making the basic point that so little is known about women's sexuality that "normal" has no meaning. Even though we know that men have more testosterone than women, there has been so little research on women's sexuality it might explain why drugs for women's low libido (unlike blood flow drugs for men) have not been effective. Katherine Rowland has written a whole book on why women are "losing their appetite for sex" and how "inhibited sexual desire" has become "the most prevalent sexual complaint of women in America."[23]

Only a hundred years ago, women were called nymphomaniacs if they desired sex at all, either with a partner or in terms of masturbation.[24] The term "nymphomaniac" is defined as excessive sexual desire by a female. There is no equivalent for men, given how normalized it is to assume that men are ready, willing, and able at any moment. They are not seen to be abnormal or "maniacs" for liking sex. In another classic double bind, women are seen to be frigid if they don't like sex and nymphos if they do. Not surprisingly, according to the article mentioned above, women reporting high sexual desire also reported more satisfying sex lives and sexual function

than other women with more "normal" levels of desire. The author concludes that women with high sexual desire "should not be made to believe
this signifies a problem, an abnormality or a dysfunction."[25] Why was this
research worthy of commentary in 2017? The myths and stereotypes about
female sexuality are so deeply engrained that we think we have to reassure
women that if they have high sexual desire they don't have to worry. They
are "normal." High sexual desire in men is seen as normal by definition.

Why Does Selling Sex Work for Lucy and the Other Escorts?

Why does sex work work for Lucy? Because she loves sex and sees it as a
calling – to be able to bring pleasure to others and have pleasure herself
doing so. Selling sex worked for the women I interviewed in large part due
to their (apparently normal, yet) high sex drives. I'd say the other important
factors were their sexual experimentation as young people and openness
about sexuality generally, their comfort with the body and their lack of (or
resistance to) socialization to be "good girls." As Maria, the former escort
doing her PhD in religious studies said, she comes from a conservative
Catholic family that wants her to feel ashamed of what she did but she does-
n't. She thought sexuality was a wonderful thing, not a shameful thing, and
she liked the work. Rather than seeing themselves as deviants or nymphomaniacs, the women I interviewed operated and had sex lives "like men"
so that they didn't feel shame for what they did, and they were not psycho-
logically harmed by the sex they had. Whereas researchers like Melissa
Farley claim that paid sex traumatizes "prostituted women," these women
definitely did not see the work that way.[26] Many of the women were bisexual, a few were polyamorous, and they were adventurous sexually. They had
no hang-ups about the body or giving someone else pleasure. They saw
their work like that of a massage therapist and they got pleasure from giving
others pleasure. The women were motivated by money, but they weren't
desperate financially. They had all worked at other jobs and had chosen sex
work. They were able to set up their businesses with strict boundaries about
when they would see clients (not after midnight) and in what condition

the clients could be (i.e., not drunk). They protected themselves by obtaining home and work information and credit card deposits and relied on regular clients. The currently working escorts relied on their own websites for their businesses and vetting clients.[27] All of these characteristics help to explain why sex work was not damaging for them and in fact was perceived by these women as a helping profession and part of their own lifestyle.

Catherine Hakim confirms this in her interview with the author of *The Diary of a Call Girl*. "In Belle du Jour's case, it was unquestionable she did have a high sex drive, because I had an argument with her once about the male sex drive and she couldn't see it, she couldn't see the male sex deficit because she had always had this high sex drive herself, which was part of the reason that she ended up thinking this is perfectly good, a kind of occupation temporarily for herself."

For the women I interviewed, then, enjoyment of sex was a big part of why they did sex work. The attraction to the work, as tainted as it was by society's standards, was largely the sex itself. The women were combining business with pleasure essentially: making money doing something they liked to do, as Benoit et al. also found in their research.[28] As Lucy related her story of her new client in Las Vegas and how he wanted the "porn star" experience, I thought about her ten to twelve orgasms:

My general sense is that he is one of the types of clients that really enjoys a woman who's sexually liberated. So he really seems to be one of the types of guys that likes a sexually adventurous and outgoing woman. And so he enjoys toys, hence him even bringing me one as a gift but he had mentioned it so I had brought some of my own toys as well. And there's a lot of guys that really enjoy a woman that embraces her sexuality, that isn't afraid to let her hair down, enjoy herself and … it's like the porn star experience type of thing because it's a woman that just is unabashed with her sexuality. So there's a fantasy about women like that, that can't get fulfilled elsewhere.

As Amanda stated, she answered an ad for private dancers in the newspaper and went for the interview: "When I got to my first 'private dance,' it turned out that it was a lot more than a private dance and I was actually really thrilled because at that time in my life I was sleeping with a lot, I was having a lot of anonymous sex, and I was finally getting paid to have anonymous sex and I thought this is like brilliant. Why didn't I think of this before, you know? Like this is just the most brilliant thing that I could have fallen into."

That was Maria's experience as well. "I feel that I have a very healthy sexuality, and I enjoy sex. This is one of the main reasons I decided to do this, not only as a helping profession, I really enjoy being sexual with men. And it was fun. It was a lot of fun." The continuing stigma surrounding sex work and stereotypes of female sexuality, however, means that the sexual pleasure of escorts themselves remains under-researched (and very controversial) and only recently have empirical studies begun to address this divisive topic.[29] Jo Doezema cites her own research on sex work and pleasure and "suggests that we move sex workers' experience of pleasure to the centre of our analysis and practice. In doing so, we can give meaning to the term 'empowerment,' by locating its source in sex workers' bodies"[30] and thereby find the conditions under which pleasure can happen. Her research has shown that the "more control the woman has, for example, to choose working hours or to choose clients, the more pleasurable her work may prove to be,[31] as the women I interviewed pointed out. Doezema concludes that "there is no contradiction between the money-making and the enjoyment aspects of providing sexual services, indeed these exist hand-in-hand for many sex workers. In my own work with sex workers, it was very common for sex workers to accept sexual pleasure as a work bonus."[32]

Sex-work activists and researchers, however, are divided on this question, and many have claimed that enjoyment of the job is "classist" or a problem for seeing sex work as work and have distanced themselves from the "empowerment" or sex positivity perspective as a motive for sex work.[33] "Ultimately, the worker is there because they are interested in getting paid, and this economic imperative is *materially different* from the client's interest in recreational sex."[34] Another sex-work-rights activist who I met during the making of the film, Audacia Ray, has written that sex workers' rights must be separated from sex positivity as the linkage takes away from accepting that sex work is a job.[35] Both examples illustrate what a double bind the women I interviewed are in: disbelieved entirely by antiprostitution activists and discounted by some sex-worker activists because they like their job. So even the people who are the most supportive of sex-worker rights don't want sex work to be about sex! While I understand why some people worry about this analysis (because so far the sex-positivity argument has not resulted in labour rights for sex workers and doesn't resonate with many people given the victim narrative of prostitution), I think it is another example of "respectability politics." It shows the tremendous bias that society has about "nymphos" and it ultimately undermines the many women who choose to work in sex work for reasons other than just money.

Women who combine business with pleasure, Milrod argues, are actually much more common than most people imagine. "There are clearly some women out there who enjoy what they're doing. Because what we're also seeing is that there are women who are continuing to do this when they're in their fifties and sixties, and that's way past menopause, and they chose to do this, and they find that they're making a good living." And as Doezema puts it, "If we are to take seriously sex workers' own reports of feeling pleasure at work, we must question an interpretation of prostitution that would make that very pleasure an impossible experience. We must accept that sex work can be pleasurable. And if we accept that sex work can be pleasurable, we must accept that sex workers have some control over their encounters with clients."[36]

Disability and the Goods of Sex

The women's comfort with their own sexuality and their knowledge of the goods of sex also meant that they were much more sympathetic to the male client's desire for sex than antiprostitution activists could likely ever be. This was illustrated most poignantly around the issue of disability. Maria told me she loved being a sex worker. Sex work, she says, gave her both financial security and meaningful work, "and if it wasn't illegal, I'd still be doing it." She advertised her services as a kind of sex surrogacy and specialized in men with disabilities.

Probably one of the most profound experiences I had was a client who was a burn victim. He was burned, [but] you couldn't tell [because] his face was fine, but underneath on his chest he had been in an accident where he was electrocuted during work and so he ha[d] scars on his body and he was afraid to go out and meet women and have them see these scars on his body and so what I was able to do was to touch him, you know, in these places where he was scarred and bring him pleasure. And so that he could begin seeing his body as something that was pleasurable rather than something that was ugly or disfigured.

All of the women interviewed had a story about someone who they helped, unrelated just to sex, to feel better about themselves and which made them feel that their work was meaningful. Even Lucy's client Jim had a story of his own about disabled men and the goods of sex.

One of the girls [at a brothel in Nevada] told a story about how she'd had a disabled guy come to her and he was in his fifties and he'd never had sex his entire life and she told the owner, she said I'm just going to take this guy and give him what he's never had and I'm not even going to charge him any money ... And so she took him back and kept him with her the whole night and you know the next morning he just couldn't thank her enough because, he was in his fifties and he had a disease that was crippling and he was going to die younger than a lot of men would and he wanted to experience that and she did that for him.

It was clear that Jim really felt strongly about this, and he had tears in his eyes when he related these stories. We might think of these men as self-interested, of course, but when you see the footage his emotion is unmistakable.

And not to go on and on but then there's another gal I know out there who got kind of popular and got well-known and literally she would have soldiers, eighteen, nineteen, twenty-year-old guys that have never been with women who come to her and say, "I'm leaving for Iraq next week, I don't want to go over there and maybe die and never have been with a woman." And once or twice she had to hear that guy

didn't make it. And it's heartbreaking ... but she's like at least he got
to experience that, he got to know that ... pleasure, that joy, that happiness and so you know it's not just sex. There's a lot more to it.

Norma Jean related a story about a disabled client and her incredulity
that anyone would think this was a bad thing:

I had a disabled client, totally, thoroughly disabled, he had polio when
he was a little boy, he had braces on his legs, he couldn't afford a lot
of money, he only saw me maybe once a month or once every other
month when he could pull up the money to pay for it, but when he
saw me, and I lifted him out of his chair and I took his leg braces off
and put him on the bed and he couldn't reciprocate. He couldn't have
a normal relationship with another woman, I mean he had to rely on
someone giving him pleasure and being the caregiver to him. So
when he saw me, he used to say, "Norma Jean I think about you all
the time. I think about coming to see you. I think about how wonderful it's going to be. After I've been here I just, I dream about it."
And how can you say to this kind of man, "you're evil, you're bad,
you want company, you want companionship, you want to feel good,
how fucking dare you, you want to feel good, you bad man." Who are
these people that think like that?

As I say in the film, rather sheepishly, these people were me, actually.
Until you meet someone who makes you see things differently it is easy to
fall into stereotypes about clients and providers. There are of course different points of view about sex and disability, but the antiprostitution activists interviewed for the film took a very hard line. Said Sylvia:

It's not about whether or not someone deserves to have a social, sexual relationship. It's whether or not there needs to be, whether or not
there should be a class of human beings set aside to service them. And
no one ever asks and people need to ask this question, what does
being prostituted do to the sexuality of the prostituted? We now know
the toll that prostitution takes on the prostituted. Remember I don't

call anyone a prostitute, we say a prostituted woman, prostituted child, prostituted man. What about the toll on the sexuality of the prostituted? We now know that we're looking at incredible trauma. So I don't believe that we should take one class of human beings, just because there may be a class of human beings that may not, for any number of reasons, have access to sex. Oh, the solution to that is to go create another class of human beings that you're going to traumatize so somebody else can have sex? This goes back to male privilege. Someone's needs are being seen as outweighing somebody else's human rights.

Laurie Shrage takes issue with the idea that sex workers who work with the disabled are not choosing to do that work or are somehow being coerced.

No one should be forced to serve anyone sexually. But the sex workers who are seeing clients like that [who are disabled] are not being forced to take those clients ... I mean I've heard sex workers who have had men who have colostomy bags and talk about how they deal with a colostomy bag and most, I think a lot of people who have not been engaged in sex work ... are I think unreasonably inhumane toward people who have disabilities and their sexuality. Men in wheelchairs, women in wheelchairs, I mean I think that the sex workers who see clients like that, to me they're wonderful ... they see the humanity in people who have these disabilities and are willing to be sexually intimate with them.

In Germany where prostitution is legal and regulated by the government, the Green Party wants the government to fund sex-work services for the disabled and elderly in order to improve the quality of life for its citizens.[37] In the UK, sex-surrogacy services are being introduced for the disabled.[38] In the Netherlands, "the disabled person can receive government funding for sex (10–15 times a year) through commercial companies (often a coalition of sex workers)."[39] For some this is a sensible suggestion because sex is a basic human desire and many people have trouble accessing sex through normal relationships. To others, this is horrifying. As antiprostitution activists have said to me, "we can't have one class of people set aside to service another class of people," and if people can't have sex naturally then they don't have a right to have sex at all.

In an article on disability and sexual inclusion, Tracy de Boer engages with prohibitionist Sheila Jeffreys's contention that disabled men going to sex workers are abusing commercial sex workers and that sex surrogacy is nothing more than prostitution. De Boer rejects the claims for several reasons but mainly because she convincingly argues that "disabled men who seek sex with sex workers are seeking the goods of sex, such as intimacy, connection, and sexual inclusion, as opposed to male domination."[40] The antiprostitution activists I interviewed, however, echoed Sheila Jeffreys's perspective that disabled men are abusing women. Says Claire,

> If you are disabled or in some way unable to have a normal, sexual relationship with another person, so you think that the right way is to buy it? Well, my answer to you is that unfortunately due to your illness and your disability you cannot have sex with another person. It's again, we're not accommodating you for some special reason, it's just the reality. It's the same way I can't drink Coca-Cola after two o'clock because it will affect me, right. But this is a much more serious issue, but the buying of a human, whether it's a child, adult, the buying of a human body for sexual gratification is a violation of that person's human rights.

Do people have a right to sex? Clearly not at the expense of people who don't choose to have sex with them. But this question brings up interesting points about the rights of the disabled and the elderly or any person who does not have easy access to sex. For the women I interviewed, saying that someone is just out of luck in terms of sex is a cold way to look at something they think is a wonderful part of life and should be enjoyed by everyone, especially since these women do not see themselves as abused by the service they provide. In many ways Maria also talked about her work as a calling: she really felt that she was doing therapeutic work. To her, men have issues: whether low self-esteem, disability, sexual abuse, workaholism, high libidos, or mismatched libidos. Thus, buying sex gave them intimacy and connection they would not otherwise have had. She did not meet clients who wanted to dominate her. They wanted sex with consenting adult women but were unable to have sex with women without money changing hands. She was helping them; she was making money; everyone's needs were being met. And what, she wondered, was the harm in that?

As I mentioned in chapter 1, I chose not to include quotes from prohibitionists interviewed for the film because I felt there was an inherent ableism in their responses. Saying that people have no right to sexual relations seemed to me to be a form of discrimination at best and dehumanization at worst, especially since I had met women who specialized in disabled men who didn't feel that they had been traumatized by the experience. I also felt the prohibitionists were underestimating the importance of the goods of sex, and, further, that this was probably why antiprostitution activists believe that the eradication of sex work is even possible. As Anna says, "When they ask us to prove that it can't be eradicated well ... I sort of don't even know how to answer that, I mean sex is a human need, it's a basic human need. It's like food and water. And so because it's a basic need, expressions of people's sexuality and their needs to fulfill them are strong. It's just never going to go away unless we get rid of sex, which isn't happening. So it's always going to be there." Norma Jean Almovadar, as usual, was even more blunt:

> I mean I laugh but it's just so horrifying to think that they think they can eradicate it. First of all, even if they were to stop every public aspect of prostitution, and they were to go after all the escort agencies that advertise and Rentboy and Craigslist and all that, there's still private prostitution going on. And as long as there are men who are willing to pay for the services of a sex worker, there will be women and men who are willing to provide those services and ... they're not going to get eradicated but what it will do, it will marginalize those people even more so that they are absolutely terrified of anybody finding out what they're doing. And they can't eliminate something that's been going on I mean for thousands of years; the churches tried to stamp out sex outside of marriage. It just isn't going to happen.

The goods of sex are why Lucy saw sex work as a calling and why Amanda saw sex work as a career that gave her pride, meaning, and rewards: a career, in other words, that "renders work itself a source of self-esteem," as Bellah et al. put it in their influential book introducing the job, career, calling model.[41] Amanda worked as an escort for both financial and lifestyle reasons and felt good about herself while doing it. "I really enjoyed the sex work actually ... I felt good about what I did, I treated my clients with respect, they treated me with respect and I felt like I was really fulfilling a deep personal need that people have, that that's just a natural feeling of the desire to have affection, the desire to have some kind of intimate contact with another human being. I mean cause that's what we're talking about."

Many sex workers believe they are selling a valuable service and that what they do involves much more than sex. Penttinen describes how sex workers spend a great deal of time listening to their clients' problems, stating, "some said that being a psychotherapist or sex therapist made their work meaningful."[42] This thought echoes Hochschild's work on women's emotional labour generally.[43]

Lucy's speech at the antitrafficking conference emphasized what she thought was the value of sex work: that all people need human touch, including the research that shows that babies will not thrive without it.

> But as humans we also need bonding and intimacy and this is shown right from the get go. We're told as a parent, anybody who's out there that has children, if you don't hold your child and they don't have the ability to bond with you, they're not going to eat properly and they're going to have failure to thrive. They're not going to take in enough nutrition, they're not going to gain enough weight, they're not going to develop on schedule for what they want to see for a newborn infant. I don't know why this is something that we only talk about with children and with infants and why this would be something that as we grow up, as adults we somehow forget that we need this too. And I'm talking about simple human contact, human touching.

She is correct about this as well and research shows that touch is important from birth to old age. An article about sexual intimacy in nursing homes between people with dementia illustrates both the importance of human touch and the ethical dilemmas surrounding the issue. Research from Lori Schindel Martin of Ryerson's School of Nursing backs Lucy up as Martin calls for nurses "to consider what human touch means for residents' well-being. 'Research tells us ... that older people will have an increased quality of life, enhanced self-esteem and will heal from their depression because they connected with someone on a level that involves their skin.'"[44] Martin claims elderly people's sexuality is censored because of ageism, "squeamishness" about sex between the elderly, and our tendency to see "elderly people as asexual beings." She argues that most people in these situations are "seeking each other out for company, belonging and warmth."[45] And as researchers Pia Konto and Alisa Grigororide write, human sexuality is a basic human need. "Sexual expression is a universal human need that transcends age and disability. It has many positive health and wellness benefits, including the opportunity to experience pleasure, decreased pain sensitivity and increased relaxation."[46]

Men get the goods of sex. They don't need to be educated about the benefits of their own sexuality. Not one man who I talked to about this research wondered about what the big deal was about not having access to sex or about how his life would be negatively impacted if he didn't have sex. Women I talked to would. Some people may genuinely be asexual. A former colleague of mine claimed she had never had sex, had no desire to have sex, and couldn't understand what the big deal was all about anyway. Is this someone who just doesn't know what she's missing? Or do some people just have no interest, as the rise in asexuality studies would suggest? When Lucy and Anna claim that sex is just like food, shelter, and water, many people object that they are very different things. We need food and water to live; we don't need sex except in the sense that without reproduction our species will die off and so there is an evolutionary advantage to having sex. But it isn't a driver in the same way as food. Perhaps. Though, perhaps, drives differ between people. We all know people who are very driven by their sexuality and those who couldn't care less. Perhaps the women I met have very high testosterone and that explains why they like sex so much and why they don't have a problem being sex workers. Perhaps it's a problem that I keep trying to explain their behaviour – I wouldn't ask myself why if it were a man who was selling sex. When I interviewed sex surrogates in Los Angeles, the man I met seemed genuinely interested in helping women with various sexual dilemmas and physical problems like vaginismus but nearly everyone else who the film editor and I talked to about male sex surrogates thought it was hilarious. In their minds, he was clearly out to have sex with women and making money was the bonus. Why not the same thinking for women selling sex?

In reality the harm (and/or value) of sex work is intimately tied to the harm (and/or value) of sex. If sex were valued in our culture and if women's sexuality were not hampered by the sexual double standard and good girl/bad girl dichotomy, then women would be able to demand the same rights to sexual pleasure as men. As Lucy says, "You know sometimes it's just about having sex. I mean it's, I think some people over romanticize it, for some of us it's really just about sex you know."

The escorts' hope was that as the stigma about female sexuality declines, the value of sex might be able to come to the fore, and we might begin to really free women's sexuality. And as women become clear about what they want and need in terms of sexuality, they will be able to hold men accountable for their behaviour. Sex won't be an entitlement for men only but about mutual pleasure.

As I have discovered, once your mind has been opened to a different story, it is very difficult to go back and force a certain narrative on something you know just isn't true. Once you know that not all women who engage in exchanging sex for money are victims and not all men who buy sex are aggressors – that many, rather than buying sexual subordination of women are buying the *goods* of sex – then it is difficult to see what good comes of criminalizing one aspect of the sex trade, i.e., the "buyers." When we see sex work practiced with respect and dignity, then it is easier to sort out when the objections to sex work are moral and ideological rather than based on empirical evidence, as many sex work organizations and activists have been trying to tell prohibitionists. When we can see how sex work is practiced with respect, shouldn't we attempt to understand how it can be done more often with respect? Surely the point should be to understand under what conditions sex work can be done with respect and dignity and to reject sex work that lacks these qualities. If someone doesn't want to sell sex for money, as one of the interviewees put it, they shouldn't do it, full stop. But, as importantly, those who want to do sex work should be given all the labour protections that other jobs have.

To that point, I return to Christine Overall's argument that prostitution is just too gendered for it to have a place in an equal society, that while it might be fine for an *individual* woman to sell sex, it is bad for women.[47]

Other scholars similarly argue that the structural issues of "violence against women (VAW) [undermine] sex workers' autonomy because it is a social threat limiting choice formation and pursuit,"[48] and therefore they do not argue in favour of decriminalization: "all forms of prostitution continue to be morally problematic."[49] In related terms, Sue Sherwin and Francoise Baylis articulate why an individual woman might want to be a commercial surrogate – "earning income," and "the experience of pregnancy more rewarding and satisfying than other economic options available to them,"[50] but in the end they argue that it should be disallowed as a social or public policy because it's bad for women as a collective. As they write, "a policy to prohibit commercial surrogacy contracts would clearly affect the lives of individual women and men in ways that may not coincide with their own deeply felt choices. Nonetheless, we support such a prohibition for its potential to promote greater gender equality."[51] Putting aside the important question of intersectionality and whether we can speak of the interests of "women" at all, I would also question whether the individual choices of individual women are that much of a threat to womanhood as a whole. Maybe it's the other way around, i.e., that preventing individual women from bodily autonomy is bad for women in general. It is "bad" because reinforcing the stigma against sex workers and reinforcing the idea that selling sex is exploitation (even when it is not) reinforces the idea that sex hurts women and that there is something wrong/deviant with women who choose to sell sex.

Antiprostitution rhetoric may be directed against the male clients now but it impacts the women too. There must be something wrong with the sex worker because no one with choice would "degrade" herself by choosing prostitution. This perspective reinforces the idea that sex harms and degrades women and that women with high sex drives are somehow deviant. How do we know what to believe when men are encouraged to be sexual and women are still discouraged from sex? Why must women be protected? We need protection from violence and assault, from going missing and no one caring. Do we need protection from consensual sex? Maybe preventing women from selling sex hurts women in general because it reinforces the stigma and marginalizes them even further by entrenching the sexual double standard and Madonna/whore binary. The argument that prostitution hurts "women" not only problematizes the normalization of men buying sex but it also restricts the rights of women to the autonomy of their bodies and sexualities. ·

As we saw in chapter 2, maybe it is a problem for girls to grow up fearing their own sexualities and therefore being gatekeepers, keeping men at bay rather than developing their own sexualities and agency. Believing that girls who have sex with multiple boys are sluts just opens girls up to more abuse – again look at the cases of girls committing suicide because they have been so slut-shamed for activities that would be hailed in boys. Even in cases where these girls were victims of assault, they have been blamed as sluts. So in order to eliminate the sexual double standard and Madonna/whore binary, we need to eliminate the stigma against sexually active women.

If we accept that sexuality is a normal part of human life then we need to make the commercialization of sex as safe as we can. Removing the stigma would better protect the providers, not just the clients. As we saw in part 1, however, this is much easier said than done. There is a whole array of forces opposing the sexual liberation of women. The stigma against sex workers is so great and deep-seated that it will take years to make changes to their status, and that's only if society can agree that the stigma should end. Centuries of whorephobia and slut-shaming continue to be barriers to the freedom of women but until we stop distinguishing women based on their sexual history or what they do for a living, none of us will be free.

Unfortunately, wanting to end the demand for prostitution without recognizing that there are women and men who want to sell sex puts the autonomy and agency of that person at risk. If someone has freely chosen to sell sex and makes a lot of money doing that without violence and exploitation, why are we saying she shouldn't be able to do it? Should we not have agency over our own bodies and sexuality? Without acknowledging women's agency, we are paternalistically saying that women cannot make decisions for themselves. And then aren't we inadvertently reinforcing slut-shaming by protecting women from sex and by the implied belief that women are hurt and degraded by sex?

The stories of the sex workers I met for my film perfectly illustrate the huge double standards of male and female sexuality that are still with us today and the stigma that exists when women's expressions of sexuality go outside the norm. Sex work is a hierarchy and continuum of experience from street-based survival sex workers to high-end escorts. It is also a microcosm for the double standards and hypocrisy surrounding sex in our society today. As the former executive director of a Halifax sex-work advocacy group said to me, "Society continues to treat sex workers as their punching bag. I also think that sex workers kind of are like this vestibule that society puts all of their stigma, their nastiness, their thoughts, their blame, their guilt, like just everything into that. So I think that the stigma has a huge part to do with it ... and not seeing sex workers as people." We project our discomfort on women who are "free" with their sexuality, like sex workers, by stigmatizing them. Although the escorts I met for the film chose to do sex work and their economic situation is much better than a survival sex worker, they face the same stigma. There's even a stigma around studying sex work.[52] As my grandmother always used to say to me, "Why can't you study something I can tell my friends about?!"

As much as misogyny still exists and the worry that women in sex work are being exploited and abused is valid in some cases, I'm amazed that it took me so long to realize that misogyny also lies in the control of women's sexuality and particularly the control of women who sell sex. Of course, I always knew about the Madonna/whore dichotomy but it was really only theoretical until I met these women. They are free from any kind of notion of being a good girl or a bad girl.

Is it, then, in eradicating sex work (and somehow forcing men to be as restricted sexually as women have always been) that we create equality or is it in destigmatizing the women who sell sex and encouraging women to explore their sexualities? Which is the more progressive act? The next two chapters examine what the next sexual revolution might look like both for sex-workers' rights and women's sexuality generally. At minimum, we need to decriminalize sex work and destigmatize sex.

PART THREE

Ending Good Girl Privilege and Bad Girl Stigma

Chapter Seven

Decriminalize Sex Work

When I worked on a sex tourism development project in the Philippines, I vividly remember my colleague and I trying to explain to a horrified Manila police officer that in Canada prostitution was (at that time, pre-2014) technically legal but solicitation for both the buying and selling of sex was illegal – meaning that men could be arrested. In the Philippines, he said, clearly incredulous at the idea of men being punished, "it's a crime for women to *be* prostitutes, not for men to *go* to them."[1] How times have changed. Canada now follows the Nordic model where it *is* a crime to go to a prostitute, not to *be* one. The unique hybrid model of the Philippines where prostitution is officially illegal but regulated by the municipal government is the worst for sex working women that I've seen, but I believe our asymmetrical model comes a close second.

For prohibitionists, however, Canada is a beacon of hope, as a large anti-trafficking organization in the US put it, because in 2014 we adopted a version of the Nordic model in which buying sex is illegal and selling sex is decriminalized under certain circumstances. Our legal framework criminalizes the sellers of sex when those sellers are in places known to be frequented by children and criminalizes third-party advertising, so it is more restrictive than Sweden's original version. The Nordic model states that prostitution is violence against women and an act of inequality, and so far Sweden, Iceland, France, Ireland, Israel, Norway, and Canada have adopted this asymmetrical framework. These countries now penalize the clients, reversing the centuries-old idea in countries like the Philippines that women are the criminals and men the unsuspecting victims of feminine wiles.

How Did This Come to Be?

In 2013 the Supreme Court of Canada ruled that the prostitution laws in Canada's Criminal Code were unconstitutional and counter to the Section 7 provision of "security of the person."[2] Basically, prostitution wasn't illegal in Canada prior to 2014 but most activities that could arguably make sex work safer were illegal (for example, bawdy houses, soliciting, and living on the avails). The court gave the government a year to come up with new laws, and the Conservative government of the time took a position that was consistent with the lobbying of prohibitionist feminists and religious groups by instituting the Canadian version of the Nordic model in its Bill C36, Protection of Communities and Exploited Persons Act.[3]

The government could have chosen to decriminalize prostitution completely, as New Zealand has done, and to use health, safety, and labour laws to regulate the industry. The government could have gone with a regulated system as in Germany and the Netherlands, where only certain types of prostitution are legal and these are regulated by the government. It chose instead to keep prostitution essentially illegal, underground, and stigmatized. The current Liberal government has said it will review those laws, but at the time of publication, well into their second mandate, there is no indication that they have any plans to do so. The stakes for the government are too low to stir the hornet's nest that is the coalition between radical feminists and the religious right. One must ask, however, whose interests does this lack of engagement, with laws that some scholars have called "draconian," serve?[4]

On the one hand, it seems right that all people should have labour and human rights protections. Nothing seems controversial about that. On the other hand, however, recognizing sex work as labour and providing health and safety protections for workers means legitimizing sex work as work. That's where people who are ideologically opposed to sex work balk. They want to eradicate prostitution, not legitimize it, and harm reduction solutions like decriminalization are a threat to the future elimination of prostitution. Western concepts of sexuality may have liberalized tremendously over the past fifty years but on the issue of selling sex Canada seems to have become more conservative. Only thirty-five years ago, the Fraser Commission of 1985, when asked to evaluate legal options for prostitution, stated that the asymmetrical model (which is now Canadian law) was fundamentally incompatible with our notions of liberty and fairness especially in light of the relatively new Charter of Rights and Freedoms of 1982.[5]

Prohibitionist Arguments in Favour of the Nordic Model

Prohibitionists support the Nordic model fully as it criminalizes the buyers of sex who they see as the fundamental problem and supports the sellers to leave the trade. As Julie Bindel writes, "Abolitionists argue that the only effective way to tackle any trade that is built on vulnerability, exploitation and desperation is to support those desperate enough to sell sexual access to themselves and ensure that those creating the demand pay the price."[6] Prohibitionists don't believe the industry can be made less dangerous because they believe prostitution is inherently violent and that risk reduction does not address the range of problems they associate with sex work. As Trisha Baptie states, "It's a delusion that clean sheets and a condom on the bedside is going to erase the emotional, psychological, physical, spiritual and emotional harm that's going to happen to that woman when she conducts that trick."[7]

The prohibitionist perspective is that decriminalizing the buyers creates two related problems: decriminalization legitimizes the commercial access to women's bodies and, secondly, increases the demand for paid sex, thereby creating more demand for sex trafficking. That is why most prohibitionists reject the distinction between voluntary and involuntary prostitution. As Bindel states unequivocally, "All men who pay for sex are exercising male power, privilege and financial control over the woman he is paying for."[8] They also believe that the vast majority of women and girls in the sex industry are there because they have been forced to be there. Says Sylvia,

> If there is someone who says that they are there by choice, well I might concede 1 per cent and then I'll also add to that, besides saying "good luck with that," I'll say "ever noticed who's doing the choosing? The

people with very few choices." So another piece of that is to understand that you make social policy off of what's happening to 99 per cent. You don't make social policy off of the 1 or 2 per cent who say it's working well for them. You create social and political legal conditions that foster real meaningful choices that honour the dignity and worth of human beings and do not create vehicles by which people can be used and exploited in this way.

I interviewed Sylvia on the same day that I first met with the organizers of the media workshop. After each interview or meeting, I went on camera to record my own thoughts about the interview and where I stood on the issues at that time. Several times in my reflections I noted that "it's too bad that those two groups can't get themselves together because they are, to a certain degree, working for the same thing." At the time my thinking centred on the fact that both groups advocated for decriminalizing the sellers of sex. I knew that the group organizing the workshop and other sex-worker rights groups did not agree with the Nordic model, which just decriminalizes the women, not the men, but at least, as I said in my on-camera reflection, "it's a step forward. It's something better than the situation now in the States where not only is solicitation illegal as it is in Canada, but in some states prostitution itself is illegal which makes it very difficult for women and criminalizes the act of prostitution." I ended again with the sentiment that "it's just unfortunate that these two very strong, powerful groups and individuals can't work together to make this happen." That was then; this is now.

Now I understand more fully the differences between the two groups and how their goals are fundamentally at odds. Prohibitionists look at the Nordic model as a way to eradicate sex work by eliminating the demand for prostitution; sex worker rights groups want to establish the right to work in safety by decriminalizing the trade itself. One model makes buying sex illegal and encourages women to find other employment, whereas the other model decriminalizes adult, consensual exchanges of sex for money and sees sex work as work which ought to be governed by the rights and regulations attached to other industries, using other elements of the criminal code to deal with violence, coercion, or exploitation. It is true that both groups want to decriminalize the sellers of sex. Bindel herself acknowledges the laws in the US are "dreadful" because the women are criminalized. "Abolitionists and pro-prostitution activists agree on this, but not on the potential solutions."[9]

In the US, criminalization of prostitution means that, technically, the only way to prove prostitution has occurred is for an undercover police officer to have sex with a sex worker, exchange money afterwards, and then arrest the sex worker. As Amanda related, this was the worst thing to ever happen to her and in her state it was actually illegal for the police to do this. Only two states in the US continue to allow this to happen, paid for by the taxpayers. Most states still have criminalization of prostitution in their laws even if it is no longer enforced. Rather, other forms of harassment are used as a deterrent including being arrested for prostitution if found carrying condoms, vagrancy claims, and police intimidation.[10]

Unfortunately, many socialist and radical feminists are caught between their ultimate goals of eliminating prostitution *and* capitalism (and its commodification of just about everything) and supporting harm-reduction policies needed by sex workers in the here and now (that antiprostitution activists believe will continue the practice of sex work). They also rely on often faulty statistics like the one used above by Sylvia that only 1 per cent of sex workers choose to do sex work. In fact, most sex workers worldwide choose to work for the money.[11]

Statistics on Sex Work

What do the statistics on sex work actually tell us? Is it true that only 1 per cent choose? Are Lucy and the other women really such outliers? Statistics are hard to come by for sex work because of the nature of the mostly illegal business and the stigma surrounding it.[12] Unfortunately, research is so polarized and politicized that the ideological position of the author presenting the stats will almost certainly determine the statistics offered or how the stats are read. So Hakim's research showing that only 10 per cent of sex workers worldwide are survival sex workers flies in the face of Bindel's research that seems to suggest that virtually no women choose to do sex work.[13] Robert Weitzer claims that 80 per cent of sex workers work indoors and that survival sex workers make up only 20 per cent of the total.[14] He and Laura Agustin have also written about the problematic methodology of antiprostitution research in terms of lacking a diversity of sex work experiences other than survival sex work.[15] Most research I have seen puts the number of survival sex workers at 10–20 per cent of the total.[16]

It seems likely, then, that there are many more Lucys out there, but stigma and criminalization keep them silent. Sex work is certainly gendered, with approximately 80 per cent of sex workers being cisgender females, and we live in a racialized, class-based society, which means that marginalized sex workers tend to be women of colour and poorer women. Naomi Sayers, for instance, reports that Indigenous women make up almost 70 per cent of the street-based industry in Canada.[17] Lever and Dolnick reported in 2000 that 70 per cent of their street sample in Los Angeles were African American women and 80 per cent of their indoor sample were white women.[18] Sex work is stratified by race and class but also by age, location of work, appearance, and "public visibility."[19] Indoor workers are less visible and therefore less likely to come into contact with the law and less likely to be harassed on the street or be victims of violence.[20] The remaining 20–25 per cent of sex workers are male and transgender female sex workers whose main clientele are males,[21] though the market for male escorts and sex tourism for women is growing.

The other statistic that some people have a hard time acknowledging is that many women who do sex work are actually quite educated and have other choices, so the fact that two of the women I interviewed were doing PhDs seems like another "special case." In research done in Vancouver on violence within the indoor sex-work industry, researcher Tamara O'Doherty found very low rates of violence and very high rates of education:

> The other piece that I think people are usually very surprised about when they look at my findings, is the number of people who had a very high education. I mean 93 per cent of my sample had at least some post-secondary education. Thirty-five per cent had a master's degree, a law degree, or a PhD because students will often work in informal labour in order to pay their tuition so as long as the federal government is continuing to give us these exorbitantly high tuition rates, you will see more women engaging in sex work.

During my research, when I told antiprostitution activists about all the women I was meeting and asked them if these women's stories complicated their antiprostitution analysis, many responded that women like Lucy and Anna are the privileged 1 per cent. This assumption made it easier for them, I guess, to discount the analytic and political relevance of their experiences. As argued by UK sex-worker rights activist Juno Mac, this puts sex workers in yet another double bind: they're either all victims so they can be discounted because they don't know what's good for themselves or they're too privileged and they can also be ignored because their experiences are not sufficiently representative.[22] In either case, their voices can be disregarded because their narrative doesn't fit into the mainstream victim narrative. Kerry Porth outlines this dilemma when sex workers testified at the Canadian PCEPA hearings before the law was proclaimed and saw their testimony dismissed: "witnesses who were critical of the proposed legislation, and who supported sex worker rights to safe and fair workplaces, were actively discredited as 'not representative.'"[23]

Part of the problem with the disbelief about women's diverse experiences, including their level of education, is the emphasis on the street-based survival sex worker as the main image of the "prostituted woman." Another, related part of the problem is the conflation of voluntary sex work between consenting adults with forced sex trafficking.

"Sex Work Is to Trafficking as Sex Is to Rape"[24]

My first experience with seeing this forced/voluntary debate up close and personal was at the United Nations 1995 World Conference on Women in Beijing. What I remember most were the fights between the pro- and antiprostitution feminists. In their drive to eliminate prostitution, antiprostitution groups did not want to make a distinction between voluntary sex work and sex trafficking and wanted the wording in the draft declaration to state that all prostitution is a violation of women's human rights. Pro-prostitution groups wanted to add in the word "forced" to indicate that not all prostitution was problematic. Norma Jean Almodovar was one of the main architects of the revised wording:

We managed to lobby the NGO delegates and we got the paragraph that dealt with prostitution, it originally said, "all pornography and prostitution are incompatible with the dignity and worth of the human person and must be eliminated." So we managed to change that paragraph by inserting one word, all *forced* and we absolutely believe that if someone is forced to do anything, whether it's prostitution or whether it's working in a sweat shop or working as a domestic servant and never being allowed out of the house, these are things that people are forced to do and we agree that people who force them, ought to be caught and punished.

This forced/voluntary distinction has been adopted by the United Nations and most other international organizations. The United Nations Protocol to Prevent, Suppress and Punish Trafficking in Persons (a protocol to the Convention against Transnational Organized Crime) defines trafficking as the use of force, fraud, or coercion for the purposes of labour or sexual exploitation across borders. Therefore, prostitution is the consensual buying or selling of sex; trafficking involves violence or coercion in the transport of people for the purposes of prostitution or other labour (though most people associate trafficking with sex trafficking and ignore the other forms of labour trafficking and exploitation). Says Laurie Shrage:

I'm against trafficking and I think we should have very stringent laws against trafficking. Trafficking is ... forced prostitution, where sex workers work under essentially slave conditions, against their will, it involves minors typically, it involves illegal migration. So for all those reasons, I'm with them when it comes to trafficking and preventing forced prostitution, forced migration for prostitution, forcing minors or anyone, adults as well, into the industry, deceiving people about the kind of work they're doing and forcing them into prostitution. We should have laws against trafficking, we should have laws against slavery, and we should have laws against the abuse of ... workers generally.

So although pro- and antiprostitution activists agree on very little, everyone recognizes that actual acts of trafficking should be criminalized for the great harm done to the victims, even if critical antitrafficking researchers are rightly sceptical of the emphasis on sex trafficking because of how damaging antitrafficking campaigns have been to sex worker's rights.[25] As Lepp and Gerasimov state, "In many countries, anti-trafficking legislation, policies, and interventions have targeted sex workers with highly detrimental impacts. This has taken the form of greater police surveillance of the sex industry, raids on sex work establishments, forced detention in rehabilitation centres, arrests and prosecutions of sex workers as traffickers, and deportations of migrant sex workers – all of which undermine and ignore sex workers' agency as well as their legitimate demands for better working conditions and human, social, and labour rights."[26] Antitrafficking groups also use what many people think are very inflated numbers to make their points and encourage the use of police resources and carceral strategies to arrest and harass sex workers who are not trafficked.[27]

By calling consensual prostitution sex trafficking, antiprostitution organizations keep the media image of the poor, trafficked victim top of mind and have successfully changed the narrative from women as criminals to women as victims. Although many might see this as a step forward, this narrative erases the women who have chosen to be sex workers and makes their lives even more invisible to those who don't know much about sex work. If all prostitution is violence against women and inherently exploitative, and if women cannot consent to their own exploitation, then if they claim to be doing sex work freely they must not know their own minds or what is good for them. As the head of an anti-child-exploitation group in Canada said to me, "adults in prostitution ... are also fuelling that demand side. I also feel terribly sorry for them. Because you're not engaging in something that's in your best interest. Simple as that. Where are you going to be when you are my age? Where's your pension, you know? What are you going to tell your grandchildren?" Because prohibitionists cannot imagine that sex work is ever done freely and consensually, they are not able to imagine a world where sex work is normalized and decriminalized.

We may think we are better off than the Philippines now with our asymmetrical model that favours the "prostituted women" but does criminalizing the consensual sexual behaviour of adults help solve the problem of sexual inequality, stigma, and violence against sex workers?

Arguments against the Nordic Model

Sex work activists generally oppose the Nordic model and support the New Zealand model because in the New Zealand legal framework prostitution has been decriminalized fully and labour laws and health and safety regulations support the workers' rights to work safely. The model is based on the idea that sex work is work and sex workers should have the same rights as other workers – that the harms of prostitution can be dealt with without making sex between two consenting adults a criminal offence. Sex workers in Amsterdam, for instance, claim that "regardless of who is targeted, customers or providers or pimps – legal restrictions drive the sale of sex underground."[28] The Dutch Union for Sex Workers is calling for full legalization because of all the rules and regulations in the Dutch system and rejects the idea that trafficking has anything to do with sex work. One is a crime; one is work. "The GNSWP [Global Network of Sex Work Projects] says sex workers should have the same rights as other workers, including to associate and organize; to be protected by the law; to be free from violence; to be free from discrimination; to privacy and freedom from arbitrary interference; to health; to move and migrate; and to work and have free choice of employment."[29]

Amnesty International has developed policy supporting the New Zealand model and advocating for the decriminalization of adult, consensual prostitution.[30] Although many antitrafficking groups and prominent celebrities have loudly condemned them for a policy they believe condones sex trafficking, pimps, and abusive johns, Amnesty International already has specific policies against sex trafficking and force, fraud, or coercion in prostitution, as they have attempted to point out. What their research showed them is that full decriminalization would be a harm-reduction strategy because even if you decriminalize the selling of sex, it is still a criminal environment if the men are criminalized.

As Laurie Shrage says about criminalizing only the buyers of sex, it still makes the work environment criminalized for the sellers as well. It "endangers the women … who work as prostitutes and so they often have to work under very unsafe conditions … And for that reason, I think more feminists should really strongly oppose the criminalization of prostitution because rather than protect the women that these laws claim to protect, it just places their lives in great danger." Using carceral strategies to try to eliminate prostitution hurts the women most of all.[31] According to Shrage, the desire to criminalize all clients is also based on erroneous assumptions about the nature of sex work. "I think that the public has the wrong idea of sex work. First of all, their clients don't have unlimited sexual access to them. The terms and the kinds of services that their clients get are often carefully negotiated."

Andrea Krusi et al. make the point that "harassing the clients is exactly the same as harassing the workers."[32] In a research project based on street-based sex workers in Vancouver they show how criminal penalties levied on the male clients hurt the women sex workers as well. They have to work longer hours and they have to take more dubious clients because the economic circumstances of their lives haven't changed. They still need their income and so the law has simply made their lives more difficult. They are out in the cold longer, so they are getting into cars quicker and taking less time to evaluate potential clients. The authors conclude that their "analysis provides strong empirical evidence that the continued criminalization and policing of clients negatively impacts sex workers' working conditions and their health and safety while reinforcing mistrust of police."[33]

Criminalization of the clients hurts marginalized women the most.[34] Indigenous women in Canada who make up a high percentage of the on-street sex worker community are divided themselves on whether the appropriate policy to help and protect Indigenous women should be de-criminalization for both clients and workers or just for the women selling. While the Native Women's Association of Canada (NWAC), for instance, joined the Women's Coalition in taking a strong criminalization stance during the Bedford decision, other Indigenous groups and individuals supported full decriminalization. As Mariana Valverde states, the support of NWAC was critical "to the credibility of the Women's Coalition in feminist circles. But this support was counter-balanced by the vocal Indigenous street workers allied with PIVOT in Vancouver ... vehemently supporting decriminalization."[35] It seems that sex working women are in favour of decriminalization because of the harm criminalization causes them as currently working sex workers. It is *ex*-sex working women and *non*-sex working women who make up the majority of the prohibitionist cause, and so I think it is important to point out that they may not have the same interest in harm-reduction strategies in the here and now as women currently doing sex work, preferring their long-term strategy of prostitution elimination. Again, whose interests does this serve? If we are interested in harm reduction in the here and now (not the imagined future), then we really do need to take seriously Durisin et al.'s claim that we should decriminalize sex work: that it is "untenable to support the criminalization of aspects of sex work when it is known to result in serious harms and violations of human rights."[36]

The desire to just stop men from buying sex is understandable but is highly unlikely to ever work. Laws prohibiting prostitution have not stopped it, just as laws against alcohol consumption did not stop the making and consuming of alcohol. When looking at the historical accounts of the problems of alcohol consumption and the movement for prohibition, we see interesting parallels with the desire to prohibit men from buying sexual services. Alcohol was seen through a moral lens and drunkenness seen as a sin to be eradicated. It was described as a scourge to humanity, and a large-scale movement to prohibit alcohol was successful in demonizing alcohol. Banning alcohol during Prohibition in the US (from 1920 until 1933) didn't stop people from drinking alcohol but it did enable gangs, rumrunners, and organized crime to thrive because the demand for alcohol did not abate; it just went underground.[37]

So other than simply not working, criminalizing the clients will also not solve the social problems that create the supply of women coerced into sex work. In a report about the child welfare system in British Columbia, entitled "Too many victims; sexualized violence in the lives of children and youth in care," Mary Ellen Turpel-Lafond reported that Indigenous children in the child welfare system are the most vulnerable and at risk for abuse and in fact "have been groomed for a lifetime of victimization."[38] These children are disproportionately trafficked or in survival sex work, and the state is failing to protect them. The roots of this are systemic – unemployment, lack of education, poor housing, and residential school trauma. Criminalizing male clients does not solve these problems.

Most Western societies are struggling over moral issues like drugs and sex work, and what to do about them. Most are still taking the criminalization route. For instance, even though evidence suggests that all drugs should be decriminalized, only Portugal has actually done so. They decriminalized the personal possession of all drugs in 2001 and now report one of the lowest rates of drug overdoses in the world.[39] In Canada the opioid crisis has led to the CMHA advocating for decriminalizing the simple possession of drugs on the evidence that criminalization stigmatizes drug users and discourages them from seeking treatment, resulting in further marginalization. Rather than see addiction as a moral failing or a crime, the CMHA argues, the more progressive way to look at it is as a public health problem. Those who are addicted are not going to be cured by criminalization; they need treatment and the removal of stigma.[40] Unfortunately, politicians do not want to be seen as promoting drug use so it is highly unlikely that drugs other than cannabis will be officially decriminalized anytime soon, though the Public Prosecution Service of Canada has "directed members to refrain from pursuing charges for drug possession" which means de facto decriminalization.[41] Even drug injection sites are controversial because they make it look like the government is sponsoring drug use – even though there is strong evidence that these safe injection sites prevent overdose deaths. Perhaps this evidence fails to sway public opinion because, like sex workers, drug users are thought of as the undeserving, having made bad choices, and are dehumanized because of that.

Canada has legalized the possession and use of cannabis, and the debates about the pros and cons of this move have strong parallels with debates over the decriminalization of sex work. Decriminalizing cannabis will help those who already use by not making them guilty of a crime and not giving them a record for possession. But legalizing will also encourage others to try cannabis or be more regular users. It will decrease stigma and increase normalization. This is the worry of antiprostitution activists: that we will normalize prostitution and encourage more men to seek out sex workers. A London School of Economics study concluded that legalized systems as in Amsterdam create more demand for paid sexual services, which increases trafficking to meet that demand. At the same time, legalized systems, the study showed, enhance the protection of workers.[42] So there is a trade off between women's individual safety as currently working sex workers and an increase in the use of sexual services and therefore perhaps of trafficking.

Women in sex work, wherever they may find themselves within the industry, do not want their activities or their clients' activities criminalized, both for the income they will lose and the danger of working in an underground economy. Banning sex work because there is abuse or fear of misuse does nothing for the workers currently in the trade. Many things have dangers, alcohol and opioids for instance, and no one is saying they should be banned. Making moral judgments about, and then criminalizing, women's consensual sexual activities helps no one. As Norma Jean states about the hypocrisy,

> But we don't … send the police out and … go house to house to see if there's a domestic servant in that house, we don't send people out to go to see if wives are being victims of domestic violence and spousal abuse. But we go out and round up prostitutes and arrest them and charge them and give them a record and destroy their lives utterly because we think they're victims. And it's like ah in what universe do we do this to a victim?

Decriminalizing sex work would help to prevent problems with police and their abuse of sex workers, like Amanda. Police are known to harass women for vagrancy, demand sexual favours for letting them stay in certain areas, and even for having sex with them in order to make arrests for prostitution.[43] As mentioned above with Amanda, this was the most humiliating experience she had ever had and it was this violation that propelled her into activism, not her experiences as an escort. Decriminalizing sex work would enable workers to go to the police and report assaults against them, and to be taken seriously, as Anna said, rather than the situation now where women can be charged for even the simple possession of condoms and "possessing an instrument of crime." Being in the industry, the women I interviewed also felt they would be in a better position than police and social workers to see abuse if it was occurring and be able to report it. The same could be said about the clients as well. One client I interviewed had a few instances where he wondered about the consent of the escort and did not follow through on accepting sexual services. He said if he hadn't been worried about being arrested himself, he would have reported it.

Decriminalizing sex work would also mean that women and men would be able to safely and legally use the internet and websites to work. FOSTA

(Allow States and Victims to Fight Online Sex Trafficking Act) and SESTA (Stop Enabling Sex Traffickers Act) have had a profoundly negative impact on the ability of women to work safely in the United States. Both acts were supported by antiprostitution groups as a way to crack down on sex trafficking and protect women, but the support of the US Congress and conservative religious groups showed it was also about curtailing sexual freedom and surveilling sex. The harassment and raids (and eventual shuttering) of websites Rentboy and Backpage means that sex workers trying to safely use the internet to book clients and avoid pimps and brothels have lost another route to employment. Prohibitionists have been huge supporters of shutting down all these adult sites because they see them as a hiding place for sex trafficking and child prostitution, though there is little evidence these sites were being used for trafficking. The reality is that eliminating online sites just eliminates another venue for selling sex and endangers consensual online dating sites by increasing the surveillance of sex online, particularly of minority sexualities. How do we best deal with the circumstances on the ground? According to Amnesty International, we decriminalize all aspects of consensual sex work (including the clients) to protect the workers. As Durisin et al. have convincingly argued there is "an irreconcilable contradiction to advocate for policy approaches in the name of feminism that have been empirically proven to cause harm to sex-working women and that current sex workers – the population most affected by such policies – have vocally opposed."[44]

What Do the Escorts Think?

For the women I interviewed, sexuality is a normal part of human life and we need to make the commercialization of sex as safe as we can because people have different needs and different access to sex. If we remove the stigma, we can better protect the providers because the harms of prostitution depend on the context and the amount of control the seller has over her situation. Not surprisingly, all of the women interviewed believed that sex work, as work, should be treated as a legal, regulated business not as a criminal enterprise. Says Lucy,

I would love to see sex work get decriminalized in the United States – well, globally actually. And the main reason is that the more [open] the worker can be and the more apparent and out of the shadows that workers can show themselves without fear of being arrested and being stigmatized for what they do, the more protection that they will have from things that can happen with the work. Right now criminalizing sex work causes us to operate behind the scenes, in the shadows, out of the way of law enforcement or judgments from society and what that does is it forces us into a criminal element.

Maria, who got out of sex work only when she had an awakening about potentially being arrested for what she was doing, agrees that sex workers should be decriminalized and argued that criminalization is the real violence:

We need to decriminalize prostitution because it's unfair. It hurts women; it's violence. Criminalizing prostitution is violence against women. That's what I think. And I can't imagine … I would be so traumatized if I was in my apartment and all these police officers came in with guns. I don't know how much therapy I would need to get over that kind of an experience. If that's not violence against women, I don't know what is.

While recognizing that violence and exploitation occurs in sex work, the women all believed that currently existing criminal laws against assault, sexual assault, fraud, trafficking, and child prostitution could be used to prevent abuses in sex work and that having labour rights and health and safety standards would do far more to protect sex workers than antiprostitution laws. They argued that decriminalizing prostitution is the first step in ensuring women's safety because then they would be able to report abuses to the police. As Anna passionately relates,

The perspective I get from most women who've had those kinds of issues [bad experiences as street-level survival sex workers] is not [to] keep this economy underground and my life hidden. It's … figure out how to help me in getting laws changed so that I don't have to lurk in the shadows in the manufacturing district, so that no one arrests me and takes away my condoms and destroys them, so that if I go to the police and say that guy hit me, they arrest him and I'm treated seriously in a court of law … [Sex work] is work. It's difficult work, it's challenging work, and it's work that is made much more challenging and dangerous because of the way that it is criminalized and because of the way it's stigmatized.

Amanda also took a strong decriminalization stance based on the harm to women who sell sex and the effect of a criminal record on self-esteem and job prospects.

The first harm is that criminalization criminalizes your identity and your body, your sexuality, your desire. It criminalizes the whole person. And that's in and of itself unacceptable. But, number two, criminalization doesn't help anyone. Arresting people and putting them in jail and making them pay fines doesn't help a single person. It doesn't protect people; it doesn't help a single person. You don't put battered women in jail because she's, to save her, to rescue her. It doesn't make any sense.

They all rejected the Nordic model because it still criminalizes the practice of sex work and keeps that part of the economy underground. As Lucy states, "I mean still with the Swedish model it's not completely decriminalized, there's still certain regulations that are in place that still do not favour sex workers' safety and their rights you know." Lucy also was critical of the underlying intention of the Swedish model, which is that "it reinforces a vilification of men's sexuality that the men are the criminals, and that's not necessarily the case either, okay, so we're not, we're trading off one stigma for another stigma and neither one [is] true."

Anna believed the New Zealand model was the best for sex workers themselves because of the emphasis on health and safety and because sex workers had been involved in the drafting of the legislation and standards.

The government in New Zealand also put out what I think is absolutely the best … health and safety manual … it's the rules by which folks that have these licences have to operate. Everything in terms of clean up, proper disposal of condoms, towel cleaning, I mean it gets really quite specific and you read the document and yah it's a lot of rules to follow, some people don't like rules. But they're all geared to protecting the health and safety of the people working there. Just like any profession has health and safety standards. And this was particularly great in New Zealand, developed in consultation of sex workers, from my understanding of reading the introduction of it. So, I mean good on them.

Anna's comments are backed up by research in New Zealand that shows there has not been any great increase in demand for sexual services but there has been a big decrease in violence against sex workers.[45]

My last question to the women interviewed was this: in your perfect world, what would sex work look like? For Norma Jean it was decriminalizing all forms of commercial sex between adults.

We would repeal all existing laws that prohibit private consenting adults [having] commercial sex, period: male, female, transgendered, makes no difference. As far as public places, I think that people have a right to say we don't want commerce in our neighbourhoods, etc. There are people who don't want to be confined to a hotel room or whatever. And I think we can accommodate them by making areas like they have in Hamburg and in various places around the world which allow red light districts to exist in safe places, they're well secured by law enforcement and people know who want to find someone in that area, know where to go and everybody's happy. We would repeal all of the ancillary laws around it including pimping and pandering and we would focus solely on coercion.

For Lucy, it was to decriminalize sex work so women could work together: "to be able to work together in a community like in a brothel situation or having a place that you share with another colleague and coworker, those are, you know when we're allowed to work together that increases our safety. We have someone that's there, that knows where we're at, that's close by and that protects us." Anna thought that the power of the government should be used to help sex workers and enable them to work legally and safely:

> I believe strongly in the ability of societies to reform and adapt and support communities. I think that there are some good regulations that we could put in place that would be really helpful. I think that there should be oversight of sex workers in establishments. I would like to see really serious attention by policy makers in a good way, being paid to making the working conditions and the health and safety concerns of sex workers a priority, without jeopardizing their rights and abilities to choose how and when they do their work. And I think that's possible. And because I think that's possible, I'm doing this [activist] work.

That is not to say that sex work is easy or for everyone. Lucy, who says sex work is her calling, is very realistic about the work itself. "Sex work isn't easy. I'm not here trying to tell anybody that sex work is an easy job and that everybody should do it. Not by any means. It takes a particular type of person and a particular type of personality to be able to do it, in part because it is very draining and you have to really know yourself and really be introspective and be a very, very strong person to survive and not get lost in it. But it is possible, and I know many people that do it." Lucy gave the example of a friend who was always short of money and who had asked her about doing sex work. Lucy knew it wasn't something the friend could do without harm to herself and never encouraged her to try it.

The Future of Sex Work

All of the escorts interviewed predicted that as women gain more economic and sexual power, they too will become clients of sex providers, both as sex tourists using their economic clout for sexual and romantic encounters with younger men in the Global South and as clients of male escorts in the Global North. They all knew of male escorts who worked with women and couples and they all said this was something that was bound to increase in the future as women gained more sexual freedom. Maria thought that a revolution was coming for women:

> I think things are really changing, I mean just in this [Desiree Alliance] conference that we've been at, one of the sessions was a male sex workers' movement. I think we're going to see a lot of change in the next ten years in terms of men out there providing sex for money with women. Women are very ... how do I put this? Women are owning their sexuality more than they ever did before in history and once you own your own sexuality and feel that's what you need and you deserve and it's important to you then I think you can go out and see a sex worker. Because it's something you feel that you need, you deserve, you want, but women still have a difficult time. I think women are still more sexually oppressed than men are.

Catherine Hakim certainly agrees with this assessment as well. "I think a lot of women have never really had a very flourishing sex life with regular orgasms, so they don't know what they're missing. Whereas men almost always orgasm if they have sex and therefore if they don't get it, they know what they're missing. Whereas so many women have difficulty reaching orgasm and a lot of women have never actually got there and learned how to do it regularly."

Prohibitionists like Sylvia think women haven't been as influenced by the sex industry or are somehow more moral in their sexual lives. As she states, thinking that women will be clients of sex workers "is nothing but a huge scam being perpetrated by the sex industry to increase their customer base and also, much more disturbingly, to erase the harm of prostitution." I think it is more likely that the reason women don't go to escorts is because of how socially unacceptable it is for women to have sexual pleasure outside love, relationships, and marriage. As Suzanne Moore writes about the right-wing reactions to New York Representative Alexandra Ocasio-Cortez dancing and her toes (!), "beneath all this is a tangible disgust and anxiety about the biggest taboo, women's pleasure."[46] It may be more unacceptable for men today to go to sex workers than it was years ago, but it has never been okay for women.

Research on women going to male escorts in Australia shows that as women become more empowered they are going to escorts too for the same reasons as men: little time for dating, it's all about them, they want to be pampered, and they want sex.[47] Our stereotypes say women have sex for emotional or romantic reasons, but women go to escorts for physical reasons too. Even with more and more women going to Ghana or the Caribbean or the Gambia (where I've participated in another development project) for sex with local men, radical feminists insist on calling this "romance" tourism,[48] not sex tourism, and that even in these (limited) situations, the women are the ones being abused, not the poor African men. Here's the double standard in reverse. Women couldn't possibly abuse men because the sex act itself means that they are being penetrated and therefore open to abuse. The idea is that either women are such a minority that this is just a deflection from men's far greater sex tourism in Asia or that they really do believe that women can never have power over men. As Melissa Ditmore says about sex tourism, "it doesn't speak to male privilege as it speaks to monetary privilege. There are situations in which the market for sex is driven by women, there are so-called beach boys in parts of Africa who sell sex and parts of the Caribbean who sell sex to women from richer countries typically."

The sex trade is more complicated than most antiprostitution activists would have us believe, and this complexity is likely to increase. As women gain more economic and social power, more women will use that power to buy leisure activities and feel themselves entitled to the goods of sex, just as men do. The dynamics of the sex trade will surely change when women become the buyers.

In a perfect world, would we have a sex trade? If it's just about men's rights to women's bodies and male domination generally then we can safely say that the sex trade will not exist in the future. Like domestic violence and sexual assault, the sex trade will fade away because it will not be socially acceptable. Patriarchy and male domination will end eventually even though feminists have been working to end male domination for at least 200 years. However, if the sex trade is not just about male domination then the answer is not so simple. If sex is a basic human need and not everyone has access to the goods of sex, then there would seem to be a built-in demand for sexual services. And as long as there is a demand, there will be women (and men) willing to supply that demand. If, in the future, sex is valued then perhaps sex work will be valued too as Lucy and the other escorts argued. If sexuality was embraced and celebrated and seen as a pleasurable and valuable part of human identity (and not only valued when it is married sex for procreation), then perhaps sex work would flourish, too.

It's hard to imagine such a future when the present is as male dominated as it is and where men's pleasure is taken for granted but not women's. It's hard to imagine what a sexual utopia would look like. I like to imagine a future in which women's autonomy and pleasure are seen as important, where the sexual double standard has disappeared, and in which women have equality with men sexually, not just in the work or political world, as I'll outline in chapter 8. The futuristic workers of Risa (from the TV show *Star Trek: The Next Generation*) come to mind:[49] men and women who work for a resort and provide (mutual) pleasure to visiting tourists. I also think of *Firefly*'s courtesan, Inara Serra, who has high status, influence, and income.[50] Although it is difficult to imagine what sex work in the future will look like that doesn't mean we can't try. And it doesn't mean that we have become collaborators to the patriarchy to think about what sex work would look like, other than that it wouldn't exist. If we can show that sex work isn't inherently good or bad, we can imagine a future in which sex work is done with respect and dignity. And if we find people, and more than just a few, who choose sex work because they like sex work and find fulfillment doing the work, then perhaps we have to change how we see sex.

How Do Prohibitionists Perpetuate Whore Stigma?

Listening to sex workers means listening to all of the various stories and narratives about sex work and accepting that there are good and bad aspects to sex work. I started this research project without an agenda except to further examine the various forms of and problems with prostitution, with a nod to the goods of sex work, after meeting Lucy. I understood the harm-reduction lens, but I was sympathetic to the Nordic model of criminalizing the clients. Not until I met Lucy and the others did I start to understand what I had been missing in my analysis: the problem was about more than preventing women from selling sex and men from buying sex. First of all, some women choose sex work over other options and don't want to leave sex work, and, just as importantly, I realized that the Nordic model is not a stopgap towards greater equality (as prohibitionists think) but rather an approach that continues women's inequality by reinforcing and therefore prolonging whore stigma.

What happens to the victimization narrative when we realize it has more than a few exceptions, when we realize that its authors are telling a single story but that this is not the story of the women I met and interviewed. If 80 per cent of sex workers choose selling sex over some other type of work, how is this "paid rape"? How does this narrative of abuse and violence actually perpetuate whorephobia? Many prohibitionist scholars and activists, as well as the media, are complicit in sensationalizing the sale of sex and creating the idea that these women are different from the rest of us. The framing of sex work as deviant or as a form of male abuse creates one narrative and it becomes a lens through which we see all forms of sex work. It then becomes even harder for the general public to sort out the issues because the stories we hear in the media are all so stereotyped and sensationalized.[51] As Lucy states,

> I think the unfortunate part of public perception of sex work is based on two factors and that's what they see sensationalized either through the trafficking stories and the horrific stories of women or children, being forced to do things against their will or the glamorized, sensationalized, high dollar hottie, high dollar call girl specials, exposés, or scandals with politicians ... Those are the spectrums, the bottom end and the high end of it, and there's this huge, I think, area in between that we never see.

Lucy's point is that there is much more to sex work than meets the eye but that the middle tier worker is made invisible because of the stigma and criminality of what they do. Anna, similarly, calls out the prohibitionists who insist upon calling her a "prostituted woman" believing that she is being "used" by men. She points out the harm caused by this framework, as prohibitionists have bought into the notion of women being "dirtied" through sex.

I dislike the word "use," you know. If you have a situation where someone is being paid for labour, I don't think that's someone being used as though they were once clean and now they're dirty. You know like a napkin that you sneeze into. I think that's pretty uncool as a way to characterize that and really disrespectful to the person who is doing that work. It's words … like "prostituted women" as though you're in the past tense and you are a verb, you're reduced to some kind of action rather than being a whole person that has a job that can be problematic, that can be challenging, that may have real issues that you should care about. It's a big difference and one is very moralistic and judgmental and frankly just not helpful.

These stereotypes are also a huge problem for seeing sex workers as competent agents. Says Laurie Shrage,

There are women who will choose to go into sex work who have other choices and they don't have a history of abuse, either sexual abuse or drug abuse and so on. So I think that those who are antiprostitution focus on the prostitute as either being sexually abused or who's a drug addict because again it just recirculates these, I think, myths and stereotypes about prostitutes. And it completely ignores the middle-class prostitute who is engaging in prostitution for different reasons … I've known sex workers who are mothers who do sex work to be able to have more time to spend with their kids. Sex work is a job you can do at night when you can hire a babysitter and then you can be home all day. I know sex workers who have been students, for the same reasons. You can do sex work at night and then go to school all day and you can earn enough money to live on. And so, you know, the typical sex worker just isn't typical. But again I think some of the feminists who are highly critical of prostitution as a practice and an industry focus on sex workers who fit the stereotype. And in a way then you know they reinforce the stereotype which is not useful.

Unfortunately, prohibitionists encourage this stereotyping and whore stigma when they decry any depiction of prostitution that is not their version of exploitation and debasement, believing such depictions to be ploys of the sex trade industry intended to normalize prostitution and glamorize it. As Sylvia states,

> We have ... an ongoing campaign against *Cathouse*. HBO is very, when you talk about normalizing prostitution, HBO is a major culprit. HBO is a major media outlet that for some strange reason seems very, I call it pimpcentric ... Very accepting of pimping of other human beings, which is trafficking, so they have a show called *Cathouse*, which they call a documentary, which actually is putting a camera in a brothel in Nevada, a brothel by the name of Cathouse, and it's presented as entertainment, laughable, the commercial selling of human beings. And it is a show that shows how cynical HBO is because if they were serious about producing a documentary about prostitution they would actually produce a documentary that tells the truth about prostitution and tells the truth about the sex trafficking that's going on in the state of Nevada.

Popular culture depictions of sex work run the gamut from realism to cliché. From *Pretty Woman* (prostitute with a heart of gold) to *Monster* (whore as victim) to *Secret Diary of a Call Girl* (glamorized and sensationalized) to *The Girlfriend Experience* and *Hustlers* (world weary and exploiter of male weakness), sex workers in popular culture have been fairly one-dimensional and unrealistic, and tend to reinforce whore stigma.[52] The treatment of sex workers in the TV show *Sons of Anarchy* is particularly bad. *Sons* is an award-winning show about a biker gang in LA. It is all about brotherhood, family, loyalty, and honour and had a huge fan base. It has been cited as a reason for a resurgence of biker clubs in the US. Women in the show, however, are dismissed as "Crow Eaters" and get no respect unless they are an "old lady" of one of the bikers. There is a great deal of name calling and slut-shaming, and the women in the show are as bad as the men for putting other women down and blaming women for their men's bad behaviour. Matriarch Gemma beats up a young sex worker who has had sex with her husband; wife Tara beats up the madam who has been sleeping with her husband, and they both treat Wendy – the main character's ex-wife and mother of his son – as the "crack whore" that she used to be. It's not pretty. Sex workers are seen as disposable and exploitable and no respectable woman would be involved in such activities. They deserve the violence against them.[53]

These stereotypes feed into whore stigma as we saw in chapter 3. Whorephobia is defined as the hatred or fear of the concept of the whore and, by extension, of women who transgress sexually according to the norms of their society. So by definition, I would argue, whorephobia affects us all. Radical feminists and conservatives think that paid sex is the problem, but it is the hatred of sexually active women that is the real problem. Criminalizing the selling and buying of consensual sex doesn't help the problem of stigma. Continuing the stigma around sex work in terms of the men buying sex will continue the stigma for the women selling sex most of all. Yet even on the issue of whorephobia, sex workers and prohibitionists cannot agree. Julie Bindel thinks that the emphasis on whorephobia is being used to silence radical feminist criticism of the sex trade.[54] She admonishes the LGBTQ+ movement for their acceptance of SlutWalks[55] and having sex-worker-rights groups march in pride parades seeing these acts as acceptance of prostitution as a "sexual preference or identity."[56]

Patriarchy does divide and conquer after all and until we can come together on sex worker's rights it is unlikely that any headway will be made; particularly when we have such vocal support for the criminalization of sex work coming from some women's groups. Prohibitionists have been extremely successful in keeping the debate about prostitution focused on male abuse in prostitution rather than worker's rights or the autonomy or sexual freedom of women, so, inadvertently or not, they have contributed to the continuation of whorephobia in society. Criminalizing sex work also does not address the question of value in sex work and the issue of the goods of sex nor does it eliminate stigma against sexually active women.

Sex is still seen in very moralistic ways by our society, and sex workers are dehumanized because they are seen to be "dirtied" by their connection to selling sex. They are looked down on by society and are seen to be irredeemable in some fundamental way. We can't associate with them because the dirtiness will wear off on us. As the former executive director of a sex work advocacy group in Halifax says, "I think society bullies prostitutes and sex workers to make them feel better about themselves. I also think it's very hypocritical; I think it's like the most hypocritical thing. It's sex. It is sex. And last time I checked there was not, you know, seven billion virgins walking around the planet, and it's tied in with, you know, the stigma around promiscuity."

The whole notion of slut-shaming and whorephobia is a way to control and police women's behaviour, as I hope I have shown. Theoretically of course most people realize that calling someone a whore or slut is not a good thing, but I don't think we really realize the unintended consequences when we continue to stigmatize sex work and sex workers. There's a fallout for everybody else too: for the "good" girls, as well as the "bad." Prolonging the stigma of sex work means that we maintain slut-shaming and whorephobia. We continue to give license to men (and women) to treat "sluts" badly, whether they are whores or not. Slut-shaming has very real consequences as it works to control and shame all women.

Sex work includes a range of experiences extending from the most vulnerable women on the planet, to high-end escorts making more than many professionals. To make policy for all means taking seriously women's experiences, the good, the bad, and the ugly. The value of sex work is clear to me now – for some of the women engaged in it. Women make more money as sex workers than at many low-income jobs. Sex work also fulfills many sexual desires, for women as well as men. While the current reality is that men are the main buyers of sexual services and women are the main sellers, can we imagine the reverse where both men and women buy and sell sex? Is the reversibility issue, as argued by Overall more than twenty-five years ago, so far from becoming reality? Women are much freer sexually than in the past. Women do go to escorts and are becoming sex tourists. Can we not imagine a world where women's sexual desires are accommodated in the same way men's are? If sex was valued, if women's sexual pleasure was valued, and if women could legally and socially go to sex workers then perhaps sex work would become valued as well.

Meeting Lucy made me realize that the misogyny that feminists are worried about is not reflected solely in the buying and selling of sex but also in the desire to punish women who embrace their sexualities. As the women interviewed continually emphasized, we need to make women more aware of the goods of sex and remove the barriers to women's sexual enjoyment: socialization to be good girls, lack of sexual education, stigma, and shame of the body. Women's lack of knowledge of their own bodies, women not understanding their own pleasure before they become sexually active, and the focus on men's pleasure is a far bigger problem for the sexual advancement of women than women selling sex.

Chapter Eight

Destigmatize Sex

Even if sex work were decriminalized tomorrow in Canada or the United States, much more work would need to be done to ensure that sex workers could work in safety and be free from stigma. Stigma is such a deep-seated problem that it could be years before the shame of working in the sex industry loses its hold on society. And that's only if society was interested in eliminating stigma in the first place. The questions posed at the beginning of this book about the debate between prohibitionists and sex work advocates were stark: according to the former, women will not be free until sex work is eliminated. According to the latter, women won't be free until their sexuality in whatever manifestation is not shamed and stigmatized. As I hope I have shown in this book, once we see the connection between controlling women's sexuality and restricting their bodily autonomy it should be evident that continuing the stigma against sex workers undermines all women's liberty.

The sexual revolution is incomplete, then, because we are still dealing with the two pillars of women's sexual inequality that must be eliminated: the sexual double standard between men and women and the good girl/bad girl dichotomy between women and girls themselves. These pillars must be confronted and challenged at every opportunity in order to promote the next sexual revolution for women: emphasizing and enhancing women's pleasure and eliminating what Katherine Rowland calls the "pleasure gap."[1] To do that, we need to destigmatize sex, especially for women. As part of the challenge to destigmatize sex, women (and men) need to confront the societal shame and stigma surrounding female sexuality, educate women (and men) about the female body and its bodily functions, ensure radical sexual education for young people, create a culture of female sex positivity, and ensure women's bodily autonomy is respected.

The "Shame" of the Female Body

I saw on Twitter that Dr Victoria Bateman, a professor at the University of Cambridge, went to a university event wearing only a sheer jumpsuit to make the point that women's bodies shouldn't be shamed or hidden or seen to be obscene.[2] She says she is against both the laws banning burqas in France and Saudi modesty laws forcing women to cover up, seeing them as much the same thing or at least with the same root cause.[3] Women's bodies have been associated with sin and shame and policed as such, in the case of the modesty laws, and women have lacked the autonomy to make decisions about what they choose to wear, in the case of the movement to ban burqas and other face covering veils. She writes that she was particularly bothered by the amount of hate she got from other women which just goes to show how internalized our own oppression is.[4] Many women can't imagine going naked in public so we condemn other women who can.

Bateman's main point was that women's bodies (more so than men's bodies) are seen to be sinful and shameful and therefore eligible to be seen as public and policed as such. Women are shamed for their bodies and then police themselves and other women's behaviours. What are the consequences of body shaming? Not surprisingly, the more uncomfortable you are with your body, the more uncomfortable you'll be with sex. A therapist once told me that you'll know you're comfortable with your body when you can play volleyball in the nude. Lucy could do this. She is very comfortable in her own skin and very comfortable with nudity. When the cameraman and I arrived to do an interview in her hotel room before she went for her date in Las Vegas she was wearing only a bra and thong as she put her makeup on. As you can hear me say in the footage, "that's too much for a public broadcaster," so I asked her if she would mind covering up. She was totally comfortable with her body and nudity. She could play volleyball in the nude and she could show up at an event at the University of Cambridge and display her nudity, no problem. I never could. Does that make her freer than me? Absolutely! Because it is a pretty fundamental freedom to feel literally comfortable in your own skin and not feel shamed by your naked body. And as much research has shown, one of the main problems for women enjoying sex is that they are not comfortable with their bodies and rather than enjoy the moment they are judging themselves negatively because of what they look like. They lack body confidence. As Edna Keeble argues, there are two ways of seeing the body: body-as-object or body-as-process. Women tend to see their bodies as objects to themselves and for others (and consequently judge their appearance harshly), while men generally see the body as related to performance or functionality (and hence "they are also more likely to have positive body esteem because they see their bodies in a more dynamic, rather than static, fashion"[5]). Both these stances "result from socialization processes that value women for their looks and men for their actions"[6] and, consequently, result in very different relations to the body and to sex. Sex becomes an out-of-body experience when you are more focused on what your thighs look like than what pleasure you are giving and receiving. In order to have good sex, therefore, you have to get out of your head and stop self-judgement. As Melinda Chateauvert says, "Shame makes sexual pleasure difficult."[7]

A big reason why Lucy and the other women were so comfortable having sex for money is that they were comfortable with sex for pleasure and, particularly, with their bodies and nudity. If you would be shamed by being naked in front of someone you don't know, sex work is not for you, as the women always pointed out. The women I interviewed also challenge beauty norms because they were not classic model types, with very thin bodies and exaggerated breasts. They were average looking, slightly overweight women – again somehow overcoming the socialization to be ashamed of their own bodies and to want "perfect" bodies. Most people who see the film seem surprised at how plump the women all are – as if this somehow made them less valuable as sex workers. And it also illustrates the ongoing problem society has with fatphobia.[8] The women were extremely comfortable with their bodies and their sexuality in a way many women will never be. There was no embarrassment, self-consciousness about their bodies or their bodily functions. They were self-confident people and they had no problem taking up space.

But many women feel alienated from their bodies and grow up thinking there is something about them that is shameful. As Lindy West, author of *Shrill*, has written, if we didn't think "vaginas are disgusting and mysterious ... Maybe everyone would have better sex."[9] Women's bodies are scrutinized, policed, and judged much more harshly than men's bodies. We learn that we don't control our bodies and we must protect ourselves from men. West writes that fatphobia in society today is the last acceptable discrimination, but her words also fit the discrimination against sex workers. Fat people are infantilized and mocked, she says, and treated as lesser people who don't deserve respect.[10] She writes about the need for fat solidarity and her critique of the infantilizing of fat people reminds me of some aspects of the prohibitionist movement's infantilizing of adult women in the sex industry. To paraphrase West, we only want to help you, to rescue you from yourself, to treat you like the children you are.

Shaming is used as a tool of oppression, West writes, when the concern is not about the health of fat people: "it's about eewww. You think fat people are icky."[11] That is the "same feeling that drives anti-gay bigots" and, I would argue, antisex-work bigots. West believes that "reclaiming fatness – living visibly, declaring, 'I'm fat and I'm not ashamed' – is a social tool so revolutionary, so liberating it saves lives."[12] Or as Lucy would say, I am a sex worker and I am not ashamed. West writes of "coming out as fat"[13] and the power of taking back her body and not being ashamed anymore. The problem is that it is not illegal to be fat anywhere in the world currently whereas it is still illegal to be a sex worker in most parts of the United States and illegal to be a client in Canada. And although Lucy is not ashamed of being a sex worker at all (to the contrary she is proud of being a sex worker), the consequences of her coming out were devastating. Until more sex workers and their clients are able to come out – as Shrage pointed out in chapter 3 about the success of the LGBTQ+ community – we will not get past the shame and blame.

We also see this body shame played out in relation to menstruation. Most women will have menstrual periods for a significant portion of their lives, and we are just now speaking more publicly about and normalizing a biological function. Scotland, some provinces in Canada, and California have begun to make menstruation products free in schools, community centres, and libraries to help with period poverty. If toilet paper is provided free of charge, why aren't menstrual products? The shame around women's periods seems to be decreasing, as it is normalized and politicized, but women and girls are still socialized to be ashamed of their bodies.[14] They are generally not encouraged to look at themselves "down there." They are not encouraged to play with themselves "down there." And in fact in many ways are actively discouraged from masturbating or learning about their bodies. Young girls are made to feel ashamed of their bodies and are reluctant to experiment even with their own bodies because to do that would be "bad," so there is a huge disconnect with their own bodies. Consider the distancing that must go into feeling that some parts of one's body are literally off limits to yourself? All of this produces a shame about the body for girls that boys just don't have.[15]

And unfortunately, because some people see the sexual differences between men and women as natural and inevitable, we get the claim that women's shame is actually a good thing. As an example in pop culture, we have rapper Lord Jamar's interview about SlutWalks and about Amber Rose's walk of (no) shame video.[16] Rose worked as an erotic dancer before she became a model and actress. She has become a successful businesswoman and entertainer, and she posted a video on YouTube that went viral spoofing the notion of the walk of shame. In the video she struts back home from a sexual encounter, not ashamed of having her pleasure too. Asked about Amber Rose, Jamar condemns her and attacks SlutWalks in general because "sluts *should* be shamed." He says equal doesn't mean identical and, because women are penetrated and men penetrate, women and men will never be equal sexually. He's not ashamed of having sex with lots of women but women *should* feel ashamed. Victims can be blamed and you certainly don't marry them, he says. They're "not wifey material."[17] So very starkly, women are different biologically in terms of sex and should be ashamed if they sleep around. You can't get more biologically determinist than that.

Women and Sex: Part III

In Jen Gunter's book *The Vagina Bible* she writes about why ideas like Lord Jamar's are so common and hard to eradicate: because of the obsession with purity, a "woman's worth is measured by her virginity."[18] It's why musician

T.I. admits taking his eighteen-year-old daughter to have her hymen checked to ensure she's still a virgin but doesn't care whether his fourteen-year-old son is sexually active.[19] Gunter is also interested in dispelling myths about the "unclean" uterus and "used" vagina that keep women ashamed of their own bodies.[20] What she calls her "vagenda" is for women to know the history of the vagina and the capabilities of the clitoris.[21]

The biology of the orgasm and clitoris has interesting implications for women. The only purpose of the clitoris is for women's pleasure, and yet for years doctors and psychologists insisted only vaginal orgasms were mature or relevant.[22] As Gunter writes, a detailed anatomy of the clitoris was done in 1844 but ignored because of a combination of Victorian-era worries about the dangers of female sexuality and Freud's notion of the "immature" orgasm.[23] "Freud's argument that girls' sexuality is clitoris-based and that the process of advancing to womanhood is achieved by 'transferring' this sensation to one's vagina ... was one of the major modern obstacles to clitoral competence. Freud's fiction took decades to be dispelled: decades of women fretting that they were having the 'wrong kind' of orgasm."[24] Even as that notion has been debunked, girls are not taught about the function of the clitoris and are discouraged from exploring it.

Even though women have the capacity to enjoy sex (and many of course do) society's beliefs have not caught up with the capacities of the clitoris. What I mean by that, of course, is that society has conveniently either denied the importance of the clitoris or has denied its very existence. In an article detailing the first conviction for FGM/C in Britain, the author highlights how representations of the crime never once used the word clitoris and she hypothesizes that this is due to the continuing discomfort we have with its function.

> The big difference here seems to be that while the vagina has an obvious functional utility, the clitoris exists entirely for female pleasure. It seems that the issue stems, not from the provocative nature of a word, but our continued societal taboos regarding women daring to enjoy sex. Sure, we can see depictions of women shrieking with pleasure plastered all over any porn site. But that is exactly the point. Female sexual enjoyment remains exclusively in the realm of the forbidden.[25]

Yet this hasn't always been the case even in North America. "From as early as the medieval period, the clitoris (as Thomas Laqueur, Naomi Wolf, Rebecca Chalker, and others have shown) was routinely part of midwifery manuals and medical models, but it began to be erased around the 18th and 19th centuries, when women started to demand political rights."[26] As Rowland puts it, "Within a century, a new doctrine of female passionlessness blanketed Western culture"[27] probably because the linkage between ovulation and female orgasm had been broken by science – the two were not connected as once thought. "As the Victorians spun a new cultural world around the ideal of virtuous wives and nurturing mothers, they shunted the female libido into the hinterlands."[28] The timing is interesting. Women's sexual power was the only limited power they had until the twentieth century, and Jean-Jacques Rousseau, for instance, felt women would lose that power if they tried to get more social and legal rights. To him, sex gives women tremendous power over men, which is why he thought women must be feared and controlled. He was an early advocate of restricting women, politically and physically. Lucy talks about the power of female sexuality in her views about why some men fear and hate women.

I think the fear of the power of sex is very deep-seated and certainly in our culture but in other cultures as well. I think female sexuality has, I mean we're the gatekeepers of life, you know we're the ones that can bring life into the world and as much as we might still have a lot of patriarchal kind of constructs in our society, nonetheless women still are the power source with their sexuality. Men seek it out, and they will, they will either worship or hate women because of the power that they have and … it's such a powerful thing and it motivates men in particular to move mountains when they want to.

But as Kate Harding points out, women's sexual power and women's supposed power over men is actually a bit more sinister. The idea that women have "'all the power' means, simply, the power to withhold consent."[29] And that power leads to some men's "frustration that not all extremely young, conventionally attractive women want to sleep with them."[30] There are online hate groups now devoted to the "incels," involuntary celibate men who blame women for not having sex with them and, in at least two cases that we know of, killing women because of this. We have seen an increase in online hate groups who threaten women generally with violence and "corrective" rape (see "Boycott American Women").[31] Does this make women powerful or vulnerable?

Many men are also very motivated sexually, partly because, as Peggy Orenstein puts it, there is no bad sex for men, barring sexual assault and harassment.[32] Men are encouraged to be sexual and are rewarded for being sexually successful. Women are not. Women are shamed for their sexuality and not encouraged to explore their bodies or their pleasure. Boys may feel shame for their wet dreams and inevitable masturbation, but they still do it. And they know it feels good. Women sometimes have to be taught to masturbate. Men do not.

Regardless of how pleasurable sex can be for women, the simple fact that there is a potential for sexual violation and pain means that sex for women is not the straightforward event that it is for males. The consequences of sex are also much greater for women, particularly before reliable contraception was available. Parents are not worried that their boys are going to be raped or get pregnant or get hurt or get shamed, though they do worry about their son getting someone pregnant or being "falsely" accused of rape.[33] Perhaps our ambivalence about, and fear for, female sexuality is because sex for women is not always mutual or pleasurable. In fact as Rowland states, for the women she interviewed "personal pleasure scarcely registered as part of their early [sexual] experiences"[34] and most of the women had at some time or another faked orgasm, put up with painful intercourse, and pretended all was well so that their partner's ego would not be injured. She believes this is because women "co-opt an external logic that holds someone else's pleasure as more urgent and more consequential than our own."[35] Changing this dynamic will require societal and individual transformations.

The Need for Radical Changes to Sex Education

A key part of the next sexual revolution has to be revolutionizing sexual education. Girls need to know their own bodies in order to know how to ensure they have pleasurable sexual experiences. They have to be taught about masturbation so they will know how to give themselves pleasure and how to help partners do the same for them. As the OMGyes website and many others now promote,[36] women need to understand their own bodies and know they have the right to orgasm in order to know what they like and then be able to demand it from their partners. Some writers have called this the "pleasure gap"[37] and a movement towards orgasm equality.[38] Rowland disagrees with the view that "women are not as libidinous or desirous or pleasure-seeking as men" naturally but rather argues that "many women do not feel free to enjoy their sexuality or know how to do so" because "they assume a second-class position in their sexual interactions."[39] Women must know their own bodies and feel entitled to pleasure.

The problem with revolutionizing sex education is that many parents and educators are so reluctant to be seen encouraging girls to be sexually active that they will prevent knowledge of pleasure from reaching the girls, ensuring that the boys' pleasure continues without mutuality. It's a vicious circle. We don't want teens to be sexually active, so we fill them with knowledge of the dangers and risks of sex. But teens are going to experiment; they are going to be watching pornography that might not adequately inform them about real women's pleasure, and yet we're not educating young women that the only thing their clitoris is for, it's only function, is for their pleasure.

Unfortunately, this is just too radical for many people and though I understand the impulse to "protect" girls, the consequences are usually the opposite of what is hoped. Abstinence programs do not actually work and just add to the shame and secrecy about girls' sexuality. What are we protecting when we don't teach girls about the function of their sexual organs, particularly the clitoris? We are showing our discomfort with the idea of girls being sexual. Many people don't have the same discomfort about boy's sexuality because it is assumed to be natural, and "boys will be boys." If girls are ashamed of their bodies and don't know the pleasures of the clitoris, then they are oblivious to the pleasures of sex itself, and the sex act becomes a performance for the boy's pleasure. Girls are to be sexy but not sexual. Why is it so problematic to imagine a frank conversation in a classroom about masturbation?

In Ontario, socially conservative parents and religious community members objected to a new sex-education curriculum that was more explicit than before and which dealt with issues of consent and discussed masturbation, though certainly was not a how-to class by any means. One of the first acts of the Conservative government in Ontario after they were elected in 2018 was to roll back this curriculum to the 1998 version, before cyberbullying was a problem or before consent issues were taught in school. Apparently, the government seriously considered suspending sex education entirely.[40] As André Picard writes, "failing to properly teach children doesn't protect them. It only breeds ignorance."[41] If schools can't do this education work and parents are unwilling to then we leave it to the internet, pop culture, and peers.

Because of our worries about young people and how they may react to information, parents, teachers, and other authority figures want the information in question banned or hidden. We fear that our children will become sexually active because they are provided information about contraception or condoms. We fear that normalizing same-sex relationships (or any other previously taboo subject) will just encourage the behaviour. As one of my students said about both sex education and prostitution:

> It just kind of reminds me of like when you're in school and your parents don't want teachers to teach you about sex because that means you're going to do it, you know what I mean ... but just being safe and knowing, protecting yourself, doesn't necessarily mean ... that we're all running out to do it right away. Chances are, like we already knew about it, if we wanted to do it, we would have done it. So it's kind of, I feel like it's kind of the same thing, just if they decriminalize it and make it safer, it doesn't necessarily mean that all these men are going to rush out and get prostitutes.

Her point was that simply giving young people information about issues will not automatically cause the problem to occur. The same applies to sexual education that does more than explain (some) body parts and advocate for abstinence. The controversies over two Netflix limited series remind me of how difficult it is to do educational work on a difficult subject matter. For instance, 13 Reasons Why is about the suicide of a young girl and unfolds as tapes she has recorded to explain her suicide are revealed.[42] The show deals with rape, bullying, and sexting. You would think the program would be applauded for being so topical. Instead, it has been condemned as glamorizing suicide. Netflix has put warning labels on the opening credits, and many schools have banned the show or have sent home notices about the dangers of the show, even though the book has been out for several years without the same concerns arising. In the same vein, another controversy for Netflix is a show called *To the Bone* about an anorexic young woman and her battle to overcome her eating disorder.[43] The same concerns are being expressed: the series will encourage more young people to become anorexic or bulimic because the show glamorizes the subject matter and gives tips on how to be anorexic. Rather than see both programs as potential tools for education and discussion about the issues, the call is for them to be banned or boycotted.

The controversy about banning TV shows relates to the concern about sex education in general. Rather than applaud schools for attempting to educate young people about a very important topic that will affect them all eventually, some parents and community members want sex education banned or curtailed or limited to abstinence and the biology of sex. Issues of consent, pleasure, and masturbation are seen to be ways of encouraging the sexual behaviour of children, when in fact these are tools that are needed if people are to have sex safely, pleasurably, and consensually. It is still a radical idea to have a sex-education curriculum that discusses masturbation and pleasure, even though the lack of these puts girls at a distinct disadvantage. Even if there is still some shame surrounding boys' masturbation, they know how pleasurable sex can be because they become experts at pleasuring themselves. Girls often don't have the same experience and so they are at a disadvantage when not able to express what they need or want because they just don't know. Add to that a shame about women's bodies generally and a sexual double standard that punishes women for their sexuality and you have a recipe for boys' sexual needs being met and girls providing for boys without reciprocity, as Peggy Orenstein and Leora Tanenbaum have both brilliantly pointed out.[44] We are doing a disservice to our daughters by not educating them about what their bodies can do and how they can feel, all of which can be done in an age-appropriate developmental way, as the revised Ontario sex-education curriculum was doing.

We are very far from accomplishing sex-positive sexual education in the North American context, since we are still debating about sex education beyond abstinence or disease and pregnancy prevention. As Peggy

Orenstein has shown, American parents emphasize risk and danger while Dutch parents, for instance, also teach joy and pleasure. The Dutch report that more good sex is happening because of this: shared pleasure, mutuality, and reciprocity. They talk to their girls about their capacity for pleasure and teach that expressing sexuality means understanding your body, expressing your wants and desires, and having that respected.[45]

The idea that young women could enthusiastically enjoy sex should be common sense, but as psychologist Lisa Damour says, "We unwittingly perpetuate a harmful boys-on-offence-girls-on-defense framework that is so atmospheric – so deeply engrained in our culture – as to be invisible."[46] This invisibility perpetuates the idea that sex is primarily a male-focused activity. "Sex is framed as something a man asks for, which a woman may either consent to or decline, rather than an experience of mutual participation, agency and pleasure. This is not to say that consent is not important; on the contrary, it is essential. But to reduce our discussions of sex to this kind of dichotomy is to fundamentally misrepresent what is an active and reciprocal enjoyment."[47] "No means no," of course, is the bare minimum. What is needed is education about the notion of enthusiastic, affirmative consent, i.e., yes means yes.[48]

Research shows that the more educated girls are, the more empowered they are to make good choices. Damour again: "I know that parents of girls, especially, worry that their daughters are more likely to get hurt if we talk about desire first and risks last. But research shows the opposite. The young women who get into bed without their own agenda are the ones most likely to make compromises."[49] This research shows that women who see themselves as sexual agents, while often being constructed as "bad girls," are less at risk for bad sexual experiences or being pressured into acts they are not interested in.

Young people's sexuality is often discursively constructed within the confines of a masculine/feminine binary that minimizes young women's sexual subjectivity (i.e., desire, pleasure, and agency) while taking young men's subjectivity for granted. Accordingly, young women who acknowledge themselves as sexual subjects are constructed as "bad girls" who incite males' purportedly uncontrollable desire and, thus, invite undesired sexual attention. However, there is reason to hypothesize that young women who view themselves as sexual subjects may be less likely than other women to engage in undesired sexual activity (i.e., sex that their partners desire, but they do not desire for themselves).[50]

Explicit sex education is therefore one of the solutions for enhancing women's pleasure in sex by ensuring that girls know their own bodies. But until women's sexuality is not something to be ashamed of, it is unlikely that women's orgasmic potential will be reached.

Female Sex Positivity

What would a "positive," authentic sexuality look like? Outlining a "healthy" sexuality is problematic, as noted in chapter 6, because the notion of "healthy" has been used by conservatives at various points in history to criminalize homosexuality, interracial marriage, and premarital sex. Defining sexuality as good or bad has consequences for those who find themselves on the "bad" side of morality, which at various points in our history was everyone having sex outside of (heterosexual) married, procreative sex – the "heterosexual conjugal bond" as described earlier.[51] That's a lot of people. But if I was going to take a stab at it, I like the definitions given by the women I interviewed. According to Lucy and the other escorts, revelling in one's sexuality leads to empowerment because people get a taste of freedom and discovering their authentic selves. As Lucy says, "When I say sex-positive I mean freedom of judgment from whatever a person might want to explore with their sexuality, not casting sexuality in a negative light or saying that one type of sexuality is okay and that another isn't. Basically, giving the freedom for people to be able to say, 'I like to do this in the privacy of my own home with other consenting adults' and not have anybody judge them."

Why don't we all recognize the goods of sex? The intimacy, touching, and emotional connection? Or the sheer physical release of sex? Some people believe that sex is not in the same realm of drives as the need for food, water, and sleep. No one would argue that not having enough food to sustain oneself is a good thing, but many people argue that although sexuality might be a quality of life issue, it is not a life or death issue. It is a privilege not a right, if you will. Many people are celibate, through choice or circumstance, and they don't die because of it, according to this argument. Unfortunately, accepting the idea that sex is not that important (and so something that shouldn't be paid for) means that only people who are "doing well in the dating game," as Milrod put it, can have sex. We have, therefore, restricted who can have sex (because only unpaid sex is legal or morally acceptable) and even whose sexuality we can see depicted. Most of the sex represented in movies and on TV is between very good looking, thin, young (usually white, heterosexual) people. No other bodies need uncover themselves. "The message is that fat people are not sexy and should not be portrayed as such on television."[52] Because we have bought into media and pornographic ideas of the perfect body, some naked bodies are seen as unworthy (see French author Yann Moix's dismissive comments about the "unlovable" nature of the bodies of women over fifty).[53] There is shame and derision about fat people having sex, about elderly people having sex, about people of the same sex having sex unless they are lesbians titillating men in porn. According to the women I interviewed, if sex was valued and seen as a basic human good for both men and women, sex work would be valued more highly too. According to their sex-positive view, if you valued your sexuality, you would pay a sex worker if you didn't have a partner because the goods of sex are to be embraced.

Research on women's sexuality is starting to back up the claims of the women I interviewed and show how the biological argument is evolving – no pun intended. "In *What Do Women Want?: Adventures in the Science of Female Desire* (2013) the American writer Daniel Bergner argues that female sexuality is as animalistic – if not more so – than male. 'We'd rather cast half the population, the female half, as a kind of stabilising force when it comes to sexuality,' he explains. The idea that monogamy is more suited to women is no more than a 'fairy tale.'"[54] The same research claims that women are as visual and as sexual as men but that shame prevents them from acknowledging or acting on their sexuality.

In one experiment in 2007 by Meredith Chivers and colleagues at the Centre for Addiction and Mental Health in Toronto, both men and women were made to watch videos of sex, ranging from heterosexual penetration to fornicating bonobo apes. The apes proved a turn-on for women, whose blood flow soared, while men reacted in much the same way to the primates as they did to mountains and lakes. But here comes the telling part: when asked, the women themselves reported less arousal than their bodies let on. At the root of this gap – between physical urges and psychological restraint – sits societal shame.[55]

As Rowland writes, any differences between the sexual desires of men and women are most likely due to three social, not biological, reasons: women "have learned to police their own eroticism," they "pay a greater social price for promiscuity," and "they have simply been taught from girlhood onward to be wary of their physicality."[56] The idea that men want to spread their seed and women want an emotional partner in order to have sex has been undermined as well. At issue is the potential for women's pleasure, not the length and depth of relationship. "In a 2011 paper, Terri Conley and colleagues at the University of Michigan found that women are not less interested in casual sex than men. But they are happier to engage if they expect the experience to be sexually satisfying and if they can remove any risk of stigma."[57] This makes sense, of course. It's the same findings reported by Orenstein and Tanenbaum. Women are as interested in hookups when they know it's going to be a pleasurable experience as opposed to being all about him and his orgasm.

Because of self-policing, worry about promiscuity, and lack of physicality, many women haven't been encouraged to experiment sexually or they have had very negative experiences of sex and don't know what all the fuss is about. Perhaps what is in order for women, as well as men, is to have positive sexual experiences with someone who knows what they're doing and cares about the other's pleasure, like a sex worker. In many countries, like Greece and the Philippines, young men go to sex workers for their initiation,[58] and perhaps young women need that, too. A sex surrogate who has been trained to show women the potential of sex could educate them about their bodies and the pleasures of sex. I realize this is in the realm of science fiction in today's society. We are a long way from that scenario when many people in the West don't agree with sex education in schools and want abstinence until marriage. And even the desire for such a woman-focused solution is highly unlikely. The problem with the

books previously mentioned that are currently focused on women's pleasure and orgasm (or websites like OMGyes) is that the women who would
benefit most are the same women who will not pick them up and read
them. If women's bodies are seen as "gross" by many women (and men –
shame on you Robert Pattinson), women are not likely to pick up that
mirror and take a look, let alone feel empowered to pleasure themselves,
and ask partners for what they want.

Even so, I think the potential for sexual equity is much greater for
women now in the twenty-first century than it was even twenty years ago.
Third (and fourth) wave feminists are much more interested in reclaiming
women's sexual power and see issues differently, including sex. Women
today, hopefully, have less shame about sex and the body, and so this revolution is now more possible than in the 1980s and 1990s. Students in university are conducting workshops on consent, rape culture, and pleasure.
Zosia Bielski reports on a new sex education program called Flip the Script
that deals explicitly with educating high school girls about their bodies'
capacity for pleasure and tries to overcome the negative consequences of
socialization to be a good girl. The workshop aims to "recondition young
women away from the old social expectations that they be people-pleasers,
and get them prioritizing self-preservation instead ... On one side of [the
diagram] are the words: 'be nice,' 'be good,' 'maintain relationships' and
'don't hurt anyone's feelings.' On the other side are the words: 'personal
integrity,' 'personal safety' and 'sexual rights.'"[59] Participants leave feeling
empowered and more confident, and for the first time see that "girls and
women are taught to put the needs of others before their own and that
this thinking can hinder them in relationships where a partner proves to
be abusive."[60]

Celebrities like Nicki Minaj and Miley Cyrus have been vocal about the
importance of their sexualities (though Cyrus was brutally slut-shamed
when she started a relationship with a female friend weeks after she left her
husband, Liam Hemsworth). But as Minaj put it, "I demand that I climax.
I think women should demand that. I have a friend who's never had an orgasm in her life. In her life! That hurts my heart."[61] Cardi B and Megan Thee
Stallion caused a stir with their song and music video "WAP," celebrating
and reclaiming women's potent sexual potential. The lyrics are raunchy
(the title refers to "wet ass pussy") and the music video has been called

pornographic but it seems to me that they know exactly what they're doing – not just being provocative and salacious to sell albums but to undermine the slut-shaming of sexually active women. It seems unlikely that the repetitive refrain of a man singing "There's some whores in this house" in the background was an accident.[62]

Women themselves are more motivated to discover their orgasmic potential, filling each and every orgasm class run by adult bookstores Good for Her in Toronto and Venus Envy in Halifax. All of these developments give me hope that sexual change (maybe a revolution) is on the way for women and men.

The Right to Bodily Autonomy and Ending Good Girl Privilege

But first … Lindy West makes the important link between fat shaming and the "repulsive campaign" to remove or reduce women's reproductive rights. "Both say: 'Your body is not yours' … Both insist: 'Your autonomy is conditional.'"[63] Sexual and reproductive rights are inextricably tied to the fundamental right to bodily autonomy, which unfortunately for women tends to depend on political ideology, not as a matter of human right. In the words of philosopher Martha Nussbaum, treating a woman as the means to someone else's ends (i.e., forcing a woman to go through with a pregnancy so that another person can adopt a child), has a long and destructive history. We can't imagine forcing men, for example, to undergo vasectomies – that would be a violation of their bodily integrity – but we can somehow imagine forcing women to bear children they don't want. Why? Because women's bodily autonomy is considered not so important. And as antichoice activists like to say, what's the big deal? We don't have the same stigma about unwed motherhood as we used to, and a lot of couples want to adopt children. There is no justification for abortion anymore.[64] Unless, of course, you believe that all people, including women, should have full autonomy over their bodies.

Unfortunately, our society still struggles with the question of who has bodily autonomy and who doesn't and with the question of whose body is it? And for women, less so than for men, that autonomy is questioned.

Women and girls are constantly under surveillance in terms of clothing and their appearance. They are judged much more harshly than men. Women's bodies are policed and essentially seen as public. Women in some cultures are assumed to be fair game in terms of groping and sexual harassment, for instance, because good women don't go out in public.[65] Dress codes, victim blaming, and sexual double standards all have their roots in the desire to control women's sexuality, as I pointed out in chapter 3. The next sexual revolution, then, must ensure that women's bodily autonomy is a matter of fact, not ideology, in terms of consent to sex, reproductive freedom, and of course sex work, if that is a woman's choice.

The final issue, as we attempt to end bad girl stigma, is how to end good girl privilege. Bad girl stigma and good girl privilege are two sides of the same coin and both must be tackled at the same time. Calling out slut-shaming and challenging our sexist depictions of sexually active women, however, might be easier than eliminating good girl privilege, at least in the short term. Even though good girl privilege is a double-edged sword (with both harms and rewards), it will not end while women benefit from being good girls and when they use those privileges to their advantage. Clearly good girls benefit from being "good girls" whether it is protection and respect from men and authority figures or the privilege of getting "helped into carriages and lifted over ditches and to have the best place everywhere."[66] Like all privileges it must be acknowledged before it can be eliminated and consciously rejected.

How does good girl privilege harm us? Through socialization, girls are taught to stay within the lines and not make a fuss, as we saw with the gymnastics abuse scandal. We accept bad behaviour that keeps us in our place so we can maintain our status as good girls. Being good girls arguably keeps us small and diminished, but we end up policing our and other women's behaviour to enforce the good girl/bad girl dichotomy. As Tanenbaum has argued, women slut-shaming each other and using the word slut even as a joke between friends is a problem for ending shaming.[67] She doesn't see a way for the word to be reclaimed in the same way as "queer" has been, for instance, because of the historic significance of the word and the gender specificity of it. This "policing" must be recognized and challenged in all our relationships.

But, of course, it's not all on the good girls to ensure this happens. Without significant societal change and the end of the sexual double standard, we can't possibly end the good girl/bad girl binary. Good girl privilege won't end until the stigma against bad girls is a thing of the past; when hopefully in the future we will look back and say, "can you believe they used to judge women based on their sexual and marital status? How strange."

Lessons Learned

All of the escorts I interviewed recognized that as humans we are all sexual beings to some extent and that sex is a basic human driver. By accepting this as fact, they all lived by the notion that women are sexual beings as well and should not be punished for expressing their sexuality. They were very knowledgeable about double standards and tried as much as possible to eliminate them from their lives. Slut-shaming had huge consequences on their lives and so of course they believed that any kind of slut-shaming should be eliminated. They also believed that sex work won't be valued until sex is valued as an intrinsic good, not related to morality or reproduction or monogamy.

Second, because they know they are sexual beings, it followed that they believed they deserved sexual pleasure. They demanded respect and accountability from others, including their clients. They expected reciprocity in their sexual relations and had firm boundaries about what behaviour they would and wouldn't accept. The escorts all owned their sexuality and embraced it. These women demonstrate what happens when freed from the social pressure to be a good girl. They have made themselves extremely knowledgeable about their bodies and take full responsibility for their sexual pleasure. Women and girls need to know their own bodies in order to know how to ensure they have pleasurable sexual experiences and not, as Orenstein and Tanenbaum have shown, be performing for men but not receiving sexual pleasure themselves.

Third, the escorts I met were remarkably tolerant people who recognized that different people have different values, and we shouldn't judge others based on our morality. They had all experienced life as a "sexual minority" both as sex workers and as either queer, polyamorous, or into BDSM. These experiences also made them more tolerant of people's differences as long as no harm was being done (i.e., non-consensually). They recognized that their life was not for everyone. Their lives were difficult in many ways, and they recognized sex work as emotionally and physically draining work.

Finally, the escorts realized that stigma and criminalization were just ways to control them and their sexualities. And they taught me that in maintaining the distinctions between good girls and bad, prohibitionists are reinforcing the stigma, making it easier to blame women for what happens to them and to label any woman who transgresses a slut. Support of antiprostitution laws and rhetoric, therefore, however inadvertently, negatively affects all women. If the day ever comes when sex workers aren't stigmatized that will be the day women will be free because then we'll be able to express ourselves sexually without shame or without fear of being harmed. The good girl/bad girl dichotomy will be no more.

Concluding Thoughts

It is difficult to change our perceptions – but it is possible. The work my colleagues and I did in the Philippines is still valid and I recognize that there are huge problems with the activities of men from the developed world going to the Global South to have sex with young girls and women. That is a legitimate concern and the worst aspects of the sex tourism and sex work industries must be addressed. What I would also say is that if I was to do the research and film again, I would be more nuanced about what was going on and I would acknowledge how much agency the women I met actually had, rather than just want to rescue them. Most did not want to be rescued, except by the Western men who were their clients. They wanted to exchange their sex work with many men for marriage and a better life abroad with one man. Engels was wrong about this one.

In one of the saddest articles I have read in a long time, Margaret Simons details the fates of several children of sex tourists in the Philippines.[68] I have not been back to the Philippines since our development project ended in 2004 but reading about Angeles City and Fields Avenue and remembering

the man who bragged to me that he had fathered ten children but supported none made me cry in rage. I read these stories and I understand why
people think sex work should be criminalized and there should be consequences for men's bad behaviour. It is outrageous that men do not support
their own children and that the children are stigmatized as children of sex
workers. There is no justice in this. But I have learned to hold two seemingly
contradictory thoughts at the same time: men who engage in this type of
behaviour should be strongly condemned (and legally held responsible for
the support of their children) and making the buying of sex illegal only
hurts the women who are selling. As Martha Nussbaum puts it, "the way
to deal with sexism, in this case as in all, is by persuasion and example, not
by removing [women's] liberty."[69] We can morally condemn men's behaviour and seek to educate them, while not legally taking away the little
support and income the women have. As Nussbaum states, the "correct response to this problem seems to be to work to enhance the economic autonomy and the personal dignity of members of that class, not to rule off
limits an option that may be the only livelihood for many poor women and
to further stigmatize women who already make their living this way."[70]

Revolutions take time and there will be backlashes but change is happening. The increased recognition of slut-shaming has led to protests about
rape culture and about society's tendency to blame victims for their own
victimization. Victim blaming is being recognized for what it is: a way to
control women's behaviour. As Catherine Hakim says, "the good girl/bad
girl, Madonna/whore stereotype is a very, very strong ideology for controlling women and their behavior and their aspirations even."[71]

In both Canada and the United States, there have been multiple sexual
harassment and assault charges stemming from incidents at major US net-
works, Canadian broadcasters, the entertainment industry, and university
campuses. The #MeToo movement has been credited with exposing serial
predators and attempting to hold them accountable. I've already mentioned
Harvey Weinstein and Larry Nassar. The film *Bombshell* describes the sexual
harassment scandal at Fox News that brought down Robert Ailes and Bill
O'Reilly.[72] Bill Cosby was convicted of sexual assault in 2018 and sentenced
to three to ten years in prison. The University of Southern California has
just settled a $215 million class action lawsuit against the actions of former

USC gynecologist George Tyndall, who sexually abused female students at USC for decades. The university knew of the claims but did nothing about them, even when more than 200 pictures of patients' genitalia were found on his computer![73] R&B star R. Kelly has been charged with ten counts of aggravated sexual abuse after decades of his abuse of young women and girls was covered up by the music industry. "The rise of #MeToo played a major role in breaking the protective culture surrounding Kelly."[74]

The #MeToo movement in general might help change the double standard of sexuality and help more women come forward with their stories of abuse and bad sex. Singer Taylor Swift won a civil suit against a man who groped her, even though she was asked the same sort of insulting victim-blaming questions every victim is: the lawyer "wanted to know why the front of her dress wasn't disturbed by the incident. She tartly replied, 'because my ass is located on the back of my body.' She triumphed over the shaming."[75] She also refused to back down or feel bad because the man lost his job over what he did. As she said in court, "I'm not going to allow you or your client to make me feel in any way that this is my fault because it isn't … I am being blamed for the unfortunate events of his life that are a product of his decision and not mine."[76] She refused to be shamed by what someone else did to her. She has more power than most women, of course, in a "he-said, she-said" battle, but it's a victory nonetheless that says men can't just put their hands on women without consent, that masturbating in front of colleagues is harassment, and that sexual comments and touching are unacceptable in workplaces or in any public place. "'Realizing' that it is unacceptable to grope, kiss, flash, talk dirty to or masturbate in front of employees, co-workers or any person who is not, by mutual consent, your sexual partner" will hopefully be a signature effect of the #MeToo movement.[77]

In Canada, courts are finally recognizing some of the rape myths, as in the idea that clothing choices imply consent, and penalizing judges who use them. "Ontario's highest court has called out a judge for saying that the way a woman dresses may indicate consent to sexual activity and for describing that notion as 'common sense.'"[78] Hopefully, the #MeToo movement is a critical turning point in making men accountable for their bad behaviour. The idea that boys will be boys as an excuse for this conduct is hopefully fading away, but, if history is anything to go by, it will take a long, long time.

The negative image of the prostitute will also take a long time to change. Sex workers are so tainted by what they do that they and others are no longer able to separate what they do from who they are. They become ruined and are seen to be irredeemable. They are somehow contaminated with a stain that can't be removed – I don't think it is a coincidence that at least three of the antiprostitution activists I've interviewed who are former sex workers are also born-again Christians. It's as if the stigma is so great that the only way to restore their "purity" and be redeemed is to become born-again.

It is now embedded in our consciousness that the prostitute is a survival sex worker, but as many scholars have shown, these workers make up less than 20 per cent of the total sex worker population. The narrative of the downtrodden, degraded sex worker is a very compelling image for many people, and it is not surprising that emotional stories of abuse and trafficking have been used very effectively to lobby for the Nordic model in policy. Images create narratives; narratives create emotion, and emotion is what moves people to make change or to see things differently.[79] It is very difficult to try to change the image when we are surrounded by a world telling us a story about sex workers' lives. But a new image could transform the story if the image is powerful enough.

If we change the narrative by showing that not all sex work is survival sex work, might we be able to change the narrative of selling sex in general and combat stigma and whorephobia? It's not about denying that the survival sex worker exists and that many services need to be put into place to alleviate cases of abuse and violence. In the Netherlands, for instance, street strolls have been enclosed with security at the entrance and panic buttons at each parking spot. We need more resources for addiction problems, social and foster care services, educational and economic opportunities. However, if we consider the stories of the women I interviewed, we see a different problem – the problem of sex. Looking at the women selling sex by choice tells us that sex work is not inherently violent, unless you think sex itself is inherently violent. It is not degrading if done with respect and dignity, as is the case with the women I interviewed. The problems of male domination and violence have more to do with society in general than prostitution in particular. Sex workers just make good targets for violent men because sex work is illegal in many places and therefore underground.

The women I met are not glamorous and they're not victims. They are the silent majority of sex workers who work out of their homes, through massage parlours or brothels, and more and more commonly through on-line ads – though even that is under attack now with the shutdown of Back-page and Craigslist. They are not survival sex workers working on the streets for food, nor are they $4,000-a-night Gentleman's Club workers. They are lower middle-class women who chose sex work over working at Starbucks and women who worked to put themselves through university or pay off credit cards or travel around Europe. They didn't start working as sex work-ers out of desperation, and they thrived in the work because of a number of commonalities: they all saw sex as a basic human need and so they weren't judgmental about men's sexual desires – they had strong sexual de-sires too and enjoyed having sex with multiple partners. This leads them to see the humanity of their clients and "understand the desire for sexual relations with another human being" as Amanda said. Crucially, they all had somehow avoided the good girl/bad girl socialization that plagues most women. They embraced their sexualities, knew and accepted their bodies as they are, and relished the "girlfriend" or "pornstar" experience as active participants. They all earned a good living having sex with men and couples and could not understand why the activities of consenting adults were il-legal as is the case in most parts of the United States.

The film ends with Lucy giving her lecture to the antitrafficking confer-ence on the value of sex work. My cameraperson and I were in the audience filming, and I was very nervous about how she would be received (as a re-minder, the audience was made up of primarily antiprostitution activists, missionaries, and law enforcement). I was worried about how hostile the audience would be (because I have seen how nasty these debates can get), but she completely won them over with her easygoing attitude and open, tolerant demeanour. She may not have changed everyone's mind that day, but she made people think and she was able to present her ideas without anyone attacking her personally or yelling and screaming at her – as I have certainly experienced.[80]

As sceptical as I was when I met her and the other women at the workshop, over time I realized that meeting Lucy had changed my perspective dramatically. She showed me that some women do choose sex work over other forms of labour, that this decision to work in what she described as her calling had not damaged her, and that for her sex work wasn't the problem. Instead, the circumstances of criminalization and stigma were the problem. She helped me to see that disbelieving women who say they enjoy sex work or even that they choose it over other forms of work only allows the stigma to continue while preventing them from working safely and from demanding protection from police and law enforcement more generally.

I know that the issues explored in this book are very difficult ones. The arguments I state so bluntly now did not come easily and are the result of many years of intellectual and emotional struggle. There are reasons why the feminist community still grapples with the sex wars, including the empirical and political complexity of this area and the difficulty of changing one's mind. In Melinda Chateauvert's history of the sex workers' rights movement she gives a poignant anecdote from 1970s New York of a female streetwalker, as they were called at the time, being called a dirty slut by a woman who was just passing by.[81] What I find interesting and sad about the story is its illustration of the internalized oppression and misogyny involved when women abuse other women for their different choices or circumstances. Some women have so internalized their own good girl/bad girl ideas that they mistreat another woman on the street without realizing how these very prejudices affect them as well, as this book has argued. The sexual double standard and good girl/bad girl dichotomies are deep-seated belief systems that won't be changed through logic and facts alone,[82] but perhaps by changing the narrative, telling different stories, and framing the issues differently we might help end the feminist sex wars. Reconciling these positions and working towards meaningful change is not easy, but it is necessary if we want to ensure all women are treated with respect and dignity. We will finish the sexual revolution by confronting sexual stigma, normalizing sexual pleasure, and empowering women in whatever choices they make.

In the lead up to the Women's March in January 2017 to protest Donald Trump's election as US president, the organizers of the march attempted to draft a vision statement for the new movement. An early draft included support for sex workers, but it was removed and replaced with "trafficked and prostituted women" because of the antiprostitution lobby. Sex-worker rights groups were understandably upset about this erasure of their rights and very existence. Eventually, sex-worker rights got put back into the vision statement but not before many women dropped out feeling that the march did not represent them. A statement put out by transgender and Black feminist activist Janet Mock, apologizing for the removal, is worth quoting in full:

> We stand in solidarity with sex workers' rights movements ... I know that underground economies are essential parts of the lived realities of women and folk. I know sex work to be work. It's not something I need to tiptoe around. It's not a radical statement. It is a fact. My work and my feminism rejects respectability politics, whore phobia, slut-shaming and the misconception that sex workers or folks engaged in the sex trades by choice or circumstance, need to be saved or that they are colluding with the patriarchy by "selling their bodies." I reject the continual erasure of sex workers from our feminism because we continue to conflate sex work with the brutal reality of coercion and trafficking. I reject the policing within and outside women's movements that shames, scapegoats, rejects, erases and shuns sex workers ... The conflicts that may have led to its temporary editing will not leave until we, as feminists, respect the rights of every woman and person to do what they want with their body and their lives. We will not be free until those most marginalized, most policed, most ridiculed, pushed out and judged are centered.[83]

The day that all feminists (and eventually all people) understand why and how this statement is important to all women, is the day that stigma against sex workers, the good girl/bad girl division, and the feminist sex wars will end.

Acknowledgments

This book took me a long time to write and so there are many people to thank. It would never have happened without the documentary production and so I thank the funders of the film and all the people who worked on it with me, especially Chris Beckett who was camera and sound person and principal sounding board throughout the whole process. I thank Sharon Franklin, the main editor of the film, for her constant support and encouragement in helping me work through the issues in the film. I thank all the interviewees for giving me their time and insights, and I wish I could name you all but for reasons of safety and security, as I write about in the book, I can only acknowledge you anonymously.

I want to gratefully recognize the funders of the film and book: the Social Sciences and Humanities Research Council (SSHRC) Research-Creation grant, SSHRC Aid to Scholarly Publications grants, Mount Saint Vincent University (MSVU) internal grants, and MSVU student work grants. I couldn't have done this book without these resources.

At Mount Saint Vincent University, I would like to thank my colleagues who supported me throughout this process. In particular, I'd like to thank the research office team including Anthony Davis, Brenda Gagne, Gayle MacDonald, Derek Fisher, and particularly Ardath Whynacht for helping me to write the grant application, librarians Sandra Sawchuck and Denyse Rodrigues, public affairs Gillian Batten and Kelly Gallant, and the financial services office, above all Alison Stark and Cathleen Madgett. I want to particularly express my gratitude to Sandra Sawchuck for her detailed work on the citations and bibliography, and to Nicole Marcoux for compiling the index.

I'd like to thank my colleague KelleyAnne Malinen for reading over the first draft of the entire manuscript and making invaluable comments, my wonderful research assistant Breagh MacDonald-Rahn and two anonymous reviewers who made the book so much better. To my Women's Studies and Political Studies colleagues and to our wonderful administrative assistants, Phoebe Smith and Angela Green, thank you!

I can't express how thankful I am to McGill-Queen's University Press, especially my editor Jacqueline Mason who championed the book from beginning to end. Thank you to copy editor Shelagh Plunkett for your amazing work. Everyone from publicists to copy writers to the designers has been a pleasure to work with. A huge thanks to Clare MacKenzie of Edgewood Communications for her work on the promotion of the book. I thank you.

Of course, I couldn't have done it without support from my family and friends who always understood when I was still working on the never-ending book! Thank you to the friends I quote in the book and who helped with the film – you know who you are. Thank you to my friend Donna Barnett for reading over the entire typeset copy and for your valuable comments. Thank you to my friend Edna Keeble who read every word and always has my back, personally and intellectually. To my dad, sisters Lisa and Alison, and my late great-aunt Audrey, thank you for everything. Love to my partner Scott, as always, my biggest supporter and sounding board. I'd be lost without you.

I owe my biggest and most heartfelt thanks to the women I interviewed who bravely showed their faces and told their stories about their lives as sex workers. They helped change my perspective on decriminalization and helped me to understand the real problems with bad girl stigma and good girl privilege. Their experiences were so enlightening and life changing for me that I dedicate the book to them.

Notes

CHAPTER ONE

1 Queally, "Weinstein Trial Is a Milestone for #metoo and a Moment of Wrenching Truth for Survivors"; Queally and Ormseth, "Harvey Weinstein Gets 23-Year Prison Sentence in His New York Trial."

2 Carr, *At the Heart of Gold.*

3 Frost, "The Cult of the Clitoris."

4 Chiu, "Five Years Gone: Remembering Rehtaeh."

5 "Pickton Trial Timeline," CBC *News*, 30 July 2010. https://www.cbc.ca/news/canada/pickton-trial-timeline-1.927418.

6 Harding, *Asking for It.*

7 Ibid., 1.

8 Ibid., 3.

9 Manne, *Down Girl.*

10 Pheterson, *The Prostitution Prism.*

11 Ralston, *Selling Sex.*

12 Goudreau, "Good Girls, Bad Girls, Sluts and Moms."

13 Grant, *Playing the Whore*, 127.

14 Orenstein, *Girls & Sex*; Tanenbaum, *I Am Not a Slut.*

15 Mottier, *Sexuality.*

16 Griffin, *The Book of the Courtesans.*

17 Wolf, *Vagina.*

18 Tanenbaum, *I Am Not a Slut.*

19 Block, *O Wow.*

20 Orenstein, *Girls & Sex*.

21 Barmak, *Closer*.

22 Davis, *The Making of Our Bodies, Ourselves: How Feminism Travels across Borders*, 25.

23 Safronova, "What's So 'Indecent' about Female Pleasure?"

24 Rowland, *The Pleasure Gap*, 21.

25 Nagoski, *Come as You Are*; Block, *O Wow*; Barmak, *Closer*; Mintz, *Becoming Cliterate*.

26 Gunter, *The Vagina Bible*.

27 Rowland, *The Pleasure Gap*.

28 Frost, "The Cult of the Clitoris."

29 Valenti, *The Purity Myth*.

30 Mottier, *Sexuality*, 13.

31 Doolittle, "Unfounded."

32 Craig, *Putting Trials on Trial*; Harding, *Asking for It*.

33 Block, *O Wow*; Orenstein, *Girls & Sex*; Rowland, *The Pleasure Gap*.

34 Coalition Against Trafficking in Women. "CATW Responds: Amnesty International Turned Its Back on Women." *Coalition Against Trafficking in Women*, 11 August 2015, https://catwinternational.org/press/amnesty-inter national-turned-its-back-on-women; Bindel, *The Pimping of Prostitution*.

35 Bindel, "Whorephobia."

36 Ralston, *Hope in Heaven*.

37 Survival sex worker is the term for street-based sex workers who lack the choice of other sex workers and work for their survival either economically or to feed an addiction.

38 Ralston, *Nobody Wants to Hear Our Truth*; Ralston, *Hope in Heaven*; Ralston and Keeble, *Reluctant Bedfellows*.

39 Durisin, Van der Meulen, and Bruckert, *Red Light Labour*; Redwood, "Myths and Realities of Male Sex Work"; Marlowe, "Thinking Outside the Box."

40 The main group I interviewed was antitrafficking *and* antiprostitution, but not all groups conflate the two terms. The Global Alliance Against Trafficking in Women for instance is antitrafficking but not opposed to sex work. All groups for and against sex work are antitrafficking as I discuss in chapter 7.

41 I first read of the term "goods of sex" in De Boer, "Disability and Sexual

Inclusion," 66. The term refers to the value of sex in terms of touch and intimacy, much as sex work was discussed by my interviewees.

42 Note on language: In reference to antiprostitution activists who call themselves abolitionists I will follow Robyn Maynard's important work where she argues that using the term abolitionist to refer to antiprostitution groups is racist and an appropriation of the moral righteousness of the antislavery campaigns of the 1800s, and so she prefers the term prohibitionist. Other scholars use the term "neo prohibitionist," but for simplicity's sake, I will use the term prohibitionist except of course in the interviewees' own direct references to being abolitionists. Maynard, "Do Black Sex Workers' Lives Matter?"; Bruckert and Parent, *Getting Past "the Pimp."*

43 Perry, "What You Can Do, What You Can't Do, and What You're Going to Pay Me to Do It"; Smith and Mac, *Revolting Prostitutes*; Brown, "Leading Male Escort Reveals What Women Really Want in the Bedroom."

44 Smith, "'It Gets Very Intimate for Me'"; Doezema, "How Was It for You?"

45 Smith, "'It Gets Very Intimate for Me'"; Doezema, "How Was It for You?"

CHAPTER TWO

1 Orenstein, *Girls & Sex.*

2 Badham, *Saturday Night Fever.*

3 A young student recounted her own experiences with the movie recently (having no idea I was using it as an anecdote in my book) and how traumatizing she found the same scene. Her mother had forgotten about the date rape incident and just saw it as a fun dance movie that her daughter should see.

4 Tanenbaum, *I Am Not a Slut*; Tanenbaum, *Slut!*

5 Orenstein, *Girls & Sex.*

6 Harding, *Asking for It.*

7 Ralston, *Selling Sex*; Tanenbaum, *I Am Not a Slut*, 38

8 Collins, "Rep. Katie Hill Resigns After Allegations of Improper Relationships."

9 Gold, "Anthony Weiner Released from Prison After Serving 18 Months for Sexting Teenager."

10 Harding, *Asking for It*, 12.

11 Tanenbaum, *I Am Not a Slut*, 37–8

12   Troncale, "Your Lizard Brain."

13   Karlamangla, "Coronavirus Memes Fill Social Media Feeds," para. 28.

14   Harding, *Asking for It*, 23.

15   Nussbaum, *Sex and Social Justice*.

16   Repard, "22 Women Win \$13 Million in Suit Against GirlsDoPorn Videos,"
     para. 24.

17   Sampert, "Let Me Tell You a Story."

18   Harding, *Asking for It*, 22.

19   Ibid., 96.

20   Craig, *Putting Trials on Trial*.

21   Ferré-Sadurní and Nir, "Judge Gets Threats After Saying Teenager in Rape
     Case Was from 'Good Family.'"

22   Craig, *Putting Trials on Trial*.

23   Valenti, *The Purity Myth*.

24   Harding, *Asking for It*, 45.

25   Ibid., 12.

26   Ibid.

27   West, *Shrill*, 198.

28   Valenti, *The Purity Myth*.

29   Ibid., 14.

30   Ibid., 164.

31   Kaiser, "Emily Ratajkowski: 'Women Must Feel Liberated, Not Constrained,
     by Feminism.'"

32   Kaiser, "Taylor Swift Releases 'Lover' Album Cover & New Single 'You Need
     to Calm Down'"; Benbow, "Dancing Virgins."

33   Benbow, "Dancing Virgins."

34   Ibid.

35   Bakare-Yusuf, "Thinking with Pleasure," 40.

36   Truth, "Ain't I a Woman?"

37   Fox, "Nice Girl," 805.

38   Ibid.

39   Valenti, *The Purity Myth*; Eltahawy, "Why Do They Hate Us"; Eltahawy,
     Headscarves and Hymens.

40   Olubanke Akintunde, "Female Genital Mutilation."

41   Fox, "Nice Girl," 806.

42   Hudson et al., *Sex and World Peace*, 8.

43 Fox, "Nice Girl," 806.

44 Ibid., 807.

45 Gilbert, "Soul Tribe Live: Make Big Magic Workshop."

46 Hymson, "How 'Portrait of a Lady on Fire' Became a 'Movie Dedicated to Love.'"

47 Manne, *Entitled*, 73.

48 Williams, "These Girls Become Perfect Prey."

49 Ibid.

50 Ibid.

51 Carr, *At the Heart of Gold*.

52 Warren, "Guelph Mom Shocked Eight-Year-Old Told to Put on Her Top at Public Pool."

53 Fox, "Nice Girl," 817.

54 Froyum, "Making Good Girls," 65.

55 Ibid.

56 Bellafante, "Poor, Transgender and Dressed for Arrest."

57 Armstrong et al., "Good Girls," 101.

58 Ibid.

59 Aksakal, "Sexual Pleasure," 58.

60 Ibid.

61 "Indonesia Clinic Gives Relief to Muslims with Tattoo Regrets," *Arab News*, 16 August 2017, https://www.arabnews.com/node/1145611/offbeat.

62 Ibid.

63 Eltahawy, "Why Do They Hate Us," 65.

64 Ibid., 66.

65 Eltahawy, *Headscarves and Hymens*, 10.

66 Ibid., 31.

67 Ibid., 120.

68 Ibid., 31.

69 Mottier, *Sexuality*, 56.

70 Ibid.

71 Ibid., 59.

72 Tong and Botts, *Feminist Thought*.

73 Mottier, *Sexuality*, 108; Tong and Botts, *Feminist Thought*, 25.

74 Vance, *Pleasure and Danger*.

75 See Sheila Jeffreys, *Anticlimax*.

76 Mottier, *Sexuality*, 57.

77 Wilson, "From 'Filthy Trash' to Iconic Resource."

78 Klatch, *Women of the New Right*.

79 Mottier, *Sexuality*, 78.

80 Keeble, *Politics and Sex*; Armstrong et al., "Good Girls"; Orenstein, *Girls & Sex*; Rowland, *The Pleasure Gap*.

81 Mottier, *Sexuality*, 83.

82 Kamer, "Can Robert Pattinson Actually Have a Vagina Allergy?"

83 Hensley, "The Problem with DJ Khaled – and All the *other* Dudes Who Won't Perform Oral Sex."

84 Moore, "If Young Women Are Dying of Shame about Their Bodies, We Need a Rethink."

85 Mor, "Laughter," 290.

86 Ibid., 292.

87 Chateauvert, *Sex Workers Unite*, 116.

88 Jolly, "Why the Development Industry Should Get Over Its Obsession with Bad Sex and Start to Think About Pleasure," 34 quoted in Undie, "Why We Need to Think About Sexuality and Sexual Well-Being," 187.

89 Frost, "The Cult of the Clitoris."

90 Blake, "Gwyneth Paltrow Got Real Women's Vulvas onto Netflix," para. 1.

91 Valenti and Friedman, *Believe Me*.

CHAPTER THREE

1 "ABC News Report on Gary Ridgway's Confession," *True Crime Magazine*, 2017, https://www.youtube.com/watch?v=ksckTZKVm90.

2 Pruden, "The Day I Met a Serial Killer," para. 25.

3 Bendery, "Donald Trump Says Transgender People No Longer Allowed to Serve in Military."

4 *Reclaiming Power and Place: The Final Report of the National Inquiry into Missing and Murdered Indigenous Women and Girls*, National Inquiry into Missing and Murdered Indigenous Women and Girls (2019).

5 Abcarian, "Trump's Legacy Will Be Brutal but Simple."

6 Taylor, "Taylor Swift Case Shows Price for Treating Women Appallingly Has Risen."

7 Pheterson, *The Prostitution Prism*, 7.

8 Ibid., 8.

9   Orchard, "In This Life," 3.
10 Pheterson, *The Prostitution Prism*, 12.
11 Ibid., 77.
12 Bash and Vazquez, "Giuliani Defends Comments about Stormy Daniels' Credibility," para. 4.
13 Mottier, *Sexuality*, 5.
14 Brownmiller, *Against Our Will*, 13–14.
15 Ryan et al., *Sex at Dawn*.
16 Brownmiller, *Against Our Will*, 16.
17 Ibid., 17.
18 Ibid.
19 Ibid., 19.
20 Ibid.
21 Bakare-Yusuf, "Thinking with Pleasure," 34.
22 Ibid.
23 Ibid., 35.
24 Anderson, *A Recognition of Being*, 52.
25 Ibid., 54.
26 Paxton and Hughes, *Women, Politics, and Power*.
27 Mottier, *Sexuality*, 14.
28 Eltahawy, *Headscarves and Hymens*.
29 Roberts, *Whores in History*; Griffin, *The Book of the Courtesans*.
30 Blackwell, "A look back at *The Globe*'s January Moment in Times."
31 Backhouse, "Nineteenth-Century Canadian Prostitution Law," 422.
32 Bourgeois, "Perpetual State of Violence," 260.
33 Ibid., 265.
34 Backhouse, "Nineteenth-Century Canadian Prostitution Law," 420.
35 Van der Meulen and Durisin, "Sex Work Policy," 29.
36 Van der Meulen, Durisin, and Love, *Selling Sex*, 82.
37 Maynard, *Policing Black Lives*, 45.
38 Pheterson, *A Vindication of the Rights of Whores*, 10.
39 Ibid., 11.
40 Scorsese, *The Age of Innocence*.
41 Rossi, *The Feminist Papers*, 252.
42 Elshtain, "Aristotle, the Public-Private Split, and the Case of the Suffragists," 60.

43 Ibid., 310n31.

44 Ibid., 62.

45 Ibid., 60.

46 Gallant and Zanin, "The Bogus BDSM Defence," 40.

47 Mottier, *Sexuality*, 35.

48 Anderson, *A Recognition of Being*, 40.

49 Rossi, *The Feminist Papers*, 252.

50 Maynard, *Policing Black Lives*, 44.

51 Tamale, "Eroticism, Sensuality and 'Women's Secrets' among the Baganda," 266.

52 Ibid.

53 Malinen, *Dis/Content*, 12.

54 Perry, "What You Can Do, What You Can't Do, and What You're Going to Pay Me to Do It," 94–5.

55 Malinen, *Dis/Content*, 14.

56 Lucy had an interesting take on Victorian hysteria and it is a counterpoint to the prevailing idea that women were relatively lacking in sex drive compared to men. "So here's a perfect example too of how not having a good sexual outlet will end up bubbling up and spilling over into your life. 1800s, women were treated for hysteria, they went to the doctor to be masturbated because they were sexually frustrated. This is how the vibrator was actually invented ... because the doctors were getting so fatigued with trying to help these women that they created something to help them stimulate women. I know it's funny but that's how it happened. And this is not even women who were chaste, these were married women, women that had a sexual outlet to some degree but not sexual release. And so they were having insomnia, depression, and a whole host of other symptoms that were alleviated once they went to the doctor and were treated for hysteria. And so there was marriage, there was actual intimacy and love maybe going on but ... the sexual release was that component that was missing." Rossi, *The Feminist Papers*, 252–3.

57 Dabhoiwala, *The Origins of Sex*.

58 Limoncelli, *The Politics of Trafficking*.

59 Yakabuski, "Opinion: Andrew Scheer Can Choose to Go Out on a High Note," para. 1.

60 Rossi, *The Feminist Papers*, 265.

61 Ibid.

62 Minaker, "Sluts and Slags: The Censuring of the Erring Female," 86.

63 Ibid.

64 Backhouse, "Nineteenth-Century Canadian Prostitution Law."

65 Ibid., 418.

66 Chateauvert, *Sex Workers Unite*, 105.

67 Hinckley, "How Mae West's Arrest for Onstage Lewdness Made Her a Star."

68 Laskow, "The Racist, Slut-Shaming History of Adultery Laws."

69 Bell, *Good Girls/Bad Girls*; Delacoste and Alexander, *Sex Work*; Vance, *Pleasure and Danger*; Silver, *The Girl in Scarlet Heels*; Belak, "Bedford V. Canada."

70 Tracy, "DC Sex Decrim Drive Divides National Organization for Women."

71 Hanson, "Columnist Calls Gunpoint Rape of Sex Worker 'Theft of Services.'"

72 Sullivan, "Rape, Prostitution and Consent"; Pauw and Brener, "You Are Just Whores."

73 Disgust is a strong word but comes up regularly in discussions of prostitu-
    tion. As an emotion disgust is associated with harsh moral judgements. In
    particular, "numerous studies have found that high levels of sensitivity to
    disgust tend to go hand in hand with a 'conservative ethos.' That ethos is
    defined by characteristics such as traditionalism, religiosity, support for
    authority and hierarchy, sexual conservatism, and distrust of outsiders."
    McAuliffe, "Liberals and Conservatives React in Wildly Different Ways
    to Repulsive Pictures," para. 8.

CHAPTER FOUR

1 Whereas some sex-work researchers now start from the point of view of
   assuming that decriminalization is the best policy for sex workers (see
   Durisin, Van der Meulen, and Bruckert, *Red Light Labour*), which I agree
   with in principle, I want to explore the prohibitionist arguments as well as
   those of sex work activists to elaborate my main points about slut-shaming
   and whorephobia and because prohibitionist arguments are gaining
   ground in their efforts to change prostitution law to the Nordic model.

2 Bindel, "Whorephobia."

3 Chisholm, "Human Trafficking Forum in Halifax Hears from Grieving
   Yarmouth Mom and Ex-Sex Workers," para. 24.

4 Green, "SNP Backs Changes to Scotland's Prostitution Laws."

5   Ibid.
6   Pateman, *The Sexual Contract*, 50.
7   Ibid., 64.
8   Ibid., 55.
9   Ibid., 69.
10 Ibid., 70.
11 Overall, "What's Wrong with Prostitution," 709.
12 Ibid., 710.
13 Ibid., 708.
14 Ibid., 717.
15 Ibid., 724.
16 Ibid., 718.
17 Ibid., 720.
18 Ibid., 723.
19 Shrage, "Comment on Overall's 'What's Wrong with Prostitution? Evaluating Sex Work,'" 569.
20 Shrage, "The Case for Decriminalization," 242.
21 Ibid.
22 Nussbaum, *Sex and Social Justice*.
23 Ibid., 276.
24 Ibid., 286.
25 Ibid., 287.
26 Ibid., 288.
27 Ibid., 287.
28 Ibid., 277.
29 Ashforth and Kreiner, "Dirty Work and Dirtier Work," 81.
30 Ashforth and Kreiner, "'How Can You Do It?'"
31 Benoit et al., "Prostitution Stigma."
32 Ibid., 457.
33 Ibid., 459.
34 Ibid., 458.
35 Ibid., 460.
36 Ibid., 463.
37 Ralston and Keeble, *Reluctant Bedfellows*.
38 Benoit et al., "Prostitution Stigma," 466.
39 Ibid., 465.

40 Ibid., 467.

41 Perry, "What You Can Do, What You Can't Do, and What You're Going to Pay Me to Do It."

42 Ibid., 132.

43 Ibid., 124.

44 Zimmerman, "No, Ashley Judd, Prostitution Is Not Paid Rape."

45 Shrage, "The Case for Decriminalization," 244.

46 Smith and Mac, Revolting Prostitutes, 28.

47 Rossi, The Feminist Papers, 479.

48 Tong and Botts, Feminist Thought, 83.

49 Rossi, The Feminist Papers, 487.

50 Ibid., 479.

51 Ibid., 488.

52 Ibid., 492.

53 Ibid., 494–5.

54 Benoit et al., "Would You Think About Doing Sex for Money," 737.

55 Mears and Connell, "The Paradoxical Value of Deviant Cases: Toward a Gendered Theory of Display Work," 333.

56 Hakim, Erotic Capital.

57 Koken, "Independent Female Escort's Strategies for Coping with Sex Work Related Stigma."

58 Chapkis, Live Sex Acts, 67, quoted in Sanders, "'It's Just Acting,'" 320.

59 Benoit et al., "Prostitution Stigma," 458.

60 Ditmore, Levy, and Willman, Sex Work Matters; Van der Meulen, Durisin, and Love, Selling Sex: Experience, Advocacy, and Research on Sex Work in Canada; Van der Meulen and Durisin, "Sex Work Policy"; Grant, Playing the Whore; Benoit et al., "Would You Think about Doing Sex for Money?"

61 Willman, "Let's Talk about Money."

62 Jeffrey and MacDonald, Sex Workers in the Maritimes Talk Back.

63 Koken, "Independent Female Escort's Strategies for Coping with Sex Work Related Stigma"; Love, "Champagne, Strawberries and Truck-Stop Motels"; Smith, "'It Gets Very Intimate for Me.'"

64 Beloso, "Sex, Work, and the Feminist Erasure of Class."

65 Ibid., 50.

66 Brewis and Linstead, "The Worst Thing Is the Screwing," 92.

67 Beloso, "Sex, Work, and the Feminist Erasure of Class," 62.

68 Stone, *The New Romantic*.

69 "The Body Economy," NTE *Impact Ethics*, 2018, https://www.dal.ca/sites/noveltechethics/projects/selling-the-body.html.

70 Ibid.

71 Underwood, "Are Human Challenge Trials for COVID-19 Research Ethical?"

72 "The Body Economy." NTE *Impact Ethics*, 2018.

73 Ibid.

74 "Milk Might Be History's Most Controversial Food, Says Author," CBC *Radio*, 8 May 2018, https://www.cbc.ca/radio/thecurrent/the-current-for-may-8-2018-1.4652073/milk-might-be-history-s-most-controversial-food-says-author-1.4652081.

75 Bienstock, *Tales from the Organ Trade*.

76 Moore, *Threadbare*.

77 Picard, "Women in Amsterdam's Red-Light District Say Safety for World-wide Sex Workers Lies in Legalization, Normalization."

78 Hakim, *Erotic Capital*.

79 Benoit et al., "Would You Think about Doing Sex for Money?"

80 Ibid., 12.

CHAPTER FIVE

1   Draaisma, "York Police Say 104 Men Arrested After Child Sex Sting."

2   Bruce, "Victim Faints during Emotional Sex Assault Sentencing"; Benoit et al., "Would You Think about Doing Sex for Money?"; Dewey and St Germain, "'It Depends on the Cop'"; Pauw and Brener, "You Are Just Whores."

3   Ralston, *Hope in Heaven*.

4   Bindel, "Whorephobia."

5   Bellafante, "Poor, Transgender and Dressed for Arrest."

6   Raymond, "Prostitution on Demand"; Barry, *Female Sexual Slavery*; Barry, *The Prostitution of Sexuality*.

7   Doezema, "How Was It for You," 258.

8   Farley, "Bad for the Body, Bad for the Heart."

9   Weitzer, *Legalizing Prostitution*; Agustin, "The (Crying) Need for Different Kinds of Research."

10 Perrin, "Oldest Profession or Oldest Oppression?"; *Bedford v. Canada* (AG), [2011] ONCA 209, (Factum of the Interveners, Women's Coalition).

11 Bittle, "Protecting Victims Sexually Exploited through Prostitution?"

12 O'Doherty, "Criminalization and Off-Street Sex Work in Canada."

13 Ryan, "Petition Demands Lindsay Buziak Murder Case Be Turned Over to New Investigators."

14 Martinez, "Mollie Tibbetts Went Jogging and Never Came Back – She's Not the First."

15 "Halifax Man Guilty of Murder in Death of Off-Duty Police Officer," *CBC News*, 21 December 2017, https://www.cbc.ca/news/canada/nova-scotia/catherine-campbell-murder-trial-jury-deliberations-1.4459936.

16 Ryan, "Woman Says Halifax Taxi Driver Raped Her While She Pretended to Be Asleep."

17 "Statistics," *National Domestic Violence Hotline* (accessed 7 September 2020), https://www.thehotline.org/resources/statistics/; "Statistics About Sexual Violence," *National Sexual Violence Resource Center*, 2015, https://www.nsvrc.org/sites/default/files/publications_nsvrc_factsheet_media-packet_statistics-about-sexual-violence_0.pdf.

18 Dick, *Invisible War*.

19 Bourgeois, "Perpetual State of Violence," 259.

20 Bourgeois, "Perpetual State of Violence"; Beattie, David, and Roy, "Homicide in Canada, 2017."

21 Craig, *Putting Trials on Trial*.

22 Dworkin, *Pornography*.

23 See Manne, *Entitled*.

24 Weitzer, *Legalizing Prostitution*, 4.

25 "Percentage of Men (by Country) Who Paid for Sex at Least Once: The Johns Chart," *ProCon.Org*, 6 January 2011, https://prostitution.procon.org/percentage-of-men-by-country-who-paid-for-sex-at-least-once-the-johns-chart/.

26 Benoit et al., "Prostitution Stigma," 457.

27 Brown, "Leading Male Escort Reveals What Women Really Want in the Bedroom"; Law, "The Women Who Hire Male Escorts."

28 Overall, "What's Wrong with Prostitution?"

29 Khan, "From Average Joe to Deviant John"; Weitzer, *Legalizing Prostitution*; Milrod and Monto, "The Hobbyist and the Girlfriend Experience"; Atchison, "Report of the Preliminary Findings for John's Voice"; Monto, "Why Men Seek Out Prostitutes."

30 Kinsey, Pomeroy, and Martin, *Sexual Behavior in the Human Male*.

31   Milrod and Monto, "The Hobbyist and the Girlfriend Experience."

32   Wilford, "That Time Charlie Sheen Brought a Sex Worker to Thanksgiving Dinner at Denise Richards' House"; Rodrigues, "It's Twenty Years Since Hugh Grant Was Arrested with a Sex Worker"; Gustin, "After Sex Scandal, Eliot Spitzer Makes a Comeback."

33   Bernstein, "Buying and Selling the 'Girlfriend Experience.'"

34   Rossi, *The Feminist Papers*.

35   "Sex Id – Testosterone," *Human Body and Mind*, 1 October 2014, https://www.bbc.co.uk/science/humanbody/sex/articles/testosterone.shtml.

36   Rowland, *The Pleasure Gap*.

37   Ibid.

38   Ibid, x.

39   Comte, "Decriminalization of Sex Work: Feminist Discourses in Light of Research," 213.

40   Koken, "The Meaning of the 'Whore,'" 40.

41   Burchill, *Damaged Goods* quoted in Grant, *Playing the Whore*, 83.

42   Ralston and Keeble, *Reluctant Bedfellows*, 162.

CHAPTER SIX

1   Bruckert and Parent, *Getting Past "the Pimp."*

2   Dines, *Pornland*.

3   Baptie, "A Public Forum to Discuss Prostitution and Creating the Conditions to End It."

4   Rowland, *The Pleasure Gap*, 5.

5   Ralston and Keeble, *Reluctant Bedfellows*, 81.

6   Orenstein, *Girls & Sex*; Tanenbaum, *I Am Not a Slut*.

7   Marlowe, "Thinking Outside the Box"; Redwood, "Myths and Realities of Male Sex Work."

8   Marlowe, "Thinking Outside the Box," 352.

9   Horn, "Yeah, You Like That, Don't You?"

10   Keeble, *Politics and Sex*.

11   Ibid., 15.

12   Ibid.

13   Gallant and Zanin, "The Bogus BDSM Defence."

14   Khan, "From Average Joe to Deviant John," 75.

15   Bielski, "Grey Area."

16 Alphonso, "NDP Vow to Fight Ford's Repeal of Sex-Ed Curriculum"; Rad-
    wanski, "Ontario's Premier Delivers on People Pleasing Promises, but Fiscal
    Plans Remain a Puzzle"; Renzetti, "Good Sex-Ed Is a Vaccine That Protects
    All Students"; "Ontario Fails Badly at Sex Education," *The Globe and Mail*,
    14 July 2018, https://www.theglobeandmail.com/news/politics/ontarios-
    education-premier-fails-on-sex-education/article4189257/.

17 Brocker, "What the Reality of Breastfeeding Looks Like."

18 Renzetti, "The Slow, Steady Fall of Abortion Access in the U.S."

19 Wagner, "Feedback."

20 Moore, "If Young Women Are Dying of Shame about Their Bodies, We
    Need a Rethink."

21 Tanenbaum, *I Am Not a Slut.*

22 Brotto, "High Sexual Desire in Women Can Be Totally Normal."

23 Rowland, *The Pleasure Gap*, 3.

24 Pawlowska, "The History of Nymphomania."

25 Brotto, "High Sexual Desire in Women Can Be Totally Normal."

26 Farley and Barkan, "Prostitution, Violence, and PTSD"; Farley, "Bad for
    the Body, Bad for the Heart"; Farley, "Prostitution Harms Women Even
    If Indoors."

27 Many other sex workers relied on public websites for the vetting of clients
    and that element of safety has been negatively affected by the US antitraf-
    ficking legislation FOSTA and SESTA, which I will discuss in chapter 7.

28 Benoit et al., "Would You Think about Doing Sex for Money?"

29 See Smith, "'It Gets Very Intimate for Me.'"

30 Doezema, "How Was It for You," 263.

31 Ibid., 260.

32 Ibid., 255.

33 Smith and Mac, *Revolting Prostitutes.*

34 Ibid., 33 (italics in the original).

35 Ray, "Why the Sex Positive Movement Is Bad for Sex Workers' Rights."

36 Doezema, "How Was It for You," 262.

37 Fuchs, "German Green Party Wants Free Prostitutes for Disabled and
    Elderly."

38 Skelton, "Sex, Sex Surrogates, and Disability."

39 Couldrick and Cowan, "Enabling Disabled People to Have and Enjoy the
    Kind of Sexuality They Want," 134.

40 De Boer, "Disability and Sexual Inclusion," 66.

41 Bellah et al., *Habits of the Heart*, 66.

42 Penttinen, "Imagined and Embodied Spaces in the Global Sex Industry," 40.

43 Hochschild, *The Managed Heart*.

44 Bielski, "Grey Area."

45 Ibid.

46 Grigorovich and Kontos, "Ethics, Sexuality, and Dementia in Long-Term Care."

47 Overall, "What's Wrong with Prostitution?"

48 Burrow and Bailey, "Sexual Autonomy and Violence against Women," 182.

49 Ibid., 183.

50 Sherwin and Baylis, "The Feminist Health Care Ethics Consultant as Architect and Advocate," 154.

51 Ibid.

52 Irvine, "Is Sexuality Research 'Dirty Work'?"

CHAPTER SEVEN

1   Ralston and Keeble, *Reluctant Bedfellows*, 19.

2   See Belak, "Bedford V. Canada." for an excellent summary of the entire court challenge starting in 2007.

3   Bill C-36 Protection of Communities and Exploited Persons Act, Criminal Code RSC 1985 § C-46 (2014).

4   Valverde, "Canadian Feminsim and Sex Work Law," 248.

5   Ibid., 252–4.

6   Bindel, *The Pimping of Prostitution*, 4.

7   Chisholm, "Human Trafficking Forum in Halifax Hears from Grieving Yarmouth Mom and Ex-Sex Workers."

8   Bindel, "Sugar-Coated Pimping."

9   Bindel, *The Pimping of Prostitution*, 334.

10 Odinokova et al., "Police Sexual Coercion and Its Association with Risky Sex Work and Substance Use Behaviors among Female Sex Workers in St. Petersburg and Orenburg, Russia"; Dewey and St Germain, "'It Depends on the Cop.'"

11 Lim, *The Sex Sector*.

12 Chateauvert, *Sex Workers Unite*, 3.

13 Hakim, *Erotic Capital*; Bindel, *The Pimping of Prostitution*.

14 Weitzer, *Legalizing Prostitution*, 22.

15 Weitzer, "Flawed Theory and Method in Studies of Prostitution"; Agustin, "The (Crying) Need for Different Kinds of Research."

16 Van der Meulen and Durisin, "Sex Work Policy," 36; Hakim, *Erotic Capital*; Kuo, *Prostitution Policy*.

17 Sayers, "Municipal Regulation of Street-Based Prostitution," 58.

18 Lever and Dolnick, "Sex for Sale," 88.

19 Weitzer, *Legalizing Prostitution*, 18.

20 Ibid.; O'Doherty, "Victimization in Off-Street Sex Industry Work"; O'Doherty, "Criminalization and Off-Street Sex Work in Canada."

21 Benoit et al., "Prostitution Stigma"; Marlowe, "Thinking Outside the Box," 349.

22 Mac, *The Laws That Sex Workers Really Want*,

23 Porth, "Sex, Lies, and Committee Hearings," 322.

24 Horn, "Yeah, You Like That, Don't You," 122.

25 Lepp and Gerasimov, "Gains and Challenges in the Global Movement for Sex Workers' Rights"; Sanghera and Pattanaik, *Trafficking and Prostitution Reconsidered*; Skrobanek, Boonpakdi, and Janthakeero, *The Traffic in Women*; Brown, *Sex Slaves*; Outshoorn, "The Political Debates on Prostitution and Trafficking of Women"; Kara, *Sex Trafficking*; Day, "The Re Emergence of 'Trafficking'"; O'Connor, "Choice, Agency Consent and Coercion."

26 Lepp and Gerasimov, "Gains and Challenges in the Global Movement for Sex Workers' Rights," 2.

27 O'Doherty et al., "Misrepresentations, Inadequate Evidence and Impediments to Justice."

28 Picard, "Women in Amsterdam's Red-Light District Say Safety for Worldwide Sex Workers Lies in Legalization, Normalization."

29 Ibid.

30 "Amnesty International Publishes Policy and Research on Protection of Sex Workers' Rights," *Amnesty International*, 2016, https://www.amnesty.org/en/latest/news/2016/05/amnesty-international-publishes-policy-and-research-on-protection-of-sex-workers-rights/.

31 Durisin, Van der Meulen, and Bruckert, *Red Light Labour*.

32 Krüsi, Belak, and Sex Workers United Against Violence, "Harassing the Clients Is Exactly the Same as Harassing the Workers," 213.

33 Ibid., 214.

34 Krüsi, Belak, and Sex Workers United Against Violence, "Harassing the Clients Is Exactly the Same as Harassing the Workers."

35 Valverde, "Canadian Feminsim and Sex Work Law," 251.

36 Durisin, Van der Meulen, and Bruckert, "Contextualizing Sex Work," 7.

37 "Prohibition Began 100 Years Ago, and Its Legacy Remains," Los Angeles Times, 14 January 2020, https://www.latimes.com/world-nation/story/2020-01-14/prohibition-began-100-years-ago-and-its-legacy-remains.

38 Turpel-Lafond, "Too Many Victims: Sexualized Violence in the Lives of Children and Youth in Care-an Aggregate Review."

39 Ingraham, "Portugal Decriminalised Drugs 14 Years Ago."

40 Picard, "Sexual Violence: The Silent Health Epidemic."

41 Lupick, "Opinion."

42 Cho, Dreher, and Neumayer, "Does Legalized Prostitution Increase Human Trafficking?"

43 Dewey and St Germain, "'It Depends on the Cop'"; Odinokova et al., "Police Sexual Coercion and Its Association with Risky Sex Work and Substance Use Behaviors Among Female Sex Workers in St Petersburg and Orenburg, Russia"; Pauw and Brener, "You Are Just Whores."

44 Durisin, Van der Meulen, and Bruckert, "Contextualizing Sex Work," 7.

45 Armstrong, "Decriminalisation Is the Only Way to Protect Sex Workers"; Chrichton, "Decriminalising Sex Work in New Zealand."

46 Moore, "Ocasio-Cortez Has Shown 'Shameless' Women Are a Powerful Force."

47 Brown, "Leading Male Escort Reveals What Women Really Want in the Bedroom"; Law, "The Women Who Hire Male Escorts."

48 Jeffreys, "Sex Tourism."

49 "Captain's Holiday," Star Trek: The Next Generation.

50 Whedon, Firefly.

51 Jessome, Somebody's Daughter; Malarek, The Natashas; Malarek, The Johns; Perrin, Invisible Chains.

52 Pretty Woman; Monster; Secret Diary of a Call Girl. (2007. London, UK. Artist Rights Group (ARG), ITV Productions, Silver Apples Media, 2007); The Girlfriend Experience; Hustlers.

53 Sons of Anarchy (2008. Los Angeles, CA: SutterInk, Linson Entertainment, Fox 21, 2008).

54 Bindel, "Whorephobia."

55 Dow and Wood, "Repeating History and Learning from It."
56 Bindel, *Pimping of Prostitution*, 293, 300.

CHAPTER EIGHT
1 Rowland, *The Pleasure Gap*.
2 Bateman, "At My #Cambridge College's End of Term Supervisor Dinner."
3 Bateman, "@UKurbanite Are You Claiming #burkinibans Don't Exist?";
    Bateman, "Standing up to the Iranian Patriarchy"
4 Bateman, "@PabloGu20888312 @billymuga Of Course – My Most Vicious
    Critics *are* Women."
5 Keeble, *Politics and Sex*, 59.
6 Ibid.
7 Chateauvert, *Sex Workers Unite*, 45.
8 West, *Shrill*.
9 Ibid., 32.
10 Ibid., 14.
11 Ibid., 101.
12 Ibid., 113.
13 Ibid., 93.
14 Rowland, *The Pleasure Gap*.
15 Orenstein, *Girls & Sex*.
16 "Walk of No Shame with Amber Rose," *Funny Or Die*, 2015, https://www.
    youtube.com/watch?v=68kmBoUru-k.
17 "Lord Jamar on Amber Rose's 'Slut Walk': It's Ridiculous, Sluts Should Be
    Shamed," *DJVlad*, 2016, https://www.youtube.com/watch?v=H-FoHjVcAJE.
18 Gunter, *The Vagina Bible*, 1.
19 Virzi, "T.I. Taking His Daughter to Get Her Hymen 'Checked' Isn't Just
    Creepy."
20 Gunter, *The Vagina Bible*.
21 Ibid., 1.
22 See Barmak, *Closer*.
23 Gunter, *The Vagina Bible*.
24 Frost, "The Cult of the Clitoris," para. 7.
25 McCormick, "The Clitoris Is a Gift," para. 4.
26 Frost, "The Cult of the Clitoris," para. 8.
27 Rowland, *The Pleasure Gap*, 20.

28 Ibid.

29 Harding, *Asking for It*, 43.

30 Ibid.

31 "Misogyny: The Sites," *Southern Poverty Law Center*, 1 March 2012, https://www.splcenter.org/fighting-hate/intelligence-report/2012/misogyny-sites, para. 4.

32 Orenstein, *Girls & Sex*. She is not saying that men cannot be sexually assaulted or violated (statistics indicate that between 4 and 16 per cent of men and boys have been sexually assaulted or abused, and these stats are probably low because men have been reluctant to report [National Sexual Violence Resource Center, "Statistics about Sexual Violence"]) but rather that in consensual heterosexual sex it is difficult for men to have a bad experience, except for performance issues, because of the fluke of biology.

33 See Harding, *Asking for It*, for some disturbing examples of the rape myths at work.

34 Rowland, *The Pleasure Gap*, 35.

35 Ibid., 37.

36 "OMGyes.Com – an Entirely New Way to Explore Women's Pleasure," *OMGyes*, 2020, https://www.omgyes.com/.

37 Rowland, *The Pleasure Gap*.

38 Block, *O Wow*; Mintz, *Becoming Cliterate*.

39 Rowland, *The Pleasure Gap*, 10.

40 Gibson, "Ontario Government Considered Removing Sex-Ed Classes Completely."

41 Picard, "Sex-Ed Critics Fear That It May 'Give Kids Ideas' but That Would Be a Good Thing."

42 *13 Reasons Why*.

43 Noxon, *To the Bone*.

44 Orenstein, *Girls & Sex*; Tanenbaum, *I Am Not a Slut*.

45 Orenstein, *Girls & Sex*.

46 Lithwick, "How to Talk to Your Teens about Sex, Climate Change, and Existential Angst," para. 8.

47 McCormick, "The Clitoris Is a Gift," para. 6.

48 Valenti and Friedman, *Believe Me*.

49 Lithwick, "How to Talk to Your Teens about Sex, Climate Change, and Existential Angst," para. 12.

50 Kettrey, "'Bad Girls' Say No and 'Good Girls' Say Yes," 685.
51 Keeble, *Politics and Sex.*
52 Gailey, "Fat Shame to Fat Pride," 115.
53 Williams, "Men Prefer Younger Women Not for Their Firmer Bodies."
54 Bergner, *What Do Women Want?* quoted in Sebag-Montefiore, "When It Comes to Buying Sex, Are Women Any Different from Men?," para. 15.
55 Sebag-Montefiore, "When It Comes to Buying Sex, Are Women Any Different from Men," para. 16.
56 Rowland, *The Pleasure Gap*, 30.
57 Sebag-Montefiore, "When It Comes to Buying Sex, Are Women Any Different from Men," 17.
58 Ralston and Keeble, *Reluctant Bedfellows*, 81.
59 Bielski, "The Pleasure Gap."
60 Ibid.
61 Sandell, "Nicki Minaj Wants All Women to Demand More Orgasms."
62 Cardi B and Megan Thee Stallion, "WAP."
63 West, *Shrill*, 15.
64 "Alabama Anti-Abortion Legislation Shows 'Abysmal Lack of Knowledge' on Trauma of Sexual Assault: Survivor," CBC, 16 May 2019, https://www.cbc.ca/radio/thecurrent/the-current-for-may-16-2019-1.5137392/alabama-anti-abortion-legislation-shows-abysmal-lack-of-knowledge-on-trauma-of-sexual-assault-survivor-1.5137422.
65 Eltahawy, *Headscarves and Hymens.*
66 Truth, "Ain't I a Woman?"
67 Tanenbaum, *I Am Not a Slut.*
68 Simons, "'Do You Ever Think about Me?'"
69 Nussbaum, *The New Religious Intolerance*, 116.
70 Nussbaum, *Sex and Social Justice*, 297.
71 Hakim, *Erotic Capital.*
72 Roach, *Bombshell.*
73 Hamilton and Ryan, "Regulators Slam USC Handling of Sex Abuse Cases as 'Reprehensible.'"
74 Ali, "Sequel 'the Reckoning' Strengthens 'Surviving R. Kelly's' Case against Disgraced Singer."
75 Taylor, "Taylor Swift Case Shows Price for Treating Women Appallingly Has Risen," para. 8.

76 Ibid., para. 9.

77 McNamara, "Column," para. 4.

78 Fine, "Attire Does Not Imply Consent."

79 See Lakoff, *The Political Mind*.

80 I showed the beginning of my film on sex workers to an audience of people at our public library. Having had several screenings of the film on university campuses and film festivals, for general and supportive audiences, I had let my guard down in terms of anticipating an angry antiprostitution response from anyone. After the mini-presentations were over, a woman in her early thirties came up to me and waited while I answered questions from others. I was not anticipating the negative response and so it took me a comically long time to realize what was going on when her interrogation started. "How could you do this?" she asked. "Do what?" I replied. "Why are you being so irresponsible? This is dangerous." I just stared at her blankly. The language became shaming and blaming and crude. "Why aren't you going after the men? That's the real story – the [disgusting] men." Her anger was palpable. Now, keep in mind that she had seen exactly four minutes and fifteen seconds of a forty-eight-minute film. If I had been thinking clearly at the time, I could have asked, "how would you know what my intentions were if you didn't watch the whole show or ask what my conclusions became?" But I was so astonished by her hostility that those questions didn't make it to the surface of my brain at the time. She just continued her rant. She wasn't interested in a dialogue. She just wanted to tell me why she thought I should be ashamed of myself for producing a documentary that purported to show women choosing sex work over other jobs and, more problematically, that some of them actually like the work. In a final flourish she yelled (loud enough that others turned around in concern and caused an organizer to come up to us to see if everything was okay), "And, furthermore, if you haven't sucked dick for a living, you have nothing to say!" Deciding that a discussion was not possible, I finally walked away.

81 Chateauvert, *Sex Workers Unite*.

82 See Lakoff, *The Political Mind*.

83 Mock, "On the Women's March 'Guiding Vision' and Its Inclusion of Sex Workers."

Bibliography

Abcarian, Robin. "Trump's Legacy Will Be Brutal but Simple: He Made It OK to Be Racist Again." *Los Angeles Times*, 21 January 2020. https://www.latimes.com/opinion/story/2020-01-21/column-trumps-legacy-will-be-brutal-but-simple-he-made-it-ok-to-be-racist-again.

Agustin, Laura. "The (Crying) Need for Different Kinds of Research." In *Sex Work Matters: Exploring Money, Power, and Intimacy in the Sex Industry*, edited by Melissa Hope Ditmore, Antonia Levy, and Alys Willman, 23–7. London, UK: Zed Books Ltd., 2010.

Aksakal, Gulsah Seral. "Sexual Pleasure as a Women's Human Right: Experiences from a Human Rights Training Programme for Women in Turkey." In *Women, Sexuality and the Political Power of Pleasure*, edited by Susie Jolly, Andrea Cornwall, and Kate Hawkins, 58–75. London, UK: Zed Books Ltd., 2013.

Ali, Lorraine. "Sequel 'the Reckoning' Strengthens 'Surviving R. Kelly's' Case Against Disgraced Singer." *Los Angeles Times*, 2 January 2020. https://www.latimes.com/entertainment-arts/tv/story/2020-01-02/surviving-r-kelly-the-reckoning-lifetime-review.

Alphonso, Caroline. "NDP Vow to Fight Ford's Repeal of Sex-Ed Curriculum." *Globe and Mail*, 14 July 2018. https://www.theglobeandmail.com/canada/article-ontario-ndp-vow-to-fight-fords-repeal-of-sex-ed-curriculum/.

Anderson, Kim. *A Recognition of Being: Reconstructing Native Womanhood*. Toronto: Canadian Scholars' Press, 2016.

Armstrong, Elizabeth A., Laura T. Hamilton, Elizabeth M. Armstrong, and J. Lotus Seeley. "'Good Girls' Gender, Social Class, and Slut Discourse on Campus." *Social Psychology Quarterly* 77, no. 2 (2014): 100–22. doi:10/f57gx4.

Armstrong, Lynzi. "Decriminalisation Is the Only Way to Protect Sex Workers –
New Zealand Has Proved It." *Independent,* 29 May 2017. http://www.indepen
dent.co.uk/voices/sex-workers-decriminalisation-of-prostitution-new-
zealand-new-law-works-research-proves-sex-workers-a7761426.html.

Ashforth, Blake E., and Glen E. Kreiner. "Dirty Work and Dirtier Work: Differences in Countering Physical, Social, and Moral Stigma." *Management and
Organization Review* 10, no. 1 (2014): 81–108. doi:10/gg895q.

– "'How Can You Do It?': Dirty Work and the Challenge of Constructing a Positive Identity." *Academy of Management Review* 24, no. 3 (1999): 413–34.

Atchison, Chris. "Report of the Preliminary Findings for John's Voice: A Study
of Adult Canadian Sex Buyers," for the Canadian Institute for Health Research
and the British Columbia Medical Services Foundation. January 2010.

Backhouse, Constance. "Nineteenth-Century Canadian Prostitution Law: Reflection of a Discriminatory Society." *Social History/Histoire Sociale* 18, no. 36
(1985): 387–423.

Badham, John, dir. *Saturday Night Fever.* 1977; Hollywood, CA: Paramount
Pictures, Robert Stigwood Organization (RSO).

Bakare-Yusuf, Bibi. "Thinking with Pleasure: Danger, Sexuality and Agency." In
Women, Sexuality and the Political Power of Pleasure, edited by Susie Jolly, Andrea Cornwall, and Kate Hawkins, 28–41. London, UK: Zed Books Ltd., 2013.

Baptie, Trisha. "A Public Forum to Discuss Prostitution and Creating the Conditions to End It." Halifax Central Library, 18 June 2018.

Barmak, Sarah. *Closer: Notes from the Orgasmic Frontier of Female Sexuality.*
Toronto: Coach House Books, 2016.

Barry, Kathleen. *Female Sexual Slavery: From Prostitution to Marriage, the Land-
mark Study of All the Ways Women Are Sexually Enslaved.* New York: Avon
Books, 1979.

– *The Prostitution of Sexuality.* New York: NYU Press, 1995.

Bash, Dana, and Maegan Vazquez. "Giuliani Defends Comments about Stormy
Daniels' Credibility." *CNN,* 7 June 2018. https://www.cnn.com/2018/06/07/
politics/rudy-giuliani-stormy-daniels-credibility/index.html.

Bateman, Victoria. "At My #Cambridge College's End of Term Supervisor Dinner Tonight Wearing Feminist Fashion by @theuniformtalks #JennaYoung –
with Some Added Marker Pen! Cambridge Supports #MyBodyMyChoice.
Do You? #feminism #liberty #DeedsNotWords." *Twitter,* 12 June 2018. https://
twitter.com/vnbateman/status/1006631063693807616.

– "@PabloGu20888312 @billymuga Of Course – My Most Vicious Critics *are* Women. And That's in Part the Internalised Male Gaze and the View That a Woman's Value Hangs on Her Modesty (One That I Challenge)." *Twitter*, 8 April 2019. https://twitter.com/vnbateman/status/1115261270335348737.

– "Standing up to the Iranian Patriarchy. A State That *Forces* Women to Cover – That Pins a Woman's Value &; Respect on Her Bodily Modesty – Is Not What I'd Call 'Civilized.' Aren't We Women Worth *More* than Our Modesty – & Can't We Be Left to Choose *for Ourselves*?" *Twitter*, 8 September 2019. https://twitter.com/vnbateman/status/1170757030551924736.

– "@UKurbanite Are You Claiming #burkinibans Don't Exist? They Come alongside #burqabans in Eg. France (with the Same Justification). If They Exist, They Are Relevant to This Issue of the State Policing How Women Dress. #MyBodyMyChoice #Liberty #FreeToChoose." *Twitter*, 12 August 2019. https://twitter.com/vnbateman/status/1160961386010349570.

Beattie, Sara, David Jean-Denis, and Joel Roy. "Homicide in Canada, 2017." Statistics Canada, 21 November 2018. https://www150.statcan.gc.ca/n1/pub/85-002-x/2018001/article/54980-eng.htm.

Bedford v. Canada (AG), [2011] ONCA 209, (Factum of the Interveners, Women's Coalition) (ONCA 2011).

Belak, Brenda. "Bedford v. Canada: A Breakthrough in the Legal Discourse." In *Red Light Labour: Sex Work Regulation, Agency, and Resistance*, edited by Elya M. Durisin, Emily Van der Meulen, and Chris Bruckert, 48–56. Vancouver: UBC Press, 2018.

Bell, Laurie. *Good Girls/Bad Girls: Sex Trade Workers & Feminists Face to Face.* Toronto: Women's Press, 1987.

Bellafante, Ginia. "Poor, Transgender and Dressed for Arrest." *New York Times*, 30 September 2016. https://www.nytimes.com/2016/10/02/nyregion/poor-transgender-and-dressed-for-arrest.html.

Bellah, Robert Neelly, Richard Madsen, William Sullivan, Ann Swidler, and Steven M. Tipton. *Habits of the Heart: Middle America Observed.* London, UK: Hutchinson, 1985.

Beloso, Brooke Meredith. "Sex, Work, and the Feminist Erasure of Class." *Signs: Journal of Women in Culture and Society* 38, no. 1 (2012): 47–70. doi:10/gg8992.

Benbow, Candice Marie. "Dancing Virgins, Ayesha Curry and the Rest of Us." *Candice Marie Benbow* (blog), 8 May 2019. https://candicebenbow.com/blog/dancing-virgins-ayesha-curry-and-the-rest-of-us.

Bendery, Jennifer. "Donald Trump Says Transgender People No Longer Allowed to Serve in Military." *HuffPost Canada*, 26 July 2017. https://www.huffpost.com/entry/donald-trump-transgender-military_n_597893a9e4b0c95f37605a35.

Benoit, Cecilia, S. Mikael Jansson, Michaela Smith, and Jackson Flagg. "Prostitution Stigma and Its Effect on the Working Conditions, Personal Lives, and Health of Sex Workers." *The Journal of Sex Research* 55, no. 4–5 (2017): 457–71. doi:10/gg9bbh.

Benoit, Cecilia, Nadia Ouellet, Mikael Jansson, Samantha Magnus, and Michaela Smith. "Would You Think about Doing Sex for Money? Structure and Agency in Deciding to Sell Sex in Canada." *Work, Employment and Society* 31, no. 5 (2017): 731–47. doi:10/gcw4vm.

Bergner, Daniel. *What Do Women Want? Adventures in the Science of Female Desire*. Edinburgh: Canongate Books, 2013.

Bernstein, Elizabeth. "Buying and Selling the 'Girlfriend Experience.'" In *Love and Globalization: Transformations of Intimacy in the Contemporary World*, edited by Mark B. Padilla, Jennifer S. Hirsch, Miguel Munoz-Laboy, Robert Sember, and Richard G. Parker, 186–202. Nashville: Vanderbilt University Press, 2007.

Bielski, Zosia. "Grey Area: The Fragile Frontier of Dementia, Intimacy and Sexual Consent." *Globe and Mail*, 14 July 2018. https://www.theglobeandmail.com/canada/article-grey-area-the-fragile-frontier-of-dementia-intimacy-and-sexual/.

– "How Canada Is Dominating the Field of Sexuality Research." *Globe and Mail*, 22 November 2017. https://www.theglobeandmail.com/life/relationships/the-big-brains-behind-canadas-goodsex/article37056097/.

– "The Pleasure Gap." *Globe and Mail*, 5 December 2020.

Bienstock, Ric Esther, dir. *Tales from the Organ Trade*. 2017; Toronto, ON: Associated Producers, Canal D, Global TV.

Bindel, Julie. *The Pimping of Prostitution*. London, UK: Palgrave Macmillan, 2017.

– "Sugar-Coated Pimping." *Truthdig*, 14 February 2020. https://www.truthdig.com/articles/sugaring-is-sugar-coated-pimping/.

– "'Whorephobia' Isn't a Threat to Feminism – but Ignoring the Abuse of Women Is." *Independent*, 15 March 2017. https://www.independent.co.uk/voices/whorephobia-queer-feminism-fourth-wave-sex-work-prostitution-a7631706.html.

Bittle, Steven. "Protecting Victims Sexually Exploited Through Prostitution? Critically Examining Youth Legal and Policy Regimes." In *Red Light Labour: Sex Work Regulation, Agency, and Resistance*, edited by Elya M. Durisin, Emily Van der Meulen, and Chris Bruckert, 134–56. Vancouver: UBC Press, 2018.

Blackwell, Richard. "A look back at *The Globe*'s January Moment in Times celebrating Canada's 150th anniversary," *Globe and Mail*, 9 January 2017.

Blake, Meredith. "Gwyneth Paltrow Got Real Women's Vulvas Onto Netflix. Here's How She Did It." *Los Angeles Times*, 27 January 2020. https://www.latimes.com/entertainment-arts/tv/story/2020-01-27/goop-gwyneth-paltrow-netflix-female-orgasm-episode.

Block, Jenny. *O Wow: Discovering Your Ultimate Orgasm*. Hoboken, NJ: Cleis Press, 2015.

Bourgeois, Robyn. "Perpetual State of Violence: An Indigenous Feminist Anti-Oppression Inquiry into Missing and Murdered Indigenous Women and Girls." In *Making Space for Indigenous Feminism*, edited by Joyce Greene, 253–73. Halifax: Fernwood Publishing, 2017.

Brewis, Joanna, and Stephen Linstead. "'The Worst Thing Is the Screwing': Consumption and the Management of Identity in Sex Work." *Gender, Work & Organization* 7, no. 2 (2000): 84–97. doi:10/bc7wwf.

Brocker, Gina Marie. "What the Reality of Breastfeeding Looks Like." *Globe and Mail*, 14 July 2018. https://www.theglobeandmail.com/opinion/article-what-the-reality-of-breastfeeding-looks-like/.

Brotto, Lori. "High Sexual Desire in Women Can Be Totally Normal." *Globe and Mail*, 10 April 2017. https://www.theglobeandmail.com/life/health-and-fitness/health-advisor/high-sexual-desire-in-women-can-be-totally-normal/article34653464/.

Brown, Louise. *Sex Slaves: The Trafficking of Women in Asia*. London, UK: Virago Press, 2000.

Brown, Vanessa. "Leading Male Escort Reveals What Women Really Want in the Bedroom." *News.Com.Au*, 15 November 2017. https://www.news.com.au/lifestyle/relationships/sex/australias-leading-escorts-reveal-what-women-and-men-really-want-in-the-bedroom/news-story/09293b5ab84cff87028d148873df83d6.

Brownmiller, Susan. *Against Our Will: Men, Women, and Rape*. New York: Simon & Schuster, 1975.

Bruce, Steve. "Victim Faints during Emotional Sex Assault Sentencing, Tells

Attacker 'I'm Not Going to Let You Win.'" *The Chronicle Herald*, 12 February
2019. http://www.thechronicleherald.ca/news/local/victim-faints-during-
emotional-sex-assault-sentencing-tells-attacker-im-not-going-to-let-you-
win-283880/.

Bruckert, Chris, and Colette Parent. *Getting Past "the Pimp": Management in the
Sex Industry*. Toronto: University of Toronto Press, 2018.

Burchill, Julie. *Damaged Gods: Cults and Heroes Reappraised*. London, UK:
Arrow Books Limited, 1987.

Burrow, Sylvia, and Chris Bailey. "Sexual Autonomy and Violence Against
Women." In *Talk About Sex: A Multidisciplinary Discussion*, edited by Robert
Scott Stewart. Sydney, NS: Cape Breton University Press, 2013.

Cardi B and Megan Thee Stallion. "WAP," 2020. https://www.youtube.com/
watch?v=hsm4poTWjMs.

Carr, Erin Lee, dir. *At the Heart of Gold: Inside the USA Gymnastics Scandal*.
2019. New York, NY: Home Box Office.

Chalmers, Chip, dir. *Star Trek: The Next Generation*. "Captain's Holiday." Aired
31 March 1990. Hollywood, CA: Paramount Television, 1990.

Chapkis, Wendy. *Live Sex Acts: Women Performing Erotic Labor*. New York:
Routledge, 2013.

Chateauvert, Melinda. *Sex Workers Unite: A History of the Movement from
Stonewall to Slutwalk*. Boston: Beacon Press, 2013.

Chisholm, Colin. "Human Trafficking Forum in Halifax Hears from Grieving
Yarmouth Mom and Ex-Sex Workers." *The Chronicle Herald*, 20 June 2018.
https://www.saltwire.com/news/human-trafficking-forum-hears-from-
grieving-mom-ex-sex-workers-219633/.

Chiu, Elizabeth. "Five Years Gone: Remembering Rehtaeh." *CBC News*, 6 April
2018. https://newsinteractives.cbc.ca/longform/five-years-gone.

Cho, Seo-Young, Axel Dreher, and Eric Neumayer. "Does Legalized Prostitution
Increase Human Trafficking?" *World Development* 41 (2013): 67–82.
doi:10/gg9j25.

Chrichton, Fraser. "Decriminalising Sex Work in New Zealand: Its History and
Impact." *OpenDemocracy*, 21 August 2015. https://www.opendemocracy.net/
en/beyond-trafficking-and-slavery/decriminalising-sex-work-in-new-zealand-
its-history-and-impact/.

Collins, Sean. "Rep. Katie Hill Resigns after Allegations of Improper Relationships." *Vox*, 28 October 2019. https://www.vox.com/policy-and-politics/2019

/10/28/20936067/katie-hill-resigns-allegations-improper-relationships-revenge-porn.

Comte, Jacqueline. "Decriminalization of Sex Work: Feminist Discourses in Light of Research." *Sexuality & Culture* 18, no. 1 (2014): 196–217. doi:10/ggmwm5.

Couldrick, Lorna, and Alex Cowan. "Enabling Disabled People to Have and Enjoy the Kind of Sexuality They Want." In *Women, Sexuality and the Political Power of Pleasure*, edited by Susie Jolly, Andrea Cornwall, and Kate Hawkins, 111–41. London, UK: Zed Books Ltd., 2013.

Craig, Elaine. *Putting Trials on Trial: Sexual Assault and the Failure of the Legal Profession*. Montreal & Kingston: McGill-Queen's University Press, 2018.

Dabhoiwala, Faramerz. *The Origins of Sex: A History of the First Sexual Revolution*. Oxford: Oxford University Press, 2012.

Davis, Kathy. *The Making of Our Bodies, Ourselves: How Feminism Travels across Borders*. Durham: Duke University Press, 2007.

Day, Sophie. "The Re-emergence of 'Trafficking': Sex Work Between Slavery and Freedom." *Journal of the Royal Anthropological Institute* 16, no. 4 (2010): 816–34. doi:10/crtk4f.

De Boer, Tracy. "Disability and Sexual Inclusion." *Hypatia* 30, no. 1 (2015): 66–81. doi:10/gg9j3c.

Delacoste, Frédérique, and Priscilla Alexander, eds. *Sex Work: Writings by Women in the Sex Industry*. Hoboken, NJ: Cleis Press, 1987.

Dewey, Susan, and Tonia St Germain. "'It Depends on the Cop': Street-Based Sex Workers' Perspectives on Police Patrol Officers." *Sexuality Research and Social Policy* 11, no. 3 (2014): 256–70. doi:10/ggpm2b.

Dick, Kirby, dir. *Invisible War*. 2012. San Francisco, CA: Roco Films.

Dines, Gail. *Pornland: How Porn Has Hijacked Our Sexuality*. Boston: Beacon Press, 2010.

Ditmore, Melissa Hope, Antonia Levy, and Alys Willman, eds. *Sex Work Matters: Exploring Money, Power, and Intimacy in the Sex Industry*. London, UK: Zed Books Ltd., 2010.

Doezema, Jo. "How Was It for You? Pleasure and Performance in Sex Work." In *Women, Sexuality and the Political Power of Pleasure*, edited by Susie Jolly, Andrea Cornwall, and Kate Hawkins, 251–64. London, UK: Zed Books Ltd., 2013.

Doolittle, Robyn. "Unfounded: Police Dismiss 1 in 5 Sexual Assault Claims as Baseless, *Globe* Investigation Reveals." *Globe and Mail*, 3 February 2017. https://

www.theglobeandmail.com/news/investigations/unfounded-sexual-assault-canada-main/article33891309/.

Dow, Bonnie J., and Julia T. Wood. "Repeating History and Learning from It: What Can Slutwalks Teach Us About Feminism?" *Women's Studies in Communication* 37, no. 1 (2014): 22–43. doi:10/gg9mr6.

Draaisma, Muriel. "York Police Say 104 Men Arrested After Child Sex Sting." CBC *News*, 21 April 2017. https://www.cbc.ca/news/canada/toronto/york-human-trafficking-investigation-arrests-1.4078982.

Durisin, Elya M., Emily Van der Meulen, and Chris Bruckert. "Contextualizing Sex Work: Challenging Discourses and Confronting Narratives." In *Red Light Labour: Sex Work Regulation, Agency, and Resistance*, 3–24. Vancouver: UBC Press, 2018.

– eds. *Red Light Labour: Sex Work Regulation, Agency, and Resistance*. Vancouver: UBC Press, 2018.

Dworkin, Andrea. *Pornography: Men Possessing Women*. New York: Perigree, 1981.

Elshtain, Jean Bethke. "Aristotle, the Public-Private Split, and the Case of the Suffragists." In *The Family in Political Thought*, edited by Jean Bethke Elshtain, 51–65. Amherst: University of Massachusetts Press, 1982.

Eltahawy, Mona. *Headscarves and Hymens: Why the Middle East Needs a Sexual Revolution*. New York: Farrar, Straus and Giroux, 2015.

– "Why Do They Hate Us?" *Foreign Policy* 193 (2012): 1–9.

Farley, Melissa. "'Bad for the Body, Bad for the Heart': Prostitution Harms Women Even If Legalized or Decriminalized." *Violence against Women* 10, no. 10 (2004): 1087–125. doi:10/djfzt9.

– "Prostitution Harms Women Even If Indoors: Reply to Weitzer." *Violence against Women* 11, no. 7 (2005): 950–64. doi:10/bhz3c8.

Farley, Melissa, and Howard Barkan. "Prostitution, Violence, and Posttraumatic Stress Disorder." *Women & Health* 27, no. 3 (1998): 37–49. doi:10/d49rgc.

Ferré-Sadurní, Luis, and Sarah Maslin Nir. "Judge Gets Threats after Saying Teenager in Rape Case Was from 'Good Family.'" *New York Times*, 8 July 2019. https://www.nytimes.com/2019/07/08/nyregion/judge-james-troiano.html.

Fine, Sean. "Attire Does Not Imply Consent, Ontario Court of Appeal Says, Calling Out Justice for Comments." *Globe and Mail*, 28 November 2019. https://www.theglobeandmail.com/canada/article-attire-does-not-imply-consent-ontario-court-of-appeal-says-calling/.

Fox, Greer Litton. "'Nice Girl': Social Control of Women Through a Value Construct." *Signs: Journal of Women in Culture and Society* 2, no. 4 (1977): 805–17.
doi:10/bfrq63.

Frost, Laura. "The Cult of the Clitoris." *Los Angeles Review of Books*, 16 June 2017.
https://lareviewofbooks.org/article/the-cult-of-the-clitoris/.

Froyum, Carissa M. "Making 'Good Girls': Sexual Agency in the Sexuality Education of Low-Income Black Girls." *Culture, Health & Sexuality* 12, no. 1
(2010): 59–72. doi:10/b4rj5j.

Fuchs, Stephen. "German Green Party Wants Free Prostitutes for Disabled and
Elderly." *German Pulse*, 9 January 2017. https://www.germanpulse.com/
2017/01/09/german-green-party-prostitutes-disabled-elderly/.

Gailey, Jeannine A. "Fat Shame to Fat Pride: Fat Women's Sexual and Dating
Experiences." *Fat Studies* 1, no. 1 (2012): 114–27. doi:10/fzjrm7.

Gallant, Chanelle, and Andrea Zanin. "The Bogus BDSM Defence: The Manipu-
lation of Kink as Consent to Assault." In *Dis/Consent: Perspectives on Sexual
Consent and Sexual Violence*, edited by KellyAnne Malinen. Halifax: Fernwood
Publishing, 2019.

Gibson, Victoria. "Ontario Government Considered Removing Sex-Ed Classes
Completely." *Globe and Mail*, 31 January 2019. https://www.theglobeandmail.
com/canada/article-hrto-case-reveals-ontario-government-considered-
removing-sex-ed/.

Gilbert, Elizabeth. "Soul Tribe Live: Make Big Magic Workshop." Halifax, Nova
Scotia, 12 October 2019.

Gold, Michael. "Anthony Weiner Released from Prison after Serving 18 Months
for Sexting Teenager." *New York Times*, 14 May 2019. https://www.nytimes.com
/2019/05/14/nyregion/anthony-weiner-prison-release.html.

Goudreau, Jenna. "Good Girls, Bad Girls, Sluts and Moms: How Women's
Identities Form." *Forbes*, 11 April 2012. https://www.forbes.com/sites/jenna
goudreau/2012/04/11/good-girls-bad-girls-sluts-and-moms-how-womens-
identities-form/.

Grant, Melissa Gira. *Playing the Whore: The Work of Sex Work*. New York: Verso
Trade, 2014.

Green, Chris. "SNP Backs Changes to Scotland's Prostitution Laws." *INews*, 17
March 2017. https://inews.co.uk/news/politics/snp-backs-changes-scotlands-
prostitution-laws-53599.

Griffin, Susan. *The Book of the Courtesans: A Catalogue of Their Virtues*. New
York: Broadway, 2002.

Grigorovich, Alisa and Pia Kontos. "Ethics, Sexuality, and Dementia in Long-Term Care." *Impact Ethics*, 12 May 2017. https://impactethics.ca/2017/05/12/ethics-sexuality-and-dementia-in-long-term-care/.

Gunter, Jennifer. *The Vagina Bible: The Vulva and the Vagina: Separating the Myth from the Medicine*. New York: Citadel Press, 2019.

Gustin, Sam. "After Sex Scandal, Eliot Spitzer Makes a Comeback." *Time*, 8 July 2013. https://business.time.com/2013/07/08/after-sex-scandal-eliot-spitzer-makes-a-comeback/.

Hakim, Catherine. *Erotic Capital: The Power of Attraction in the Boardroom and the Bedroom*. New York: Basic Books, 2011.

Hamilton, Matt and Harriet Ryan. "Regulators Slam USC Handling of Sex Abuse Cases as 'Reprehensible.'" *Los Angeles Times*, 27 February 2020. https://www.latimes.com/california/story/2020-02-27/regulators-slam-usc-handling-of-sex-abuse-as-shocking-and-reprehensible-order-federal-oversight.

Hanson, Hillary. "Columnist Calls Gunpoint Rape of Sex Worker 'Theft of Services.'" *HuffPost Canada*, 14 September 2015. https://www.huffingtonpost.ca/entry/sun-times-mary-mitchell-rape-sex-worker_n_55f6bb73e4b042295e36b959.

Harding, Kate. *Asking for It: The Alarming Rise of Rape Culture – and What We Can Do about It*. New York: Da Capo Lifelong Books, 2015.

Hensley, Laura. "The Problem with DJ Khaled – and All the *Other* Dudes Who Won't Perform Oral Sex." *Flare*, 7 May 2018. https://www.flare.com/celebrity/dj-khaled-going-down-on-women/.

Hinckley, David. "How Mae West's Arrest for Onstage Lewdness Made Her a Star." *New York Daily News*, 14 August 2017, sec. New York. https://www.nydailynews.com/new-york/mae-west-arrest-onstage-lewdness-made-star-article-1.787845.

Hochschild, Arlie Russell. *The Managed Heart: Commercialization of Human Feeling*. Berkeley: University of California Press, 1983.

Horn, Tina. "Yeah, You Like That, Don't You? The Unnecessary Pleasures of Sexual Labor." In *Believe Me: How Trusting Women Can Change the World*, edited by Jessica Valenti and Jaclyn Friedman. New York: Seal Press, 2020.

Hudson, Valerie M., Bonnie Ballif-Spanvill, Mary Caprioli, and Chad F. Emmett. *Sex and World Peace*. New York: Columbia University Press, 2012.

Hymson, Paige. "How 'Portrait of a Lady on Fire' Became a 'Movie Dedicated to Love.'" *Los Angeles Times*, 14 February 2020. https://www.latimes.com/

entertainment-arts/story/2020-02-14/how-portrait-of-a-lady-on-fire-became-a-movie-dedicated-to-love.

Ingraham, Chris. "Portugal Decriminalised Drugs 14 Years Ago – and Now Hardly Anyone Dies from Overdosing." *Independent*, 7 June 2015. https://www.independent.co.uk/news/world/europe/portugal-decriminalised-drugs-14-years-ago-and-now-hardly-anyone-dies-from-overdosing-10301780.html.

Irvine, Janice M. "Is Sexuality Research 'Dirty Work'? Institutionalized Stigma in the Production of Sexual Knowledge." *Sexualities* 17, no. 5–6 (2014): 632–56. doi:10/f6j4kj.

Jeffrey, Leslie Ann, and Gayle MacDonald. *Sex Workers in the Maritimes Talk Back*. Vancouver: UBC Press, 2011.

Jeffreys, Sheila. *Anticlimax: A Feminist Perspective on the Sexual Revolution*. London, UK: Women's Press, 1990.

– "Sex Tourism: Do Women Do It Too?" *Leisure Studies* 22, no. 3 (2003): 223–38. doi:10/cc33jh.

Jenkins, Patty, dir. *Monster*. 2004; Los Angeles, CA: Media 8 Entertainment, Newmarket Films, DEJ Productions.

Jessome, Phonse. *Somebody's Daughter: Inside the Toronto/Halifax Pimping Ring*. Halifax: Nimbus Publishing, 1996.

Jolly, Susie. "Why the Development Industry Should Get Over Its Obsession with Bad Sex and Start to Think about Pleasure." In *Development, Sexual Rights and Global Governance*, edited by Amy Lind, 41–56. New York: Routledge, 2010.

Kaiser. "Emily Ratajkowski: 'Women Must Feel Liberated, Not Constrained, by Feminism.'" *Cele|bitchy*, 18 October 2018. https://www.celebitchy.com/595247/emily_ratajkowski_women_must_feel_liberated_not_constrained_by_feminism/.

– "Taylor Swift Releases 'Lover' Album Cover & New Single 'You Need to Calm Down.'" *Cele|bitchy*, 14 June 2019. https://www.celebitchy.com/624863/taylor_swift_releases_lover_album_cover_new_single_you_need_to_calm_down/.

Kamer, Foster. "Can Robert Pattinson Actually Have a Vagina Allergy?" *Gawker*, 14 February 2010. http://gawker.com/5471506/can-robert-pattinson-actually-have-a-vagina-allergy.

Kara, Siddharth. *Sex Trafficking: Inside the Business of Modern Slavery*. New York: Columbia University Press, 2009.

Karlamangla, Soumya. "Coronavirus Memes Fill Social Media Feeds. Here's

Why It's Making Young People So Anxious." *Los Angeles Times*, 5 February 2020. https://www.latimes.com/california/story/2020-02-05/coronavirus-anxiety-youth-memes.

Keeble, Edna. *Politics and Sex: Exploring the Connections Between Gender, Sexuality, and the State.* Toronto: Women's Press, 2016.

Kettrey, Heather Hensman. "'Bad Girls' Say No and 'Good Girls' Say Yes: Sexual Subjectivity and Participation in Undesired Sex during Heterosexual College Hookups." *Sexuality & Culture* 22, no. 3 (2018): 685–705. doi:10/gg9x5s.

Khan, Ummni. "From Average Joe to Deviant John: The Changing Construction of Sex Trade Clients in Canada." In *Red Light Labour: Sex Work Regulation, Agency, and Resistance*, edited by Elya M. Durisin, Emily Van der Meulen, and Chris Bruckert, 67–81. Vancouver: UBC Press, 2018.

Kinsey, Alfred C., Wardell B. Pomeroy, and Clyde E. Martin. *Sexual Behavior in the Human Male.* Bloomington: Indiana University Press, 1948.

Klatch, Rebecca. *Women of the New Right.* Temple University Press, 1988.

Koken, Juline A. "Independent Female Escort's Strategies for Coping with Sex Work Related Stigma." *Sexuality & Culture* 16, no. 3 (2012): 209–29. doi:10/cqgrw6.

– "The Meaning of the 'Whore': How Feminist Theories on Prostitution Shape Research on Female Sex Workers." In *Sex Work Matters: Exploring Money, Power, and Intimacy in the Sex Industry*, edited by Melissa Hope Ditmore, Antonia Levy, and Alys Willman, 28–64. London, UK: Zed Books Ltd., 2010.

Krüsi, Andrea, Brenda Belak, and Sex Workers United Against Violence. "'Harassing the Clients Is Exactly the Same as Harassing the Workers': Street Based Sex Workers in Vancouver." In *Red Light Labour: Sex Work Regulation, Agency, and Resistance*, edited by Elya M. Durisin, Emily Van der Meulen, and Chris Bruckert, 213–23. Vancouver: UBC Press, 2018.

Kuo, Lenore. *Prostitution Policy: Revolutionizing Practice Through a Gendered Perspective.* New York: NYU Press, 2002.

Lakoff, George. *The Political Mind: Why You Can't Understand 21st-Century Politics with an 18th-Century Brain.* New York: Viking, 2008.

Laskow, Sarah. "The Racist, Slut-Shaming History of Adultery Laws." *Atlas Obscura*, 21 August 2015. http://www.atlasobscura.com/articles/the-racist-slut-shaming-history-of-adultery-laws.

Law, Benjamin. "The Women Who Hire Male Escorts." *The Sydney Morning*

Herald, 31 January 2014. https://www.smh.com.au/lifestyle/life-and-relation ships/the-women-who-hire-male-escorts-20140203-31wtv.html.

Lepp, Annalee, and Borislav Gerasimov. "Gains and Challenges in the Global Movement for Sex Workers" Rights." *Anti-Trafficking Review*, no. 12 (2019): 1–13. doi:10/gg9zgr.

Lever, Janet, and Deanne Dolnick. "Clients and Call Girls: Seeking Sex and Intimacy." In *Sex for Sale: Prostitution, Pornography, and the Sex Industry*, edited by Ronald Weitzer, 85–100. New York: Routledge, 1999.

Lim, Lin Lean. *The Sex Sector: The Economic and Social Bases of Prostitution in Southeast Asia*. International Labour Organization, 1998.

Limoncelli, Stephanie A. *The Politics of Trafficking: The First International Movement to Combat the Sexual Exploitation of Women*. Palo Alto, CA: Stanford University Press, 2010.

Lithwick, Dahlia. "How to Talk to Your Teens about Sex, Climate Change, and Existential Angst." *Slate Magazine*, 20 February 2019. https://slate.com/human-interest/2019/02/navigating-teen-anxiety-with-lisa-damour.html.

Love, Victoria. "Champagne, Strawberries and Truck-Stop Motels: On Subjectivity and Sex Work." In *Selling Sex: Experience, Advocacy, and Research on Sex Work in Canada*, edited by Emily Van der Meulen, Elya M. Durisin, and Victoria Love, 58–64. Vancouver: UBC Press, 2013.

Lupick, Travis. "Opinion: Decriminalization Is Just the Start of Real Reform – and Drug Users Need to Be Part of the Conversation." *Globe and Mail*, 21 August 2020. https://www.theglobeandmail.com/opinion/article-on-decriminal ization-lets-hear-from-drug-users/.

Mac, Juno. *The Laws That Sex Workers Really Want*. TEDxEastEnd, 2016. https://www.ted.com/talks/juno_mac_the_laws_that_sex_workers_really _want.

MacKinnon, Catharine A. *Feminism Unmodified: Discourses on Life and Law*. Cambridge, MA: Harvard University Press, 1987.

Malarek, Victor. *The Johns: Sex for Sale and the Men Who Buy It*. New York: Arcade Publishing, 2009.

– *The Natashas: The Horrific Inside Story of Slavery, Rape, and Murder in the Global Sex Trade*. New York: Skyhorse Publishing, 2003.

Malinen, KellyAnne, ed. *Dis/Consent: Perspectives on Sexual Consent and Sexual Violence*. Halifax: Fernwood Publishing, 2019.

Manne, Kate. *Down Girl: The Logic of Misogyny*. Oxford: Oxford University Press, 2017.

– *Entitled: How Male Privilege Hurts Women*. New York: Crown, 2020.

Marlowe, Julian. "Thinking Outside the Box: Men in the Sex Industry." In *Prostitution and Pornography: Philosophical Debate about the Sex Industry*, edited by Jessica Spector, 349–58. Palo Alto, CA: Stanford University Press, 2006.

Marshal, Garry, dir. *Pretty Woman*. 1990. Hollywood, CA: Touchstone Pictures, Silver Screen Partners IV.

Martinez, Peter. "Mollie Tibbetts Went Jogging and Never Came Back – She's Not the First." *CBS News*, 22 August 2018. https://www.cbsnews.com/news/mollie-tibbetts-dead-investigation-jogging-killers-murder-cases-crime/.

Maynard, Robyn. "Do Black Sex Workers' Lives Matter? Whitewashed Anti-Slavery, Racial Justice, and Abolition." In *Red Light Labour: Sex Work Regulation, Agency, and Resistance*, edited by Elya M. Durisin, Emily Van der Meulen, and Chris Bruckert, 281–92. Vancouver: UBC Press, 2018.

– *Policing Black Lives: State Violence in Canada from Slavery to the Present*. Halifax: Fernwood Publishing, 2017.

McAuliffe, Kathleen. "Liberals and Conservatives React in Wildly Different Ways to Repulsive Pictures." *The Atlantic*, March 2019. https://www.theatlantic.com/magazine/archive/2019/03/the-yuck-factor/580465/.

McCormick, Lucy. "The Clitoris Is a Gift, so Why Is There an Ingrained Fear of Talking About It?" *Guardian*, 20 February 2019. https://www.theguardian.com/commentisfree/2019/feb/20/clitoris-gift-ingrained-fear-fgm-tackle-outdated-mysogynistic-views-sex.

McNamara, Mary. "Column: Plácido Domingo Has Apologized, Sort of, but I Do Not Buy It." *Los Angeles Times*, 27 February 2020. https://www.latimes.com/entertainment-arts/story/2020-02-26/column-placido-domingo-has-apologized-but-i-do-not-buy-it.

Mears, Ashley, and Catherine Connell. "The Paradoxical Value of Deviant Cases: Toward a Gendered Theory of Display Work." *Signs: Journal of Women in Culture and Society* 41, no. 2 (2016): 333–59. doi:10/gg9zg9.

Milrod, Christine, and Martin A Monto. "The Hobbyist and the Girlfriend Experience: Behaviors and Preferences of Male Customers of Internet Sexual Service Providers." *Deviant Behavior* 33, no. 10 (2012): 792–810. doi:10/gg9zhb.

Minaker, Joanne. "Sluts and Slags: The Censuring of the Erring Female." In *Criminalizing Women: Gender and Injustice in Neo-Liberal Times*, edited by

Gillian Balfour and Elizabeth Comack, 79–92. Halifax, NS: Fernwood Publishing, 2006.

Mintz, Laurie. *Becoming Cliterate: Why Orgasm Equality Matters – and How to Get It*. London, UK: HarperCollins, 2017.

Mock, Janet. "On the Women's March 'Guiding Vision' and Its Inclusion of Sex Workers." *Janet Mock on Tumblr*, 17 January 2017. https://janetmock.tumblr. com/post/156017232338/womens-march-sex-worker-inclusion.

Monto, Martin A. "Why Men Seek Out Prostitutes." In *Sex for Sale: Prostitution, Pornography, and the Sex Industry*, edited by Ronald Weitzer, 67–83. New York: Routledge, 1999.

Moore, Anne Elizabeth. *Threadbare: Clothes, Sex, and Trafficking*. Portland, OR: Microcosm Publishing, 2016.

Moore, Suzanne. "If Young Women Are Dying of Shame about Their Bodies, We Need a Rethink." *Guardian*, 27 January 2019. https://www.theguardian. com/commentisfree/2019/jan/27/shame-women-smear-tests-porn-feminism-bodies.

– "Ocasio-Cortez Has Shown 'Shameless' Women Are a Powerful Force." *Guardian*, 10 January 2019. https://www.theguardian.com/commentisfree/ 2019/jan/10/alexandra-ocasio-cortez-shameless-women.

Mor, Ana Frances. "Laughter, the Subversive Body Organ." In *Women, Sexuality and the Political Power of Pleasure*, edited by Susie Jolly, Andrea Cornwall, and Kate Hawkins, 286–307. London, UK: Zed Books Ltd., 2013.

Mottier, Véronique. *Sexuality: A Very Short Introduction*. Oxford: Oxford University Press, 2008.

Nagoski, Emily. *Come as You Are: The Surprising New Science That Will Transform Your Sex Life*. New York: Simon and Schuster, 2015.

Noxon, Marti, dir. *To the Bone*. 2017; Los Angeles, CA: AMBI Group, Sparkhouse Media, Mockingbird Pictures.

Nussbaum, Martha C. *Sex and Social Justice*. Oxford: Oxford University Press, 1999.

– *The New Religious Intolerance: Overcoming the Politics of Fear in an Anxious Age*. Cambridge, MA: Belknap Press, 2012.

O'Connor, Monica. "Choice, Agency Consent and Coercion: Complex Issues in the Lives of Prostituted and Trafficked Women." In *Proceedings of the Women's Studies International Forum*, 62:8–16, 2017.

Odinokova, Veronika, Maia Rusakova, Lianne A. Urada, Jay G. Silverman, and

Anita Raj. "Police Sexual Coercion and Its Association with Risky Sex Work and Substance Use Behaviors among Female Sex Workers in St Petersburg and Orenburg, Russia." *International Journal of Drug Policy* 25, no. 1 (2014): 96–104. doi:10/f5thrv.

O'Doherty, Tamara. "Criminalization and Off-Street Sex Work in Canada." *Canadian Journal of Criminology and Criminal Justice* 53, no. 2 (2011): 217–45. doi:10/fq92nm.

– "Victimization in Off-Street Sex Industry Work." *Violence Against Women* 17, no. 7 (2011): 944–63. doi:10/fvxxw2.

O'Doherty, Tamara, Hayli Millar, Alison Clancey, and Kimberly Mackenzie. "Misrepresentations, Inadequate Evidence and Impediments to Justice: Human Rights Impacts of Canada's Anti-Trafficking Efforts." In *Red Light Labour: Sex Work Regulation, Agency, and Resistance*, edited by Elya M. Durisin, Emily Van der Meulen, and Chris Bruckert, 67–81. Vancouver: UBC Press, 2018.

Olubanke Akintunde, Dorcas. "Female Genital Mutilation: A Socio-Cultural Gang Up against Womanhood." *Feminist Theology* 18, no. 2 (2010): 192–205. doi:10/bgz97m.

Orchard, Treena. "In This Life: The Impact of Gender and Tradition on Sexuality and Relationships for Devadasi Sex Workers in Rural India." *Sexuality & Culture* 11, no. 1 (2007): 3–27. doi:10/cpxd6h.

Orenstein, Peggy. *Girls & Sex: Navigating the Complicated New Landscape*. New York: Simon and Schuster, 2016.

Outshoorn, Joyce. "The Political Debates on Prostitution and Trafficking of Women." *Social Politics: International Studies in Gender, State and Society* 12, no. 1 (2005): 141–55. doi:10/bvtt3x.

Overall, Christine. "What's Wrong with Prostitution? Evaluating Sex Work." *Signs: Journal of Women in Culture and Society* 17, no. 4 (1992): 705–24. doi:10/fgvvtw.

Pateman, Carole. *The Sexual Contract*. Palo Alto, CA: Stanford University Press, 1988.

Pauw, Ilse, and Loren Brener. "'You Are Just Whores – You Can't Be Raped': Barriers to Safer Sex Practices among Women Street Sex Workers in Cape Town." *Culture, Health & Sexuality* 5, no. 6 (2003): 465–81. doi:10/czjvvb.

Pawlowska, Maria. "The History of Nymphomania." *Blast Magazine*, 13 October 2011. https://blastmagazine.com/2011/10/13/the-history-of-nymphomania/.

Paxton, Pamela Marie, and Melanie M. Hughes. *Women, Politics, and Power: A Global Perspective*. 3rd ed. Washington, DC: CQ Press, 2017.

Penttinen, Elina. "Imagined and Embodied Spaces in the Global Sex Industry." *Gender, Work & Organization* 17, no. 1 (2010): 28–44.

Perrin, Benjamin. *Invisible Chains: Canada's Underground World of Human Trafficking*. Toronto: Penguin Canada, 2010.

– "Oldest Profession or Oldest Oppression? Addressing Prostitution after the Supreme Court of Canada Decision in *Canada v. Bedford*." *Macdonald-Laurier Institute Commentary Series*, 2014.

Perry, Debra Paris. "What You Can Do, What You Can't Do, and What You're Going to Pay Me to Do It." In *Dis/Consent: Perspectives on Sexual Consent and Sexual Violence*, edited by KellyAnne Malinen. Halifax: Fernwood Publishing, 2019.

Pheterson, Gail. *The Prostitution Prism*. Amsterdam: Amsterdam University Press, 1996.

– *A Vindication of the Rights of Whores*. New York: Seal Press, 1989.

Picard, André. "Sex-Ed Critics Fear That It May 'Give Kids Ideas,' but That Would Be a Good Thing." *Globe and Mail*, 15 January 2019. https://www.theglobeandmail.com/opinion/article-sex-ed-critics-fear-that-it-may-give-kids-ideas-but-that-would-be-a/.

– "Sexual Violence: The Silent Health Epidemic." *Globe and Mail*, 6 February 2017. https://www.theglobeandmail.com/opinion/sexual-violence-the-silent-health-epidemic/article33915008/.

– "Women in Amsterdam's Red-Light District Say Safety for Worldwide Sex Workers Lies in Legalization, Normalization." *Globe and Mail*, 10 August 2018. https://www.theglobeandmail.com/canada/article-the-story-behind-amster dams-infamous-red-light-district/.

Porth, Kerry. "Sex, Lies, and Committee Hearings." In *Red Light Labour: Sex Work Regulation, Agency, and Resistance*, edited by Elya M. Durisin, Emily Van der Meulen, and Chris Bruckert. Vancouver: UBC Press, 2018.

Pruden, Jana G. "The Day I Met a Serial Killer." *Globe and Mail*, 10 August 2018. https://www.theglobeandmail.com/opinion/article-the-day-i-met-a-serial-killer/.

Queally, James. "Weinstein Trial Is a Milestone for #metoo and a Moment of Wrenching Truth for Survivors." *Los Angeles Times*, 19 January 2020. https://www.latimes.com/california/story/2020-01-19/weinstein-trial-is-a-milestone-for-metoo-and-a-moment-of-wrenching-truth-for-survivors.

Queally, James, and Matthew Ormseth. "Harvey Weinstein Gets 23-Year Prison Sentence in His New York Trial." *Los Angeles Times*, 11 March 2020. https://www.latimes.com/california/story/2020-03-11/harvey-weinstein-case-sentence-life.

Radwanski, Adam. "Ontario's Premier Delivers on People Pleasing Promises, but Fiscal Plans Remain a Puzzle." *Globe and Mail*, 14 July 2018. https://www.the globeandmail.com/canada/article-premier-doug-ford-delivers-on-people-pleasing-promises-but-fiscal/.

Ralston, Meredith. *Nobody Wants to Hear Our Truth: Homeless Women and Theories of the Welfare State*. Westport, CT: Greenwood Publishing Group, 1996.

– dir. *Hope in Heaven*. 2007; Halifax, NS: Ralston Productions Ltd.

– dir. *Selling Sex*. 2016; Halifax, NS: Ralston Productions Ltd.

Ralston, Meredith, and Edna Keeble. *Reluctant Bedfellows: Feminism, Activism and Prostitution in the Philippines*. Sterling, VA: Kumarian Press, 2009.

Ray, Audacia. "Why the Sex Positive Movement Is Bad for Sex Workers' Rights." Audacia Ray, 31 March 2012. https://audaciaray.tumblr.com/post/20228032 642/why-the-sex-positive-movement-is-bad-for-sex.

Raymond, Janice G. "Prostitution on Demand: Legalizing the Buyers as Sexual Consumers." *Violence against Women* 10, no. 10 (2004): 1156–86. doi:10/b6smpq.

Redwood, River. "Myths and Realities of Male Sex Work: A Personal Perspective." In *Red Light Labour: Sex Work Regulation, Agency, and Resistance*, edited by Elya M. Durisin, Emily Van der Meulen, and Chris Bruckert, 167–80. Vancouver: UBC Press, 2018.

Renzetti, Elizabeth. "Good Sex-Ed Is a Vaccine That Protects All Students: The Health Curriculum in Ontario Was Miraculous for a Minute and Then Vanished in a Puff of Paranoia and Backward Thinking." *Globe and Mail*, 14 July 2018. https://www.theglobeandmail.com/opinion/article-good-sex-ed-is-a-vaccine-that-protects-all-students/.

– "The Slow, Steady Fall of Abortion Access in the U.S.: Trump's Pick for Top Court Nominee Has Ignited Concerns Over *Roe v. Wade*, but the Threat to Reproductive Rights Is Not New." *Globe and Mail*, 14 July 2018. https://www.theglobeandmail.com/opinion/article-what-the-reality-of-breastfeeding-looks-like/.

Repard, Pauline. "22 Women Win $13 Million in Suit Against GirlsDoPorn

Videos." *Los Angeles Times*, 3 January 2020. https://www.latimes.com/california/story/2020-01-02/lawsuit-girlsdoporn-videos.

Roach, Jay, dir. *Bombshell*. 2019; Hollywood, CA: Creative Wealth Media Finance, Annapurna Pictures, BRON Studios.

Roberts, Nickie. *Whores in History: Prostitution in Western Society*. London, UK: HarperCollins, 1992.

Rodrigues, Jason. "It's Twenty Years Since Hugh Grant Was Arrested with a Sex Worker." *Guardian*, 26 June 2015. https://www.theguardian.com/film/from-the-archive-blog/2015/jun/26/hugh-grant-arrest-prostitute-divine-brown-20-1995.

Rossi, Alice S, ed. *The Feminist Papers: From Adams to de Beauvoir*. New York: Bantam Books, 1973.

Rowland, Katherine. *The Pleasure Gap: American Women and the Unfinished Sexual Revolution*. New York: Seal Press, Hachette Book Group, 2020.

Ryan, Christopher, Cacilda Jethá, Allyson Johnson, and Jonathan Davis. *Sex at Dawn: How We Mate, Why We Stray, and What It Means for Modern Relationships*. New York: Harper Perennial, 2011.

Ryan, Denise. "Petition Demands Lindsay Buziak Murder Case Be Turned Over to New Investigators." *Vancouver Sun*, 1 March 2020. https://vancouversun.com/news/local-news/petition-demands-lindsay-buziak-murder-case-be-turned-over-to-new-investigators/.

Ryan, Haley. "Woman Says Halifax Taxi Driver Raped Her While She Pretended to Be Asleep." *CBC News*, 20 February 2020. https://www.cbc.ca/news/canada/nova-scotia/halifax-sexual-assault-taxi-driver-1.5469995.

Safronova, Valeriya. "What's So 'Indecent' About Female Pleasure?" *New York Times*, 18 January 2019. https://www.nytimes.com/2019/01/18/style/sex-toys.html.

Sampert, Shannon. "Let Me Tell You a Story: English-Canadian Newspapers and Sexual Assault Myths." *Canadian Journal of Women and the Law* 22, no. 2 (2010): 301–28. doi:10/frprdw.

Sandell, Laurie. "Nicki Minaj Wants All Women to Demand More Orgasms." *Cosmopolitan*, 29 May 2015. https://www.cosmopolitan.com/entertainment/a41113/nicki-minaj-july-2015/.

Sanghera, Jyoti, and Bandana Pattanaik. *Trafficking and Prostitution Reconsidered: New Perspectives on Migration, Sex Work, and Human Rights*. Edited by Kamala Kempadoo. New York: Routledge, 2011.

Sayers, Naomi. "Municipal Regulation of Street-Based Prostitution and the Impacts on Indigenous Women: A Necessary Discussion." In *Red Light Labour: Sex Work Regulation, Agency, and Resistance*, edited by Elya M. Durisin, Emily Van der Meulen, and Chris Bruckert, 57–66. Vancouver: UBC Press, 2018.

Scafaria, Lorene, dir. *Hustlers*. 2019; Hollywood, CA: Annapurna Pictures, Gloria Sanchez Productions, Nuyorican Productions.

Scorsese, Martin, dir. *Age of Innocence*. 1993; Hollywood, CA: Columbia Pictures, Cappa Production.

Sebag-Montefiore, Clarissa. "When It Comes to Buying Sex, Are Women Any Different from Men?" *Aeon*, 12 November 2014. https://aeon.co/essays/when-it-comes-to-buying-sex-are-women-any-different-from-men.

Sherwin, Susan, and Françoise Baylis. "The Feminist Health Care Ethics Consultant as Architect and Advocate." *Public Affairs Quarterly* 17, no. 2 (2003): 141–58.

Shrage, Laurie. "Comment on Overall's 'What's Wrong with Prostitution? Evaluating Sex Work.'" *Signs: Journal of Women in Culture and Society* 19, no. 2 (1994): 564–70. doi:10/cbrrbh.

– "The Case for Decriminalization." In *Prostitution and Pornography: Philosophical Debate about the Sex Industry*, edited by Jessica Spector. Palo Alto, CA: Stanford University Press, 2006.

Silver, Rachel. *The Girl in Scarlet Heels: Women in the Sex Business Speak Out.* London, UK: Arrow Books Limited, 1993.

Simons, Margaret. "'Do You Ever Think About Me?': The Children Sex Tourists Leave Behind." *Guardian*, 2 March 2019. https://www.theguardian.com/society/2019/mar/02/children-sex-tourists-leave-behind-fathers-visited-philippines.

Sissons, Claire. "What Are Normal Testosterone Levels? Ages, Males, Females, and More." *Medical News Today*, 17 September 2018. https://www.medicalnewstoday.com/articles/323085.

Skelton, Anthony. "Sex, Sex Surrogates, and Disability." *Practical Ethics*, 9 April 2013. http://blog.practicalethics.ox.ac.uk/2013/04/sex-sex-surrogates-and-disability/.

Skrobanek, Siriporn, Nattaya Boonpakdi, and Chutimā Janthakeero. *The Traffic in Women: Human Realities of the International Sex Trade*. London and New York: Zed Books Ltd., 1997.

Smith, Elizabeth Megan. "'It Gets Very Intimate for Me': Discursive Boundaries of Pleasure and Performance in Sex Work." *Sexualities* 20, no. 3 (2017): 344–63. doi:10/f9w8qf.

Smith, Molly, and Juno Mac. *Revolting Prostitutes: The Fight for Sex Workers' Rights*. New York: Verso Trade, 2018.

Soderbergh, Steven, dir. *Girlfriend Experience*. 2009; New York, NY: Magnolia Pictures, 2929 Productions, Extension 765.

Stone, Carly, dir. *New Romantic*. 2018; Los Angeles, CA: Drive Films, Independent Edge Films, JoBro Productions & Film Finance.

Sullivan, Barbara. "Rape, Prostitution and Consent." *Australian & New Zealand Journal of Criminology* 40, no. 2 (2007): 127–42. doi:10/bjkbqv.

Tamale, Sylvia. "Eroticism, Sensuality and 'Women's Secrets' Among the Baganda." In *Women, Sexuality and the Political Power of Pleasure*, edited by Susie Jolly, Andrea Cornwall, and Kate Hawkins, 265–85. London, UK: Zed Books Ltd., 2013.

Tanenbaum, Leora. *I Am Not a Slut: Slut-Shaming in the Age of the Internet*. New York: Harper Perennial, 2015.

– *Slut! Growing up Female with a Bad Reputation*. New York: Harper Perennial, 2000.

Taylor, Kate. "Taylor Swift Case Shows Price for Treating Women Appallingly Has Risen." *Globe and Mail*, 15 August 2017. https://www.theglobeandmail.com/arts/music/taylor-swift-case-makes-clear-price-for-appalling-treatment-of-women-has-risen/article35992265/.

Tong, Rosemarie, and Tina Fernandes Botts. *Feminist Thought: A More Comprehensive Introduction*. 5th ed. New York: Routledge, 2017.

Tracy, Matt. "DC Sex Decrim Drive Divides National Organization for Women." *Gay City News*, 1 November 2019. https://www.gaycitynews.com/dc-sex-decrim-drive-divides-national-organization-for-women/.

Troncale, Joseph. "Your Lizard Brain." *Psychology Today*, 22 April 2014. http://www.psychologytoday.com/blog/where-addiction-meets-your-brain/201404/your-lizard-brain.

Truth, Sojourner. "Ain't I a Woman?" Presented at the Women's Convention, Akron, Ohio, 1851. https://www.sojournertruth.com/p/aint-i-woman.html.

Turpel-Lafond, Mary Ellen. "Too Many Victims: Sexualized Violence in the Lives of Children and Youth in Care-an Aggregate Review." Representative for Children and Youth, 2016. https://cwrp.ca/sites/default/files/publications/r_for_c_and_y_toomanyvictims_2016.pdf.

Underwood, Nora. "Are Human Challenge Trials for COVID-19 Research Ethical?." *Globe and Mail*. 12 November 2020, A20.

Undie, Chi-Chi. "Why We Need to Think about Sexuality and Sexual Well-Being: Addressing Sexual Violence in Sub-Saharan Africa." In *Women, Sexuality and the Political Power of Pleasure*, edited by Susie Jolly, Andrea Cornwall, and Kate Hawkins, 184–99. London, UK: Zed Books Ltd., 2013.

Valenti, Jessica. *The Purity Myth: How America's Obsession with Virginity Is Hurting Young Women*. New York: Seal Press, 2010.

Valenti, Jessica, and Jaclyn Friedman, eds. *Believe Me: How Trusting Women Can Change the World*. New York: Seal Press, 2020.

Valverde, Mariana. "Canadian Feminsim and Sex Work Law: A Cautionary Tale." In *Red Light Labour: Sex Work Regulation, Agency, and Resistance*, edited by Elya M. Durisin, Emily Van der Meulen, and Chris Bruckert, 247–55. Vancouver: UBC Press, 2018.

Van der Meulen, Emily, and Elya M. Durisin. "Sex Work Policy: Tracing Historical and Contemporary Developments." In *Red Light Labour: Sex Work Regulation, Agency, and Resistance*, edited by Elya M. Durisin, Emily Van der Meulen, and Chris Bruckert, 27–47. Vancouver: UBC Press, 2018.

Van der Meulen, Emily, Elya M. Durisin, and Victoria Love. *Selling Sex: Experience, Advocacy, and Research on Sex Work in Canada*. Vancouver: UBC Press, 2013.

Vance, Carole S., ed. *Pleasure and Danger: Exploring Female Sexuality*. Kitchener, ON: Pandora Press, 1984.

Virzi, Juliette. "T.I. Taking His Daughter to Get Her Hymen 'Checked' Isn't Just Creepy – It's Abusive." *The Mighty*, 6 November 2019. https://themighty.com/2019/11/ti-daughter-hymen-check-virgin/.

Wagner, John. "Feedback: James Taylor beyond the Persona, Shakira and Jennifer Lopez More Than Skin Deep." *Los Angeles Times*, 7 February 2020. https://www.latimes.com/entertainment-arts/story/2020-02-07/reader-feedback-james-taylor-parasite-american-dirt-lacma-higgins-clark.

Warren, May. "Guelph Mom Shocked Eight-Year-Old Told to Put on Her Top at Public Pool." *Record*, 23 June 2015. https://www.therecord.com/news/waterloo-region/2015/06/23/guelph-mom-shocked-eight-year-old-told-to-put-on-her-top-at-public-pool.html.

Weitzer, Ronald. "Flawed Theory and Method in Studies of Prostitution." *Violence against Women* 11, no. 7 (2005): 934–49. doi:10/d5znn5.

— *Legalizing Prostitution: From Illicit Vice to Lawful Business.* New York: NYU Press, 2012.

West, Lindy. *Shrill: Notes from a Loud Woman.* New York and Boston: Hachette Book Group 2016.

Whedon, Joss, dir. *Firefly.* 2002; Hollywood, CA: 20th Century Fox Television.

Wilford, Denette. "That Time Charlie Sheen Brought a Sex Worker to Thanksgiving Dinner at Denise Richards' House." *Etalk,* 8 August 2019. https://www.theloop.ca/that-time-charlie-sheen-brought-a-sex-worker-to-thanksgiving-dinner-at-denise-richards-house/.

Williams, Mary Elizabeth. "'These Girls Became Perfect Prey': The Women Who Ended Larry Nassar's Abuse Tell Their Stories." *Salon,* 14 September 2019. https://www.salon.com/2019/09/14/these-girls-became-perfect-prey-the-women-who-ended-larry-nassars-abuse-tell-their-stories/.

Williams, Zoe. "Men Prefer Younger Women Not for Their Firmer Bodies – but Their Greater Admiration." *Guardian,* 9 January 2019. https://www.theguardian.com/commentisfree/2019/jan/09/men-prefer-younger-women-not-for-their-firmer-bodies-but-their-greater-admiration.

Willman, Alys. "Let's Talk about Money." In *Sex Work Matters: Exploring Money, Power, and Intimacy in the Sex Industry,* edited by Melissa Hope Ditmore, Antonia Levy, and Alys Willman, 143–6. London, UK: Zed Books Ltd., 2010.

Wilson, Jacque. "From 'Filthy Trash' to Iconic Resource: 'Our Bodies, Ourselves' at 40." *CNN,* 5 October 2011. https://www.cnn.com/2011/10/05/health/our-bodies-ourselves-40th-anniversary/index.html.

Wolf, Naomi. *Vagina: A Cultural History.* New York: Ecco, 2013.

Yakabuski, Konrad. "Opinion: Andrew Scheer Can Choose to Go Out on a High Note." *Globe and Mail,* 27 November 2019. https://www.theglobeandmail.com/opinion/article-andrew-scheer-can-choose-to-go-out-on-a-high-note/.

Zimmerman, Amy. "No, Ashley Judd, Prostitution Is Not Paid Rape." *Daily Beast,* 28 November 2018. https://www.thedailybeast.com/sex-workers-blast-ashley-judds-anti-prostitution-crusade-you-are-harming-people.

Index